T0345038

# Social Media and Crowdsourcing

Social media and crowdsourcing are important tools for solving complex problems. The benefit of crowdsourcing is that it leverages the power of human intelligence cost effectively and with less time. *Social Media and Crowdsourcing: Application and Analytics* examines the concepts of social media and crowdsourcing as well as their analytical aspects. It explores how these technologies contribute to the real world and examines such applications as promoting social good, agriculture, healthcare, tourism, disaster management, education, crime control, and cultural heritage. The book also looks at ethical issues in crowdsourcing and future scenarios and challenges for policy. Highlights of the book include the following:

- A crowdsourcing application in agriculture
- Crowdsourcing outline for a contemporary aided medicinal backup system
- Crowdsourcing-based recommendation in the tourism industry
- Crowdsourcing mechanisms for reviving cultural heritage

Expanding the overarching concept of utilizing social media and crowdsourcing to solve various real-life problems, this book discusses how to bring together the wisdom of crowds for various decision-making problems in agriculture, disaster management, and healthcare. It addresses the various ethical issues arising out of various crowdsourcing-based applications. It puts forward diverse methodologies to involve crowdsourcing in education to implement new strategies to enhance learning outcomes. This book also addresses various problem-solving techniques for recommender applications in the travel and tourism industry.

Providing a systematic discussion of the many sectors using crowdsourcing as an essential part of social innovation, this book is a theoretical and methodological look at the application of social media.

**Dr. Sujoy Chatterjee** is an assistant professor, Department of Computer Science and Engineering, Amity University, Kolkata, India.

**Dr. Thipendra P. Singh** is currently a professor at the School of Computer Science Engineering and Technology, Bennett University, Greater Noida, NCR, India.

**Dr. Sunghoon Lim** is currently an Associate Professor in the Department of Industrial Engineering and the Graduate School of Artificial Intelligence, Ulsan National Institute of Science and Technology (UNIST), Ulsan, Republic of Korea.

**Dr. Anirban Mukhopadhyay** is currently a professor at the Department of Computer Science and Engineering, University of Kalyani, Kalyani, West Bengal, India.

# Advances in Computational Collective Intelligence

*Edited by Dr. Subhendu Kumar Pani*
*Principal, Krupajal Group of Institutions, India*

**Published**
*Technologies for Sustainable Global Higher Education*
By Maria José Sousa, Andreia de Bem Machado, and Gertrudes Aparecida Dandolini
ISBN: 978-1-032-262895

*Social Media and Crowdsourcing*
By Sujoy Chatterjee, Thipendra P Singh, Sunghoon Lim, and Anirban Mukhopadhyay
ISBN: 978-1-032-386874

**Forthcoming**
*Artificial Intelligence and Machine Learning for Risk Management of Natural Hazards and Disasters*
By Cees van Westen, Romulus Costache, Dimitrios A. Karras, R. S. Ajin, and Sekhar L. Kuriakose
ISBN: 978-1-032-232768

*Computational Intelligence in Industry 4.0 and 5.0 Applications: Challenges and Future Prospects*
Joseph Bamidele Awotunde, Kamalakanta Muduli, and Biswajit Brahma
ISBN: 978-1-032-539225

*Deep Learning for Smart Healthcare: Trends, Challenges and Applications*
K. Murugeswari, B. Sundaravadivazhagan, S. Poonkuntran, and Thendral Puyalnithi
ISBN: 978-1-032-455815

*Edge Computational Intelligence for AI-Enabled IoT Systems*
By Shrikaant Kulkarni, Jaiprakash Narain Dwivedi, Dinda Pramanta, and Yuichiro Tanaka
ISBN: 978-1-032-207667

*Explainable AI and Cybersecurity*
By Mohammad Tabrez Quasim, Abdullah Alharthi, Ali Alqazzaz, Mohammed Mujib Alshahrani, Ali Falh Alshahrani, and Mohammad Ayoub Khan
ISBN: 978-1-032-422213

*Machine Learning in Applied Sciences*
By M. A. Jabbar, Shankru Guggari, Kingsley Okoye, and Houneida Sakly
ISBN: 978-1-032-251721

For more information about this series, please visit: https://www.routledge.com/Advances-in-Computational-Collective-Intelligence/book-series/ACCICRC

# Social Media and Crowdsourcing
## Application and Analytics

Edited by
Dr. Sujoy Chatterjee
Dr. Thipendra P. Singh
Dr. Sunghoon Lim
Dr. Anirban Mukhopadhyay

CRC Press
Taylor & Francis Group
Boca Raton  London  New York

CRC Press is an imprint of the
Taylor & Francis Group, an **Informa** business

AN AUERBACH BOOK

First edition published 2024
by CRC Press
2385 Executive Center Drive, Suite 320, Boca Raton, FL 33431

and by CRC Press
4 Park Square, Milton Park, Abingdon, Oxon, OX14 4RN

*CRC Press is an imprint of Taylor & Francis Group, LLC*

© 2024 Taylor & Francis Group, LLC

ISBN: 978-1-032-38687-4 (hbk)
ISBN: 978-1-032-38690-4 (pbk)
ISBN: 978-1-003-34632-6 (ebk)

DOI: 10.1201/9781003346326

Typeset in Minion
by MPS Limited, Dehradun

# Contents

**Chapter 3**    Crowdsourcing Applications in Agriculture .................... 49

*Achala Shakya, Gaurav Tripathi,*
*and Devarani Devi Ningombam*

**Chapter 4**    Crowdsourcing Outline for Contemporary
Aided Medicinal Backup Systems ............................. 71

*Sonali Vyas, Shaurya Gupta, and Vinod Kumar Shukla*

*Sujoy Chatterjee and Thipendra P. Singh*

*Gyana Ranjana Panigrahi, Nalini Kanta Barpanda,*
*Prabira Kumar Sethy, and Debabrata Samantaray*

*Sulaiman O. Abdulsalam, Rafiu A. Ganiyu, Elijah O. Omidiora,*
*Stephen O. Olabiyisi, and Micheal O. Arowolo*

# Preface

Recently, due to the development of the internet and mobile devices, such as smartphones and tablets, it has been easy to share information and communicate across the globe. Especially social media and crowdsourcing have significantly contributed to various traditional and new industries, such as manufacturing, social good, agriculture, healthcare, tourism, disaster management, education, crime control, and cultural heritage, as efficient and effective platforms for individuals and organizations to share information and communicate with each other.

Social media is defined as online platforms that allow users to communicate with each other, share information and knowledge, and express their opinions on various topics, regardless of their physical locations, in real time. Social media users can use texts, images, videos, and URLs to create content and communicate with each other as well as create their personal profiles. Over the last couple of years, social media platforms have been used not only for individual users but also for communities and enterprises for marketing and business purposes. Types of social media include social networking sites, blogs, photo-sharing sites, video-sharing sites, instant messaging, podcasts, and virtual worlds as well as social media users can use their computers and mobile devices. Popular social media platforms are Twitter, Facebook, Instagram, YouTube, Yelp, and LinkedIn and they have been widely used as powerful platforms for crowdsourcing recently.

Crowdsourcing is defined as a sourcing model in which individuals and/ or organizations obtain goods, services, ideas, and finances from a large group of online users through an open call. Crowdsourcing is also considered a way to use the Internet to outsource work to a crowd, either paid or unpaid. It has been widely used for individuals and organizations to have collective knowledge and skills as well as create global communities to achieve the common goals. Especially, it contributes to create encyclopedias, fund projects, and address real-world complex problems, which traditional approaches struggle to solve. Crowdsourcing is based on the wisdom of crowds, which is the process of considering the collective opinion of a group of individuals, rather than a single expert to answer a question, as well as requires a diversity of opinions, independence, decentralization, and aggregation. While outsourcing is commissioned from a specific and named group, crowdsourcing comes from a less specific and more public group. Compared to outsourcing, it is known that the advantages of crowdsourcing include improved profits, speed, quality, flexibility, scalability, and diversity. It is demonstrated that proper utilization of non-expert human beings can reduce the overall cost of hiring the experts while maintaining quality.

Types of crowdsourcing include collecting information, labor markets, collaborative creation, and smartest in the crowd and their popular examples are online commerce websites' reviews, Amazon Mechanical Turk, Wikipedia, and online contests, respectively. In addition, crowdfunding is one of the example of crowdsourcing, which is the collective effort of individuals who network and pool their money, usually via the Internet, to support efforts initiated by other people or organizations. Crowdfunding includes disaster relief, start-up company funding, free software development, and scientific research that supports individuals, non-profit organizations, start-ups, and small companies. Popular crowdfunding websites are GoFundMe and Kickstarter.

Social media can be used as an efficient and effective platform for crowdsourcing. Through social media platforms, individuals and organizations can use knowledge and opinions that are collected from the crowd in real time and can be supported to make decisions. For example, social media platforms, especially online communities, can be used for idea generation and brainstorming. Social media platforms including online communities also enable individuals and/or organizations to use online polls and surveys, which are necessary for crowdsourcing. Social media platforms can be used for collecting various contents, including texts, photos, and videos, which are generated by online users and used for marketing and/or business as well. In addition, social media platforms can be a powerful source for crowdfunding.

In this book, we have discussed the concept of social media and crowdsourcing as well as their analytical aspects. We have also explored their contributions to the real world, such as social good, agriculture, healthcare, tourism, disaster management, education, crime control, and cultural heritage. In addition, we discussed ethical issues in crowdsourcing and future scopes and challenges for policy makers who use social media and crowdsourced opinions. Due to the limited scope of this book, some concepts and procedures have been introduced without theoretical explanations.

We would like to thank all the authors of this book for their valuable contributions. We hope that this book will provide practical knowledge and valuable insights to readers. In addition, we hope this book will contribute to the development of this research area.

# 1

# Introduction to Crowdsourcing

*Bikram Pratim Bhuyan[1,2] and Manisha Singh[3]*
[1]School of Computer Science, University of Petroleum and Energy Studies (UPES), Dehradun, India
[2]LISV Laboratory, University of Paris Saclay, Velizy, France
[3]Sarvottam International School, Greater Noida, India

## 1.1 INTRODUCTION

Crowdsourcing is the practice of sourcing products, services, or ideas from a large group of people, often via the use of the Internet, rather than through more conventional means such as hiring or contacting a supplier or vendor [1]. It's a common practice to hire outsiders to do work that would otherwise be done in-house or by outside vendors. Crowdsourcing has been around for millennia, but it has only recently become a familiar and effective strategy for gathering needed services, ideas, or information thanks to the proliferation of the Internet. Organizations may now more efficiently and effectively reach a wider audience through the Internet [2]. More than ever, businesses in fields as disparate as IT, the media, and advertising employ crowdsourcing [3].

Over the years, software development processes have shifted from being done in small, tightly knit teams using more conventional approaches like the Waterfall technique to being done by massive, loosely affiliated groups utilizing the more recent and successful Agile methodology [4]. More recent software development paradigms are being investigated in response to today's software projects' growing complexity and short timelines [5]. Crowdsourcing is one example of such a notion. Some vast projects may now be open to crowdsourcing thanks to the fast growth of Internet technology and the collaborative computing idea. In a 2006 piece for *Wired*, Jeff Howe first used the term "crowdsourcing" [6]. The following

DOI: 10.1201/9781003346326-1

*1*

definition was suggested by Jeff Howe: To "crowdsource" is to outsource a formerly in-house function to an unspecified (and often huge) network of individuals via an open call for participation. In this light, the strengths of crowdsourcing, such as its open call structure and extensive network of prospective workers, become more apparent. Crowdsourcing is a method in which a significant number of individuals, rather than just one person, collaborate online to find solutions to a problem. When compared to more conventional approaches, this one is an improvement. The crowdsourcing term as a word cloud is shown in Figure 1.1.

Companies that want to take advantage of crowdsourcing must adopt platforms that provide the necessary infrastructural support. Crowdsourcing has become a reality because of recent advancements in distributed cloud computing and online social networking. The widespread use of Web 2.0 and the shifting landscape of web technology have paved the way for the creation of distributed problem-solving apps that rely on input from users worldwide [7].

Although Web 2.0 made it easier to mobilize the "knowledge of the crowd," the concept has been around for quite some time. In 1879, for instance, James Murray, a philologist and the editor of the Oxford English Dictionary, encouraged his English-speaking readers to submit references for uncommon as well as ordinary terms [8]. That's because someone wanted to compile a dictionary of English terms and their histories. The creators of the Oxford English Dictionary quickly under-stood that they would need the aid of many people to complete their monumental project. The volume of responses was so high that they were able to spur the creation of the largest and most influential English dictionary ever.

The Internet has made previously inefficient types of crowdsourcing obsolete. One clear advantage is the ease with which a large number of Internet users may be mobilized quickly. Wikipedia users share their

**FIGURE 1.1**
Crowdsourcing as a word cloud.

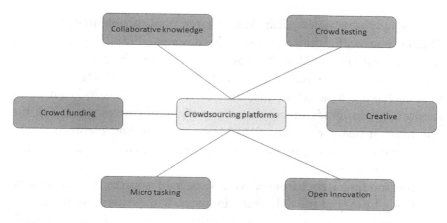

**FIGURE 1.2**
Major types of crowdsourcing platforms.

expertise with one another [9]; WikiLeaks users leak confidential papers about public issues [10]; and Kickstarter users may donate to their favorite projects [11]. The major types of crowdsourcing platforms are shown in Figure 1.2. We shall discuss in detail each type in the next section.

## 1.2 MAJOR TYPES OF CROWDSOURCING PLATFORMS

### 1.2.1 Crowdfunding as a Type of Crowdsourcing

By pooling together relatively modest contributions from several backers, crowdfunding enables startups to get much-needed investment. Crowdfunding is raising money for a good or service by tapping into preexisting social networks and online communities to match investors with those seeking to start or grow a business. This can increase entrepreneurship by widening the investor base beyond the usual suspects of business owners, friends and family, and VC firms [12].

Most legal systems typically limit the number and types of people who may invest in a start-up and the amounts they can put in. These rules are meant to prevent inexperienced or low-wealth investors from losing all their money, much as the limits on investing in hedge funds. Investors in start-up companies risk losing their first investment because of the prevalence of company failures [11]. Thanks to crowdfunding, business owners may now access cash from a large pool of potential investors. Thanks to crowdfunding, everyone who has a good idea now has a place to share it with potential backers. Someone's request for funds to develop a new tomato salad recipe is one of the funniest initiatives funded. Despite having a target of just $10, he collected $55,000 from 6,911 supporters. Hundreds of projects are available for investment, and the minimum investment is just $10. Most crowdfunding platforms make money by taking a cut of the total amount donated. Figure 1.3 clearly shows the difference.

Crowdfunding stems from a wide variety of sources. Crowdfunding has a long history in the publishing industry, with writers and publishers promoting upcoming works via subscription models. If enough people signed up to get updates on the book, it would be written and released. Since the natural flow of money does not start until the product arrives, the subscription business model cannot be considered crowdfunding. Investors' confidence is essential to risk publishing, but the list of subscribers may inspire that trust.

Startups raising money to launch a product or service and people raising money to cover unexpected expenses are the two most common examples of "traditional" crowdfunding. Due to crowdfunding websites, many victims of disasters, expensive medical bills, or other tragedies like home fires have been able to get the help they need financially. In recent years, however, crowdfunding sites like Patreon and Substack have broadened the scope of crowdsourcing to allow artists, authors, singers, and podcasters to earn a regular income [13].

Crowdfunding begins with contributions from people who also affect the value of the campaign's services and results. People suggest, choose,

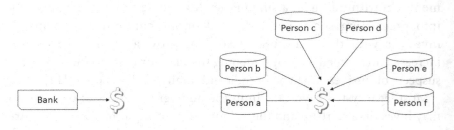

a. Traditional way of bill acquirement          b. Crowd funding way of bill acquirement

**FIGURE 1.3**
(a) Traditional method vs. (b) crowdfunding.

and advocate for initiatives in which they have invested interest. At times, they take on the role of benefactors, whose focus is on funding humanitarian initiatives. When they believe in the product enough to become shareholders, they can help it mature and expand. To rally others behind causes they believe in, people often share information about such causes with their online networks (promoters).

Feeling at least somewhat responsible for the success of others' endeavors (desire for patronage), wanting to be a part of a collaborative social initiative (desire for social participation), and hoping to reap some financial reward from one's financial contributions all motivate consumers to get involved (passion for investment). Crowdfunding allows people to get their hands on novel things before the general public. In many cases, early access gives backers a better chance to have input on the product's evolution. Family and friends of a creative are other groups that find crowdfunding appealing. It helps facilitate communication between the parties and settle disagreements over the project's budget and scope.

Crowdfunding participants typically share three distinguishing characteristics: an innovative orientation (which motivates them to try new ways of interacting with firms and other consumers); a social identification (with) the content, cause, or project selected for funding (which motivates them to want to be a part of the initiative); and (monetary) exploitation (which motivates them to participate because they expect to be exploited in some way). To make money, crowdfunding sites need to attract interesting projects and willing backers. These websites are attempting to get extensive exposure for their services and products.

Crowdfunding's most notable benefit for a new business or person is the increased likelihood of receiving financial backing from a wide variety of people. Because of the widespread use of social media, crowdfunding platforms provide a fantastic opportunity for companies and individuals to reach a larger audience and get much-needed financial backing.

In addition, many crowdfunding initiatives provide benefits to backers, such as early access to a product or a special gift. A company that develops a bacon fat soap may give out samples to its investors. Gamers often participate in video game development projects via crowdfunding platforms in exchange for early access copies of the game.

Crowdfunding via the sale of equity is becoming more popular as a means for startups to get finance without ceding control to traditional investors like venture capitalists. It may also provide investors with a chance to gain ownership of the business. Equity crowdfunding in the United States is governed by the Securities and Exchange Commission (SEC) [14].

Crowdfunding has a number of potential drawbacks, including the possibility of damage to our or our company's reputation due to "resorting" to crowdfunding, fees associated with the crowdfunding site, and, at least on some platforms, the return of all pledged funds to investors if we don't meet our funding goal.

Many popular and profitable companies and products were first financed by Kickstarter backers. One American firm that specializes in VR gear and software, Oculus VR, received funding from the platform. Palmer Luckey, the company's creator, used Kickstarter to help bring virtual reality gaming headgear to developers in 2012. Ten times the initial target of $250,000 was raised via the crowdsourcing effort [15].

As of March 2014, Facebook, now known as Meta (META), has paid $2.3 billion in cash and shares to buy Oculus VR. M3D, a manufacturer of tiny 3D printers created by two friends, is another example of a firm that achieved success with the aid of Kickstarter campaigns [16]. Micro 3D printer creators David Jones and Michael Armani earned $3.4 million on Kickstarter in 2014. The portable 3D printer, sold at Staples, Amazon.com, Inc. (AMZN), Brookstone, and others, comes with a selection of long-lasting 3D inks [16].

In April, the newest animated special for Critical Role, a weekly live-streamed tabletop role-playing game starring a collection of notable voice actors, earned $4.7 million in only 24 hours. No other 30- to 60-day fundraising effort on Kickstarter in 2019 came close to that amount [17].

## 1.2.2 Microtasking as a Type of Crowdsourcing

Microtasking is the practice of dividing a massive task into many smaller ones so that it may be distributed among several people. This is often done through the Internet to an enormous workforce. These responsibilities fall on human shoulders; they are often referred to as "HITs" (Human Intelligence Tasks) [18]. As a result, they can't be delegated to robots or executed by computers. In the first place, we need to think about the general duties. Large-scale jobs that can be broken down into smaller, more manageable chunks and require a human viewpoint are ideal candidates for automation [18].

Micro jobs are short-term jobs often arranged on the fly through the Internet. The work may take place in a virtual space, including creating articles, sorting comments, or translating. On the other hand, offline jobs include being a handyman, babysitter, or dog walker. In this glossary article, we'll be referring to the online version. Microwork sites such as clickworker.com are plentiful these days [19]. There is a need for many of these positions so that artificial intelligence (AI) may be developed, which has broad business and societal implications. Micro jobs differ from conventional jobs in that they are repetitive, may be finished in 5–10 seconds, and pay a predetermined sum [19]. Although micro jobs don't need any particular credentials, they may be subdivided into individuals who possess a specific talent, native language, or other qualities valued by the customer.

After signing up for a service like clickworker.com, workers may use the site's microtasks [20]. The system will determine which jobs should be assigned to which employees. This may rely on language, population, expertise, interests, experience level, and more. Microtasks are often done on a personal computer or laptop at home. Of course, these days, plenty of businesses also have applications. To provide just one example, the clickworker app is excellent for tasks requiring employees to record themselves or household objects on camera. Since certain microtasks need workers in the field, a reliable mobile website and app are essential. Pictures of storefront displays, vehicles, landscapes, and other things of interest may be required for such jobs [21]. This is because there are several approaches to doing the same activities, allowing a larger pool of potential employees to participate. Projects can be finished on schedule as a result.

Many customers use platforms to learn new information, improve their software and AI, test new ideas, and get feedback and final goods. One method of data collection is to have employees visit certain websites in search of a desired feature or piece of information. There are many various ways in which AI is progressing at the moment, one of which is the ability to teach voice-activated products to recognize and respond to variations in accent. This might go as far as having software in an autonomous vehicle display potential roadside obstacles. Simple surveys or in-depth product analyses might be used to gather comments and suggestions. On the other hand, it may also be obtained via mystery shopping or site visits. Some customers may need personnel to develop customized solutions. By having many employees contribute to the same blog, for instance [22].

As a result, micro-tasking will be implemented differently across various platforms. However, the best systems will provide users with several customization possibilities. Some customers choose a self-service model for their smaller, more straightforward tasks. Here, the customer may manually enter the necessary tasks and any relevant specifications and directions. The platform administration may have a peek at the micro-tasking project to make sure everything is functioning well, but they won't have much say otherwise. Another option is to lay out the project's specifics and work closely with the platform's management to develop a unique solution that meets all client's needs.

After thoroughly trying and testing the product, it may be made available to employees online. The employees will be provided with detailed guidelines and examples to follow. Sites like clickworker.com have several checks and balances to ensure the highest quality of labor. We may use a few different approaches to ensure quality control in this area. To ensure everything is done precisely, a quality control worker or team will randomly inspect the work of numerous other employees. It's essential to examine our work since specific customers insist on it [22]. For this reason, finished microtasks are sent to a queue where they await approval or rejection from a higher-up. Workers are sometimes allowed to revise and resubmit work flagged for correction. Compilation, formatting, and delivery to the client will occur when all checks have been performed.

It has been determined that before the implementation of lockdowns and curfews due to the COVID epidemic, around one-third of online crowd workers were female. Gender disparities in pandemic lockdowns are unclear, although women continue to be primarily responsible for caring for infants, young children, the disabled, and the elderly. These tasks are not amenable to strict scheduling, are not readily (if at all) delegatable, and may make it impossible to maintain a career outside the house. People are more likely to get their work done when children are at school or when other dependents are sleeping.

Swagbucks is an online community where users may do little tasks for SB points. It's easy for anybody to get by simply submitting comments after using their search bar, viewing movies, playing games, or completing surveys [23]. Typically, respondents must answer a few qualifying questions to prove they are regular purchasers of a particular product or brand before moving on to the actual duties. SB points are redeemable for gift cards to stores such as Amazon, Target, Starbucks, and PayPal and may even be earned by referring friends who join up [23]. Those who are financially motivated may easily make $100 or more monthly.

TaskRabbit is one of the most well-known online marketplaces for hiring people to help us with physical labor at home or in the office [24]. It is available at around 50 U.S., Canadian, and U.K. locations. Users needing help will publish their requests along with a rough budget estimate. They will be notified if the offered rate meets the "Tasker's" salary expectations [24]. There might be some haggling about each activity's relative ease or difficulty, the amount of time and distance involved, and the resources they'll require. From the bids provided by potential Taskers, the task owner selects the best one.

Seventy percent of Taskers have bachelor's degrees, 20 percent have master's degrees, and 5 percent have doctorates, according to Wikipedia. As a result of taking on several little jobs, some people can make a living solely via TaskRabbit. Manufacturers of flat-pack furniture in Sweden IKEA began suggesting the site to customers in the United Kingdom who were interested in having someone else build their table. As a result of the company's high level of customer satisfaction, IKEA purchased TaskRabbit in 2017 [24].

Although computers are becoming better at tasks like data deduplication and research, there are still plenty of jobs that humans do considerably better. We call them "HITs" [25]. For example, marking receipts is a simple, mundane chore.

Established in 2005, Amazon Mechanical Turk (MTurk) [26] is a frontrunner in the micro-tasking industry. It facilitates using a remote, dispersed workforce to carry out routine, repetitive activities for organizations and people.

Around half a million people use MTurk every month to do millions of jobs, including labeling photographs, filling out surveys, transcribing receipts, and crowdsourcing 0.01 dollars. A 2018 academic research looked over 3.8 million Amazon MTurk activities done by 2,676 employees and concluded that they earned an average of $2 per hour using the site. However, only around 20 percent of Turkers complete the site's jobs regularly [26]. These individuals accomplish their work more quickly and efficiently than the rest of the Turking community by using various tools and browser extensions. This MTurk gig has the potential to be a respectable side business for many Turks.

### 1.2.3 Open Innovation as a Type of Crowdsourcing

We may maintain our business on the leading edge of product and service innovation without breaking the bank by using either open innovation (also known as a user, cumulative, mass, or distributed innovation or as know-how trade) or crowdsourcing. However, their work falls short of our expectations if we don't use them correctly. First, we must know when to use open innovation and when crowdsourcing is the best choice. After that, success will come from using the appropriate channels at the right moments. These innovative approaches will get us to the end zone.

To innovate openly is to draw in the oration for new ideas from inside and outside a company. Conventional wisdom is that crowdsourcing means asking the public for suggestions. In most cases, it's best to welcome thoughts from all directions. Employees are our finest resource for ideas that fit perfectly inside our present company model and goals, and we may not have to pay for them (though we should be open to offering a bonus for exceptional ones).

Ideas from outside sources may come from anywhere, and their diversity and originality can enrich any project. However, they lack in-depth familiarity with our current product line. Unfortunately, these suggestions don't always gel with our established procedures. One of the characteristics of a creative company is its members' openness to new ideas and strategies. It would be best to consider whether our company's innovation has to be handled by an inside team, an external group like a crowdsourcing combination of the two, or open innovation.

Crowdsourcing is ideal when there is time to wait for ideas to come in, go through and pick the finest views, and bring the concept into production and testing before it enters the market. The issue is that many companies resort to crowdsourcing when they have an urgent need. Crowdsourcing that an open community won't have time to do its homework and provide well-considered, carefully planned solutions if we work under a tight deadline. Either push out the due date or hire staff from inside to work under pressure.

While both mTurk and 99designs provide crowdsourcing opportunities, they couldn't be more different [27]. To paraphrase an adage, "crowdsourcing sites are like dating sites and social networking platforms," submit our project to one of the knowledgeable professionals about our particular sort of project. Avoid becoming too specialized unless necessary.

That is to say; we shouldn't provide a simple task to a team of experts willing to work on it for free via crowdsourcing. We shouldn't post a highly technical, specialized project on a crowdsourcing platform when most users are in their early 20s.

Some companies utilize crowdsourcing platforms to collect a mountain of ideas they never plan to deploy. There are several problems with this strategy. To begin with, it's not right. Those who use crowdsourcing fronts to share ideas they feel, they deserve serious attention; are doomed to disappointment. Don't make those eager to pitch in and assist out feel like their contributions to good ideas are being wasted. Second, we're just being wasteful. Waste neither crowdsourcing companies by proposing and gathering ideas for projects that will never result in a saleable product. Third, we risk gaining a reputation as a time-waster, making it impossible to return to the crowdsourcing groups we've already exploited in times of genuine need. If feasible, submit only requests for ideas we intend to implement.

Make sure we're asking for a solution to a real issue or a genuine need if we want our submitted ideas to be taken seriously. If we wish to help me to help, we need to be specific. Don't make queries that are too broad if we want particular answers to help us; weaning fresh innovation ideas isn't the only benefit of open innovation and crowdsourcing. They are also an intelligent strategy for enhancing established concepts—attempts at a design that fell short for one reason or another. We discarded development projects that didn't make it through the testing phase. Products that failed to gain traction in the market were subsequently pulled off shelves. Open innovation and crowdsourcing may give new life to outdated or undefined endeavors, saving them from the excellent gadget cemetery.

We may become an innovation success story by releasing a steady stream of novel items to the market and strategically using the priceless mass innovation resources at our disposal. Are we prepared to get the instruments necessary to oversee the innovation procedure internally and externally?

Several significant advantages of open innovation may be seen when compared to more conventional forms of research and development in corporations: Open innovation helps businesses to reap the benefits of a wider variety of creative solutions to problems because it invites and encourages input from a broader range of skills and experience. A common problem with conventional product development is that it is carried out in isolated silos, with different parts of an organization (or even other teams within the same department) reluctant to work together or exchange information. This resistance may be overcome with the support of open innovation. Reduce the price of innovation: The expense of producing new goods and services from scratch sometimes exceeds the cost of acquiring the necessary level of expertise. Open innovation may save businesses money on brainstorming by enlisting the help of people outside the company. More quickly moving from proof of concept to pilot and testing, thanks to open innovation's broader pool of expertise. Why? Because addressing problems, and crowdsourcing large groups of people is much faster. Collaboration outside the company is a terrific approach to increasing innovation and bringing attention to the final product. That's because an enthusiastic band of supporters is already working hard on the end product. Raising interest from every wing company, and available innovative crowdsourcing tools for doing just that. When a start-up wants to prove its market presence and get attention, it might invite people outside the company to join in the innovation process.

To maintain its position as a global leader in technology, Samsung must continually develop innovative new products and services. Open innovation is an essential strategy used by Samsung in this regard [28]. Because of this need for access to cutting-edge knowledge and ideas for new goods and services, Samsung is a member of 13 international industrial consortiums. Through its academic alliances, Samsung has strong links with several schools. This is shown in Figure 1.4.

Such a varied strategy for open innovation exemplifies that good ideas may come from anyone. With the support of academics and other professionals, Samsung can strengthen its competitive position and prepare for the next major shift in the industry.

Google's rise to prominence as one of the world's leading corporations may be attributed in no little part to the company's persistent dedication to the crowdsourcing model [29]. Google is aware that valuable data may be found in many places. This is why the corporation offers rewards for such contributions; they help the organization improve its goods' quality, timeliness, and utility.

Google Maps is a superb illustration of the company's dedication to crowdsourcing [29]. The platform is built with a dedication to crowd-sourcing as a foundational tenet, with each user's input included in the

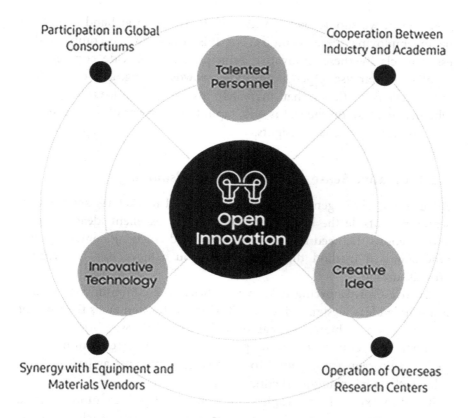

**FIGURE 1.4**
Samsung's open innovation strategy prioritizes collaboration with research institutions.

system to maintain the accuracy of journey data. Since it has crowdsourcing in place, many people probably no longer recognize it as crowdsourcing.

Lego is one of the most well-known toy manufacturers in the world, with a sizable fan base that is always willing to provide constructive criticism and innovative suggestions for new products [30]. The crowdsourcing of this group, Lego launched its Ideas portal, whereby supporters may submit ideas and vote on the best ones to be produced by the company.

Over a million Lego enthusiasts have used this site to suggest new products in the ten years since it crowdsourced. Lego's worldwide popularity has been strengthened, and the brand has received positive coverage thanks to the platform. These methods will help us accelerate the creation of new ideas, launch crowdsourcing innovation initiatives, and tap into the potential of our online fan base and clientele.

However, we should have an idea of the situation at hand before we begin employing these methods. For this reason, we've compiled this essay to clarify these innovative principles, and provide concrete examples of their use. Open innovation, crowdsourcing, and co-creation are excellent methods that may help us with crowdsourcing goals, whether to shake up the status quo, tap into the power of the masses, or generate novel, valuable insights.

### 1.2.4 Creative Sense as a Type of Crowdsourcing

Advertisers (both agency employees and brand marketers) should start searching outside the box to efficiently obtain excellent ideas, designs, and videos as the need for more authentic and engaging content grows. One standard method that might help you achieve this is "creative crowdsourcing."

Creative crowdsourcing is known as briefing a community to source innovative ideas, designs, videos, and material. It often takes the form of a competition with an open call or an invite-only/closed brief. For this context, "the crowd" refers to professional creative communities or people who regularly respond to creative requirements as part of their jobs in the advertising/marketing sector.

Brand-intoxicated catastrophes (for example, Pepsi) are more possible when a company puts all its resources into one area, such as hiring people to drink the company's kool-aid. If you're having trouble coming up with a solution to a problem, try using creative crowdsourcing to solicit input from a diverse group of people who aren't invested in the outcome (like consumers) but who will respond if inspired, won't be afraid to disagree with their executive creative director , and will submit ideas that are on-brand and effective.

That final point may seem apparent, but most agencies will agree that after a long time has passed working with a client, the agency becomes adept at producing thoughts and work that the client would like rather than what the customer needs.

We may enjoy the benefits of creative crowdsourcing by giving people a say in what they want. If you provide the same brief to a hundred skilled creatives, you'll get a hundred unique solutions, each of which will be on brand and adhere to the brief in its unique way. We are turning the status quo on its head by having just one intermediary between you and hundreds of creative brains rather than twenty agency employees.

Marketers may save a lot of money by not having to pay for those 20 agency employees (and short filters). The overhead expenses of conventional methods only rise yearly; by appealing to the correct audience with a well-defined brief and reward, you may avoid this. Many agencies don't employ creative crowdsourcing, even if it would benefit their bottom lines and the quality of their work.

When we want to try out a new creative source or media channel, it's hard to be innovative and surprising if we stick to our typical ways. Every day brings new inventions and tools; why not consult the artists who are already fluent in them or eager to expand their skill set?

Similar to outsourcing, crowdsourcing involves tapping the general public's talents to create new ideas, collect data, or carry out other activities. Taking a task that would usually be performed by a designated agent (typically an employee) and outsourcing it to an undefined, generally large group of people in the form of an open call, commonly using the Internet, is what crowdsourcing is, according to Jeff Howe, king of crowdsourcing and contributing editor at *Wired*. "Undefined" and "open call" are the two main concepts. There are instances when an "open call" is the best option rather than going with the first person who comes to mind as most qualified for the position. Due mainly to the company's co-creation of Crash, the Super Bowl campaign, Doritos commercials have consistently rated in the top five of USA Today's Ad Meter rankings for the best Super Bowl advertisements for the last nine years. When appropriately executed, crowdsourcing may be an excellent strategy for connecting with your target demographic and broadening the scope of your project.

Crowdfunding isn't a sure thing. The National Environment Research Council (NERC) held a public naming contest for their new Antarctic research vessel in March 2016 [31]. Over 120,000 people had voted for RRS Boaty McBoatface by the time the poll closed in April. Ultimately, a smaller auto-ship was given the winning moniker, and the research ship was renamed after Sir David Attenborough [31], despite widespread support for Boaty McBoatface. Angry reactions were heard from the general populace.

It's similar to Walkers's "Choose Me or Lose Me" ad campaign. Walkers Crisp's customers were given the option of trying either a new or a traditional flavor. Traditional British flavors were pitted against the 'new' ones, which were already well-liked in other countries. Walker's 'Choose Me or Lose Me' branded crisps were sold individually, or consumers could vote in a poll on the company's website. After ten weeks and 778,636 votes, the campaign increased value sales of the core class flavors by 19 percent [32].

The victory of British flavors was met with widespread approval. By limiting available choices, Walkers were able to maintain their authority. Crowdsourcing curation is crucial, and if you can't do that, at least try to embrace crowd creativity, even if it doesn't turn out exactly as planned.

Using crowdsourcing, businesses can tap into the collective brainpower of their target audience. It's not just an excuse to avoid responsibility. Andy Nairn, the co-founder of Lucky General, says, "if it were that simple, the crowd would be starting up their agency" [32]. There is a narrow line between asking your audience to do work for free and asking them to do work for no reward, and we should keep that in mind while engaging in crowdsourcing. When customers participate in crowdsourcing, they feel they have a voice. Understanding your audience's true desires might be a matter of life and death in certain situations. In any case, crowdsourcing is an excellent method that will only grow in popularity in the years to come.

Until recently, company owners who lacked an in-house creative team had to hire a pricey agency full of copywriters, art directors, and strategists. They know what they're doing and have run campaigns previously, but their experience and training unavoidably constrain their view. In the wake of blunders like Pepsi's Kendall Jenner fiasco, many have wondered, "How did this ever get approved?" Veterans of the advertising business understood why: the agency model is constrained by antiquated systems, rigid protocols, and dogmatic managers. Many people are afraid to dissuade their customers from poor decisions for fear of losing business.

Crowdsourcing has become a common way to get things done, whether for finding innovative solutions or writing content. For example, Write Label is driven by a network of thousands of authors worldwide. You shouldn't feel wrong about being afraid to go in headfirst. Here, we listed three main advantages company owners may reap by tapping into the power of crowdsourcing creativity to give you that additional push.

Write Label's concept is so effective that it draws from a "brain bank" of individuals with different opinions, worldviews, and experiences to influence their own. Agencies will always have problems including all voices as long as most of their employees are white-collar workers and college grads with degrees in communications. Crowdsourcing allows you to get the wide range of opinions necessary to effectively communicate in today's multiethnic society and connect with customers from traditionally underserved communities.

As a company owner, the bottom line is always on your mind, regardless of how much you care about the goods or services you provide. And how could it not be in these economically unstable times? The bottom line is that using a crowd for creative work saves money without lowering quality. Using a "team" of prescreened, self-selected creatives may save expenses and provide high-quality results. Crowdsourcing is an alternative advertising approach that is particularly attractive to small company owners due to its low cost.

Anyone who has seen *Mad Men* knows that pitching an advertising campaign may take a long time, often months. By comparison, analyzing crowdsourced ideas, copy, design, etc., may take just a few hours from the time you hit "send" on a brief with copy points. Advertising campaigns rely heavily on their creative execution, and crowdsourcing is a fast, straightforward approach to finding original ideas.

## 1.2.5 Crowd Testing as a Type of Crowdsourcing

Crowdtested, also known as crowdsourced testing, is a method of testing that uses the expertise and resources of a large group of people. In this method, customers undertake various real-world tests on various real-world services using real-world devices. As a result, crowdsourced testing not only aids in detecting defects and errors but also provides you with helpful input on user experience, which is something that conventional automated testing or testing with MTurk cannot accomplish.

Recent years have seen a meteoric rise in the popularity of mobile applications. Whether for business or play, there's an app for anything now. The software thoroughly tested and released quickly is more important than ever in today's cutthroat business climate. Business success depends on how quickly companies can provide reliable, well-designed software. They put new products through extensive quality assurance (QA) testing to ensure their dependability, security, and usability.

However, conventional testing methods are inadequate due to the wide variety of hardware, software, and web browsers in use today. Crowdsourced testing may provide a quicker and cheaper alternative to traditional QA testing.

In QA, crowdsourced testing (or crowdtesting) is a novel technique. It integrates human expertise with technological means to remedy issues with traditional testing.

Crowdsourcing is an alternative to in-house testing that employs a temporary, distributed team of independent testers. In-house testing teams can't keep up with the speed and efficiency of this on-demand community of testers. With crowdtesting, businesses can have their goods evaluated by consumers worldwide using their own devices.

Since crowd testers come from around the world, they can provide continuous service. By having more individuals test under a wider variety of settings, developers increase the likelihood that any problems will be found and fixed.

In-house QA teams have vital product expertise and are aligned with the company's values and objectives; community testers cannot replace them. To better respond to fluctuations in demand, we want to use crowdsourced testers to improve our current capabilities.

Companies like Global App Testing [33] specialize in managing teams of crowd testers on clients' behalf. Throughout the product development process, they may pair you with expert testers who fit your target audience.

The concept of a system or product devoid of flaws is idealistic and unrealistic. While experienced testers do their best to cover all bases, there is no such thing as "full" testing.

One reason is that an endless amount of potential inputs to a program makes it impossible to test all of them. The limited number of test cases available to testers may not be enough to uncover all input-related flaws. There is no way to simulate every scenario that might occur in the program, nor can you test for every possible failure, such as those resulting from complicated design flaws or inadequate requirements analysis. And since the system's behavior is contingent on the actual world, simulating every conceivable setting is not practical. Even the simplest of programs rely on an operating system, making them vulnerable to flaws.

However, adopting crowdsourced testing increases the likelihood of finding flaws, as more people will be looking for crowdsourcing techniques like exploratory testing (which involves learning, test design, and test execution all at once) and regression testing (which consists in re-evaluating the whole application after any change has been made to ensure it hasn't broken anything) may be instrumental [33].

Crowdsourced and outsourced testing have specific characteristics. Thus, it's understandable that they might be mistaken for one another. Both approaches let companies finish niche jobs that would be too expensive or time-consuming in-house.

When you outsource testing, you work with an outside business to conduct your evaluations. Everything, from crowdsourcing resources to managing the project and gathering feedback, will be handled by this firm. When working with sensitive information, non-disclosure agreements (NDAs) are often required [33]. As we've seen, the testing portion of crowdsourcing is carried out by many people in many places. It's easier to scale than outsourcing, but you may have to take care of the administration yourself. The key benefit is having access to testers whenever you need them without the cost of maintaining a full-time in-house group. Crowd testers are usually crowdsourced on the number of flaws they uncover, whereas outsourced testers are always paid the same amount.

Crowdtesting is an option if your QA team is short on time and you need to release a new product. But before you jump, you should weigh the benefits and drawbacks. Crowdsourced testing is beneficial for augmenting smaller QA teams since it allows input from various individuals. For groups with fluctuating testing demands, crowdsourcing may increase testing resources as needed, such as before a major release.

Crowdtesting allows businesses with limited testing resources to expand their testing breadth and coverage while employing a crowdsourcing platform for routine QA chores will enable them to use their available workforce better. Meanwhile, it works well in later phases of development when the product has become too complicated for a crowdsourcing team to test every scenario.

Software development approaches like continuous integration (CI) and continuous delivery (CD) are essential when releasing new applications and features. As we said before, crowdsourcing improves efficiency since more people are testing the product, and they can do so at any time. Therefore, they can provide outcomes considerably more rapidly than in-house groups.

In-house testing involves finding, interviewing, hiring, training, and onboarding employees, whereas crowd testers are already trained and ready to go the moment you need them. Because of this, you won't have to spend as much on administrative expenditures, employee hiring and training, paid time off, medical leave, or retirement plans. Additionally, crowdsourcing's scalability makes it more adaptable than human and automated testing. You can keep a stable in-house crew most of the time and augment them with community testers when needed.

Tests that rely on the public tend to be more thorough. If the in-house team is overly invested in the project, they may miss issues that a more extensive network of testers would catch testers. Since most crowd testers do not work for a particular company, their opinions are objective.

New applications, websites, and SaaS products must be tested across various devices (PCs, tablets, wearables, smart TVs, and appliances) and operating systems before being released to the public (Android, iOS, Windows, Linux) [33]. A more varied pool of testers is an obvious way to increase the number of devices tested. For the same reason, usability testing is a perfect fit for crowdsourcing, improving UX, and providing invaluable insight. The success of a new piece of software hinges on its ability to meet the needs of the target audience, which may be achieved by drawing on the broadest possible spectrum of expertise and insight. In conclusion, crowdsourced testing uses people from around the world, speaking many languages. Any testing has potential drawbacks. Confidentiality is a significant concern in crowdsourcing projects since it might be more challenging to maintain with a distributed team. When looking for a crowdtesting service, it's ideal to prioritize those that provide guarantees like NDAs. Still, applications that need a high degree of security may not be the most outstanding candidates for crowd-sourced testing.

Crowdsourced testers' dependability is another potential drawback that should be investigated before contracting with them. Due to the testers' geographical dispersion, it may be more challenging to have an open line of communication and avoid misunderstandings or partial findings.

Keep in mind that you may need to take on the role of project manager as well to oversee the remote testers and ensure they are meeting all of their objectives. Having a QA team whose members are acquainted with the company's procedures and the software being tested would make this process smoother. If a tester's salary is contingent on the number of defects discovered, they mustn't put quantity before quality. A crowd-sourced testing group may not have the same emotional investment in the project's success or the company's overall mission as an in-house team would.

There are many benefits to using remote labor; however, challenges must be considered, such as the impact of time zones and cultural variations on the testing process. Assuring that everyone is on the same page requires some deft maneuvering.

## 1.2.6 Collaborative Knowledge as a Type of Crowdsourcing

The Internet has made available a plethora of programs, services, instructional materials, and networking venues where consumers and experts in various fields may interact with one another. It has made the world smaller by eliminating physical distance as a barrier to communication, participation, and remote employment. The Internet has made it possible for organizations to form interdisciplinary work teams whose members are spread throughout the country or even the world but who can collaborate on a single project and share their expertise as if they were all in the same room.

The Internet has become the backbone of many new businesses, facilitating communication and cooperation among employees. In addition, it serves as a hub for those who want to share their excitement and ideas with others and work together on a project that may have its roots in online resources such as human and financial capital.

Human experts must put much time and effort into the knowledge organization's work. According to a recent review [34], it is now widely accepted that communities should be in charge of building and maintaining knowledge bases and ontologies [35] with the help of tools that serve as collaboration platforms and allow ontology stakeholders [36] to talk to one another about their concerns and share their ideas. This is why several ontology frameworks [37] for expert-level ontology generation, and integration have been developed in recent years [38].

Professional grade knowledge organization schemes and ontologies can only be built by specialists, who are both challenging to discover and costly to hire. Furthermore, [39] claim that consumer-oriented apps cannot get enough support when coupled with specialist medical terminologies like SNOMED CT since these terminologies do not contain the profane language necessary for these applications.

The evolution of Internet technology has allowed regular people to produce content, contribute to the community, share that content, and connect with others. Collective intelligence occurs when users learn to maximize the benefits of networked communications. This allows for a transition from individual to group efforts and the possibility of a more nuanced and comprehensive representation of cultural heritage. Cultural heritage institutions have long been seen as the go-to places for information on how cultural artifacts should be represented and organized and for creating norms, standards, and procedures for doing so. However, the massive expansion of cultural heritage holdings and the urge to make these collections available to the public have recently emerged as driving factors behind crowdsourcing initiatives.

Many online museums and archive initiatives use the "wisdom of crowds" [40] to assign tags to items based on the public's common knowledge. Steve [40], and Powerhouse museums let visitors freely tag museum artifacts on their websites. Together, users of these projects may add tags to museum artifacts and see both the curator-supplied information and the user-assigned tags. These initiatives use a tag-based resource discovery system that makes it easy to get data through a cloud of tags. Because many of the menus are handwritten or feature creative fonts and layouts that are not identifiable by automatic translation techniques, the New York Public Library (NYPL) has launched a crowdsourcing effort to have individuals transcribe its historical menu collection.

Researchers will benefit from having access to a searchable menu collection that includes information on items, pricing, and the structure of meals.

Without professional oversight or curation, the most crucial part of crowdsourcing is getting people who disagree to agree on something. You may do this in three ways: There are three ways to create a unified ontology: 1) by intersection, where only the commonalities between users' ontologies or classification schemes are included; 2) by the union, where all the components built by different users are included; and 3) by revision, where users may independently revise each other's ontological components to arrive at a consensus ontology version [41].

Harmonious multi-perspective knowledge representations obtained via collaborative efforts face several challenges. Acknowledging and capitalizing on such variety requires understanding the underlying barriers that must be overcome. The difficulty of identifying and agreeing upon the components of such representations, particularly in the context of new forms and genres, is fundamental. Knowledge representation is therefore said to be subject to context, as in the case of the model of biological ideas in biology and forensics. Also, just as with any translation, there is always the risk that some fundamental concepts may be lost in communicating across languages and cultures. Last but not least, even "universal" terms, like those describing kinship, vary greatly, even if the phenomena itself is understood in roughly the same manner in different cultures. Finding a method for incorporating (rather than hiding or disregarding) this variety will result in systems that respect and value everyone's input while keeping everyone's unique qualities intact.

Using technology for selecting and controlling knowledge organization schemes created by crowd work is an alternate technique to capitalizing on crowdsourcing without needing professional curation. The basic concept is to hire a swarm of unidentified people to do a certain tiny microtask using a crowdsourcing website like MTurk or CrowdFlower [26]. Each employee is given a list of tasks to do, such as questions with many responses, from which they must choose the one they believe to be most accurate. Site employees may be given a preliminary exam on a subset of qualifying questions to raise the bar for the quality of their responses, with only "the trusted workers," or those who scored well on the test, moving on to participate in the main experiment.

There is no requirement for obtaining an inter-worker agreement in technologically regulated crowd work, in contrast to collaborative social crowdsourcing, since employees complete a succession of basic tasks autonomously without interacting with one another. Instead, the collective choice is computed automatically by applying aggregation measures or algorithms to the individual employees' inputs. In several fields, including economics, healthcare, and cultural heritage, such aggregated group judgments have been proven to be as excellent as the answers provided by the subject expert but at a significantly lower cost.

To accommodate open access to crowdsourced collections, cultural heritage organizations must rethink their authoritative stance. Given the limitations of crowdsourced data (such as missing or incorrect information or misspelled words), the challenge becomes how to make the most of the collective brainpower to make accurate data available. It is time to reconsider the role of cultural institutions in crowdsourcing initiatives, given that the primary goal of knowledge representation and organization systems is to provide a user with the "best textual means to his aim". The audience in a project like the NYPL's "What's on the menu?" is limited to transcribing and editing the data provided. At the same time, the library's representatives retain complete control over the project's monitoring and QA. In Foucault's theory of power, the ubiquitous panoptical system in our civilization reduces all individuals to the submissive role of the gazed-upon subject. However, crowdsourcing might pose a threat to the current social order. The extensive nature of contributions made to cultural heritage crowdsourcing projects necessitates a reevaluation of authority structures and a switch from a centralized to a decentralized division of labor, with authority being delegated to passionate contributors backed by "intelligent" technological advancements.

---

## 1.3 THE GOOD, BAD, AND UGLY OF CROWDSOURCING

In all likelihood, crowdsourcing has become more divisive in the wake of its success than ever before. Over 2,000 different crowdsourcing platforms are listed on crowdsourcing.org, which bills itself as a nexus for the sector. When discussing the ethical concerns associated with crowdsourcing, it's easy to make blanket remarks because of the wide variety of platforms. One criticism, however, stands out as particularly pervasive, and it is the charge of exploitation, which is often leveled against crowdsourcing. Not surprisingly, Jimmy Wales is a leading opponent of crowdsourcing. He calls crowdsourcing a "vile phrase" and thinks the economic model it's based on is just a ploy to "trick people into doing labor for nothing" [26].

Given that Wikipedia relies entirely on unpaid volunteers, why is it seldom accused of exploitation? Common sense tells us much about what constitutes exploitation, but putting specific words to the concept may be difficult. This is especially true when the exploited person can click "yes" from the comfort of their own home without fear of physical coercion or when free labor is mainly seen as a joyful activity, despite someone else making a significant profit from it. Marx conducted the most comprehensive academic investigation of exploitation [40]. Still, his work is so fundamental and technical that it diverts attention away from the innate sense of justice that every one of us has. Robert Mayer, a philosopher, and political theorist offers a new way of looking at the issue of exploitation in his book *What's Wrong With Exploitation* [39]. Even when the two parties profit from one another's company, he argues that exploiters nonetheless do damage by neglecting to assist their victims as fairness demands. Mayer makes it apparent that employees are exploited when they do not obtain a fair part of the value they generate, even if they are, in absolute terms, somewhat better off (for example, by earning around $1.50 per hour on Amazon's MTurk instead of earning nothing). According to Mayer, coercion is a distinct evil and not a prerequisite for exploitation; hence, forced labor is not required for the word to apply [42].

It is not necessary to debate what constitutes fair treatment of others; it is sufficient to mistreat individuals. Another problematic issue that Robert Mayer raises is the use of legal sanctions [43]. Abolishing exploitative working circumstances may make people's lives worse in the near term because they lose the little money they get from being exploited rather than gradually improving conditions toward greater justice. An issue that crowd workers often raise when laws to prevent the use of crowdsourcing are being debated.

Some recent outside initiatives have addressed these issues in commercial crowdsourcing. Christopher Otey has sued CrowdFlower, one of the world's most powerful cognitive piecework platforms, in a class action lawsuit in California [44]. Whether or not crowd workers are independent contractors who are not entitled to the minimum pay under the Fair Labor Standards Act is at the heart of the dispute. The lawsuit might determine whether or not crowd workers in the United States would be required to pay the federal minimum wage of $7.25 per hour, up from the current average of $1.25 to $2.50 [45]. The lawsuit casts doubt on the viability of the crowdsourcing sector in the United States.

When viewed internationally, though, national labor regulations don't pose much of a threat to crowdsourcing. Initiatives by workers to foster cohesion and combat information inequality seem more promising in this setting. One such tool is Turkopticon [46], a browser extension created by Lilly Irani to empower Amazon's so-called "Turkers" by letting them "report and avoid unethical personnel." Since no one else appears to be looking out for the crowd in crowdsourcing, the site asserts that it will.

Many people's time and effort are donated online for the common benefit rather than for financial gain. Wikipedia is the model of "commons-based peer production," as Yochai Benkler terms it, in which many people work together for the benefit of everyone [47]. Despite being supported by unpaid labor, Wikipedia is not often seen as exploitation for the reasons stated above.

Therefore, is it preferable to not compensate donors rather than to compensate them inadequately? If you assist in solving tough design challenges for IDEO's customers on OpenIDEO, all you'll get in return is some gamification points, some experience, and maybe some visibility [48]. It is not clear to donors who exactly benefits from the work done on this platform, even if the projects often address problems that appear helpful for the greater good. When Singapore, for instance, contracts the for-profit design consultancy IDEO to crowdsource sustainable and community-oriented ideas for the city, this is an example of a town using OpenIDEO. IDEO undoubtedly spends a great deal of time and resources managing its creative volunteer population, but it is not clear to the participants what IDEO receives in return.

The Reality Drop crowdsourcing site created by Al Gore employs gamification to encourage users to "Spread Science regarding Climate Change, Global Warming." Human spam bots may stock up on weapons and ammunition here before being sent to "spread the truth" and "demolish denial." This group earns points by cutting and pasting brief, pre-written arguments into Internet debates and then linking back to the fuller versions of these arguments on the website Reality Drop [49]. Articles that raise doubts about global warming are the intended target. Such organized propaganda battle in the comment sections highlights the manipulative power of crowdsourcing, even if the aim is just and pure.

There has been a rise in the utilization of volunteer crowd work to combat what is seen as misconduct and even criminality. The German website Guttenplag uses crowdsourcing to expose plagiarism in dissertations, especially those written by prominent politicians. The Metropolitan Police in London uses a crowdsourcing app called Facewatch ID to identify rioters, and an American company called BlueServo has pioneered real-time crowdsourced surveillance by letting anyone act as a "virtual sheriff" and keep an eye on the Texas border to report illegal immigrants. Finally, Internet Eyes in the United Kingdom "gamifies" the process of finding shoplifters by charging the public to watch CCTV footage from stores. Though crowdsourcing has the potential to combat specific types of undesirable behavior effectively, it also raises several ethical questions about the motivations of those who are keeping an eye out and reporting suspicious activity, the impact on those who should be compensated for their efforts, and the fate of those who are unjustly named and shamed by an overly vigilant cyber mob.

The crowdsourcing sector must publicly confront these ethical challenges from within to become more reputable and sustainable for all stakeholders. When one examines the crowdsourcing sector as presented at conferences, in papers, and online, one is struck by the lack of mature ethical discourse, especially regarding the issue of exploitation. A recent study [49] is an exception to this rule. Can we imagine a crowded future workplace where we want our children to participate? This is a crucial issue posed by the authors of *The Future of Crowd Work*, who are all deeply engaged in creating crowdsourcing technologies. By posing the topic in this manner, they successfully sidestep the lengthy and convoluted history of moral philosophy and get down to the meat of the matter in the most exciting and accessible way.

The very nature of the issue suggests that something is not quite right in the crowdsourcing sector at present, namely, providing participants with enough justice, respect, and financial sustainability. The first step in developing new ethical norms for the future of crowdsourcing is to recognize this [50]. For example, in contest-based crowd work, the financial resources for payment are restricted, but the number of participants in the crowd is not; hence, exploitation is intrinsic to crowdsourcing. One might argue that exploitation arises whenever the results of a group are privatized and turned into profit without benefiting the crowd members themselves. To ensure that this new mode of production does not destroy hard-won achievements of fair labor standards, the criteria which constitute fair use of crowd work must be developed through negotiation between all stakeholders, including those who make the tools, those who use them, those who work in the crowd, and those in politics who have the mandate to protect the rights of the people. Fair Trade Mark is one possible framework for this thinking [51]. Crowdsourcing has the capability and desire to tackle global issues on a big scale, but first, it must overcome the challenge of being itself.

## 1.4 CONCLUSION

The area of crowdsourcing is young but quickly expanding. Researchers have not yet settled on a standard definition or criteria for determining whether a particular activity constitutes "practice" in this area since the field is still so new. Nevertheless, a few prominent features have evolved. To qualify as crowdsourcing, an organization must release a job through a malleable open call to gain insight, ideas, or value via a similar but not outsourced approach. However, the Internet is not required for crowdsourcing. Both professionals and novices may come together to create a crowd, and that crowd's members can be compensated money, socially or professionally. The data is aggregated in some instances, while the optimal answer is selected in others. As a result, it's not unexpected that scholars have struggled to develop a comprehensive definition of crowdsourcing, given the wide variety of its uses.

The most noticeable change in how crowdsourcing is conducted in the future is likely to be the increased use of AI/(machine learning) ML technologies. To begin, there will be abundant data on both successful and unsuccessful crowdsourcing initiatives. Data analysis will reveal which issues are most suited to being solved by tapping into the collective intelligence of a large group of people. Further, algorithms may be designed to help users convert their technical or commercial problems into targeted, high-probability issue statements. The same algorithms will advise users on what data they should be prepared to share with the community in order to improve the likelihood of a successful solution being found.

The second is that algorithms will be available to find the "best" crowdsourcing service for any given issue. Someday soon, it will be able to automatically compile a list of the most promising platforms to handle any specific issue by assessing a collection of problems each platform has dealt with in the past, the claimed solution rate, and the size and makeup of the crowd behind the platform. Finally, AI/ML systems that enable the quick production of suitably big and diversified crowds ("crowds-on-demand") are anticipated to be created.

## REFERENCES

[1] E. Estellés-Arolas and F. González-Ladrón-de Guevara, "Towards an integrated crowdsourcing definition," *Journal of Information Science*, vol. 38, no. 2, pp. 189–200, 2012.

[2] L. Hammon and H. Hippner, "Crowdsourcing," *Business & Information Systems Engineering*, vol. 4, pp. 163–166, 2012.

[3] M. Hossain and I. Kauranen, "Crowdsourcing: a comprehensive literature review," *Strategic Outsourcing: An International Journal*, vol. 8, no. 1, pp. 2–22, 2015.

[4] J. Howe, et al., "The rise of crowdsourcing," *Wired Magazine*, vol. 14, no. 6, pp. 1–4, 2006.

[5] Y. Tong, Z. Zhou, Y. Zeng, L. Chen, and C. Shahabi, "Spatial crowdsourcing: a survey," *The VLDB Journal*, vol. 29, pp. 217–250, 2020.

[6] S. Stumpp, "Crowdsourcing (Jeff Howe)," in *Social Media Handbuch*, pp. 257–268, Nomos Verlagsgesellschaft GmbH & Co. KG, 2021.

[7] M. Moradi, "Crowdsourcing for search engines: perspectives and challenges," *International Journal of Crowd Science*, vol. 3, no. 1, pp. 49–62, 2019.

[8] R. V. Gundur, M. Berry, and D. Taodang, "Using digital open source and crowdsourced data in studies of deviance and crime," *Researching Cybercrimes: Methodologies, Ethics, and Critical Approaches*, pp. 145–167, 2021.

[9] F. Leal, B. M. Veloso, B. Malheiro, H. González-Vélez, and J. C. Burguillo, "Scalable modelling and recommendation using wiki-based crowdsourced repositories," *Electronic Commerce Research and Applications*, vol. 33, p. 100817, 2019.

[10] P. Di Salvo and P. Di Salvo, "Wikileaks: an inspiration, a reference, a model?," *Digital Whistleblowing Platforms in Journalism: Encrypting Leaks*, pp. 137–153, 2020.

[11] G. Allon and V. Babich, "Crowdsourcing and crowdfunding in the manufacturing and services sectors," *Manufacturing & Service Operations Management*, vol. 22, no. 1, pp. 102–112, 2020.

[12] Z. J. Liu, E. Panfilova, A. Mikhaylov, and A. Kurilova, "Assessing stability in the relationship between parties in crowdfunding and crowdsourcing projects during the Covid-19 crisis," *Journal of Global Information Management (JGIM)*, vol. 30, no. 4, pp. 1–18, 2021.

[13] D. P. Sakas and D. P. Reklitis, "The impact of organic traffic of crowdsourcing platforms on airlines' website traffic and user engagement," *Sustainability*, vol. 13, no. 16, p. 8850, 2021.

[14] K. A. Kommel, M. Sillasoo, and Á. Lublóy, "Could crowdsourced financial analysis replace the equity research by investment banks?," *Finance Research Letters*, vol. 29, pp. 280–284, 2019.

[15] T. Inamura, Y. Mizuchi, and H. Yamada, "VR platform enabling crowdsourcing of embodied HRI experiments – case study of online robot competition," *Advanced Robotics*, vol. 35, no. 11, pp. 697–703, 2021.

[16] C. R. de Souza, L. S. Machado, and R. R. M. Melo, "On moderating software crowdsourcing challenges," *Proceedings of the ACM on Human-Computer Interaction*, vol. 4, no. GROUP, pp. 1–22, 2020.

[17] X. Zhang, E. Xia, C. Shen, and J. Su, "Factors influencing solvers' behaviors in knowledge-intensive crowdsourcing: a systematic literature review," *Journal of Theoretical and Applied Electronic Commerce Research*, vol. 17, no. 4, pp. 1297–1319, 2022.

[18] M. Zulfiqar, M. N. Malik, and H. H. Khan, "Microtasking activities in crowdsourced software development: a systematic literature review," *IEEE Access*, 2022.

[19] R. Lukyanenko and J. Parsons, "Beyond micro-tasks: research opportunities in observational crowdsourcing," *Crowdsourcing: Concepts, Methodologies, Tools, and Applications*, pp. 1510–1535, 2019.

[20] Y. Tong, Y. Zeng, B. Ding, L. Wang, and L. Chen, "Two-sided online micro-task assignment in spatial crowdsourcing," *IEEE Transactions on Knowledge and Data Engineering*, vol. 33, no. 5, pp. 2295–2309, 2019.

[21] S. Kim and L. P. Robert Jr, "Crowdsourcing coordination: a review and research agenda for crowdsourcing coordination used for macro-tasks," *Macrotask Crowdsourcing: Engaging the Crowds to Address Complex Problems*, pp. 17–43, 2019.

[22] G. S. K. Leung, V. Cho, and C. Wu, "Crowd workers' continued participation intention in crowdsourcing platforms: an empirical study in compensation-based micro-task crowdsourcing," *Journal of Global Information Management (JGIM)*, vol. 29, no. 6, pp. 1–28, 2021.

[23] R. Qarout, *Novel Methods for Designing Tasks in Crowdsourcing*. PhD thesis, University of Sheffield, 2019.

[24] P. Cheng, L. Chen, and J. Ye, "Cooperation-aware task assignment in spatial crowdsourcing," in *2019 IEEE 35th International Conference on Data Engineering (ICDE)*, pp. 1442–1453, IEEE, 2019.

[25] J. Ramírez, M. Baez, F. Casati, and B. Benatallah, "Understanding the impact of text highlighting in crowdsourcing tasks," in *Proceedings of the AAAI Conference on Human Computation and Crowdsourcing*, vol. 7, pp. 144–152, 2019.

[26] J. C. Strickland and W. W. Stoops, "The use of crowdsourcing in addiction science research: Amazon mechanical turk," *Experimental and Clinical Psychopharmacology*, vol. 27, no. 1, p. 1, 2019.

[27] M. Piazza, E. Mazzola, and G. Perrone, "How can I signal my quality to emerge from the crowd? A study in the crowdsourcing context," *Technological Forecasting and Social Change*, vol. 176, p. 121473, 2022.

[28] H. P. Lee, S. Garg, and K. M. Lim, "Crowdsourcing of environmental noise map using calibrated smartphones," *Applied Acoustics*, vol. 160, p. 107130, 2020.

[29] J. Hyyppä, J. P. Virtanen, A. Jaakkola, X. Yu, H. Hyyppᵃa, and X. Liang, "Feasibility of Google Tango and Kinect for crowdsourcing forestry information," *Forests*, vol. 9, no. 1, p. 6, 2017.

[30] D. Schlagwein and N. Bjorn-Andersen, "Organizational learning with crowdsourcing: the revelatory case of lego," *Journal of the Association for Information Systems*, vol. 15, no. 11, p. 3, 2014.

[31] S. Grant, R. Marciano, P. Ndiaye, K. E. Shawgo, and J. Heard, "The human face of crowdsourcing: a citizen-led crowdsourcing case study," in *2013 IEEE International Conference on Big Data*, pp. 21–24, IEEE, 2013.

[32] H. J. Ye and A. Kankanhalli, "Solvers' participation in crowdsourcing platforms: Examining the impacts of trust, and benefit and cost factors," *The Journal of Strategic Information Systems*, vol. 26, no. 2, pp. 101–117, 2017.

[33] E. Bari, M. Johnston, W. Wu, and W. T. Tsai, "Software crowdsourcing practices and research directions," in *2016 IEEE Symposium on Service Oriented System Engineering (SOSE)*, pp. 372–379, IEEE, 2016.

[34] Y. Feng, Z. Yi, C. Yang, R. Chen, and Y. Feng, "How do gamification mechanics drive solvers' knowledge contribution? A study of collaborative knowledge crowdsourcing," *Technological Forecasting and Social Change*, vol. 177, p. 121520, 2022.

[35] B. P. Bhuyan, "Relative similarity and stability in FCA pattern structures using game theory," in *2017 2nd International Conference on Communication Systems, Computing and IT Applications (CSCITA)*, pp. 207–212, IEEE, 2017.

[36] B. P. Bhuyan, R. Tomar, M. Gupta, and A. Ramdane-Cherif, "An ontological knowledge representation for smart agriculture," in *2021 IEEE International Conference on Big Data (Big Data)*, pp. 3400–3406, IEEE, 2021.

[37] B. P. Bhuyan, J. S. Um, T. Singh, and T. Choudhury, "Decision intelligence analytics: making decisions through data pattern and segmented analytics," *Decision Intelligence Analytics and the Implementation of Strategic Business Management*, pp. 99–107, 2022.

[38] B. P. Bhuyan, A. Karmakar, and S. M. Hazarika, "Bounding stability in formal concept analysis," in *Advanced Computational and Communication Paradigms: Proceedings of International Conference on ICACCP 2017*, Vol. 2, pp. 545–552, Springer, 2018.

[39] J. M. Mortensen, M. A. Musen, and N. F. Noy, "Crowdsourcing the verification of relationships in biomedical ontologies," in *AMIA Annual Symposium Proceedings*, vol. 2013, p. 1020, American Medical Informatics Association, 2013.

[40] M. G. Martinez and B. Walton, "The wisdom of crowds: the potential of online communities as a tool for data analysis," *Technovation*, vol. 34, no. 4, pp. 203–214, 2014.

[41] B. P. Bhuyan, R. Tomar, and A. R. Cherif, "A systematic review of knowledge representation techniques in smart agriculture (urban)," *Sustainability*, vol. 14, no. 22, p. 15249, 2022.

[42] I. Ullah, U. U. Hassan, and M. I. Ali, "Multi-level federated learning for industry 4.0: a crowdsourcing approach," *Procedia Computer Science*, vol. 217, pp. 423–435, 2023.

[43] A. Cuevas, E. Hogan, H. Hibshi, and N. Christin, "Observations from an online security competition and its implications on crowdsourced security," *arXiv preprint arXiv:2204.12601*, 2022.

[44] H. Xia and B. McKernan, "Privacy in crowdsourcing: a review of the threats and challenges," *Computer Supported Cooperative Work (CSCW)*, vol. 29, pp. 263–301, 2020.

[45] M. Alrizah, S. Zhu, X. Xing, and G. Wang, "Errors, misunderstandings, and attacks: analyzing the crowdsourcing process of ad-blocking systems," in *Proceedings of the Internet Measurement Conference*, pp. 230–244, 2019.

[46] D. Kondziella, M. Amiri, M. H. Othman, E. Beghi, Y. G. Bodien, G. Citerio, J. T. Giacino, S. A. Mayer, T. N. Lawson, D. K. Menon, *et al.*, "Incidence and prevalence of coma in the UK and the USA," *Brain Communications*, vol. 4, no. 5, p. fcac188, 2022.

[47] K. Hansson and T. Ludwig, "Crowd dynamics: conflicts, contradictions, and community in crowdsourcing," *Computer Supported Cooperative Work (CSCW)*, vol. 28, pp. 791–794, 2019.

[48] A. Piper, "Digital crowdsourcing and public understandings of the past: citizen historians meet criminal characters," *History Australia*, vol. 17, no. 3, pp. 525–541, 2020.

[49] S. Mishra and J. M. Rzeszotarski, "Crowdsourcing and evaluating concept driven explanations of machine learning models," *Proceedings of the ACM on Human-Computer Interaction*, vol. 5, no. CSCW1, pp. 1–26, 2021.

[50] H. Lu and Y. Lin, "Enabling citizen participation with the planning support system: empirical evidence from crowdsourcing greenway planning," in *Proceedings of the Fábos Conference on Landscape and Greenway Planning*, vol. 7, p. 2, 2022.

[51] W. Payne, "Crowdsourcing before the smartphone," *The Performance Complex: Competition and Competitions in Social Life*, p. 144, 2020.

# 2

## Crowdsourcing through a Digital Ecosystem: A Futuristic Tool of Remote Behavior Modification

*Rajesh Verma*
FGM Government College Adampur, Hisar, Haryana, India

**Assumption** – High virtual engagement results in rapid behavior modification.

**Operational definition** – The crowdsourcing is defined as volunteer non-paid contribution through digital means, specifically social media platforms.

Interestingly, the advent of new ways of sharing things prompted human beings to share extensively. The digital ecosystem (DE) has provided convenient means for highly engaging interpersonal virtual interaction sans limitations. The high engagement with information communication technology (ICT) tools [touch screen mobile phone] of the virtual world is due to the simultaneous involvement of three sense modalities. The DE offers spontaneous freedom from on-the-spot evaluation and perceived safety of cognizance to the contributor. The availability of DE has made the idea of crowdsourcing more relevant. The crowdsourcing being a cyclic process weighed more towards data seeker. The information collected is processed at the seeker's end and the outcomes are published and served to the very source from where raw information originated. The served and inferenced information has inherent features that significantly contribute to behavior modification, which is commonly known as remote behavior regulation (RBR). The marketers search the potential customers through crowdsourcing and use crowdsourcing to modify their behavior for

DOI: 10.1201/9781003346326-2

making targeted purchases. Politicians achieve vote swings through crowdsourcing, intelligence strategists look for potential targets through crowdsourcing, researchers look for trends, policymakers seek opinion, etc. The final idea that rests in the core of crowdsourcing is behavior modification through remote regulation. Crowdsourcing has a wider scope in behavior modification through reverse crowdsourcing (RC) as well as improving the predictive accuracy in the context of human behavior. Additionally, artificial intelligence (AI), the futuristic technology tool, is striving to enhance its accuracy for being perfectly effective. This can be achieved by crowdsourcing, which can contribute to the pool of existing big data that has inherent potential of improving AI accuracy.

## 2.1 INTRODUCTION

### 2.1.1 Definition

Crowdsourcing is operationally defined as 'Volunteer paid/non-paid contribution through digital means, specifically social media platforms.' It is an 'open innovation practice and co-creation support tool' (Ghezzi et al. 2017). Social media, the largest source of crowdsourcing, silently became the integral part of human beings on the pretext of providing connectivity and entertainment. Interestingly, the social media designers might not have ever imagined even in their dreams its wide-ranging impact and deep penetration into almost all human domains.

Since 2006, when the term *crowdsourcing* was coined by Howe, the researchers have not yet reached the final version of its definition. Estelles–Arolas et al. (2012) reviewed various definitions and attempted to define it, in the following terms: 'Crowdsourcing is a type of partic-ipative online activity in which an individual, and institution, a non-profit organization, or company proposes to a group of individuals of varying knowledge, heterogeneity, and number, via a flexible open call, the voluntary undertaking of a task. The undertaking of the task, of variable complexity and modularity, and in which the crowd should participate bringing their work, money, knowledge and/or experience, always entails mutual benefit. The user receives the satisfaction of a given type of need, be it economic, social recognition, self–esteem, or the development of individual skills, while the crowdsourcer will obtain and utilize to their advantage what the user has brought to the venture, whose form will depend on the type of activity undertaken'.

In this comprehensive definition, the authors attempted to include all potentialities the word *crowdsourcing* could embrace. The analysis reveals that crowdsourcing is a psycho-physiological phenomenon where crowdsourcing reaches out to sizable contributors through online means for seeking something new and novel.

### 2.1.2 Crowdsourcing: Concept Note

The idea of crowdsourcing is based upon the following assumption:

**Assumption** – Average response is found to be more effective, creative, and efficient than the individual response.

Crowdsourcing is the modern data collection technique of survey-based research (Whitaker et al. 2015) that piggy-backs information communication technology (ICT) tools, where the Internet is the primary vehicle (Ghezzi et al. 2017). The pivot of success of crowdsourcing is an average response. Average response refers to the inferenced information from the large collection of received responses. For example, in the famous Indian quiz show '*Kaun Banega Crorepati*' (KBC), the participant has access to several life lines. In '50-50 Audience Poll' the participant can opt to have the audience participate in a poll to help him in finding out the correct option. Though this is not crowdsourcing, it reflects the essence of average response. The wisdom of a crowd is tapped and the crowdsourcer arrives at a conclusive outcome that is usually found to be suitable and effective.

Crowdsourcing has accelerated the rate of communication and connectivity in terms of sharing and generation of ideas (Huang et al. 2014). Nothing is more interesting than the virtual world where we seem to own everything with nothing in hand except a round-cornered rectangular hand-held machine. The contribution of this machine is no less significant in managing and regulating our behavior. Amid other numerous functions, this machine has a feature of sharing. The advent of new ways of sharing things prompted human beings to share extensively and receive in similar proportion. It operates in the digital ecosystem (DE), which made the idea of crowdsourcing more relevant. It has provided convenient means for highly engaging interpersonal virtual interaction sans limitations. The DE offers spontaneous freedom from instantaneous evaluation and perceived safety of cognizance to the contributor. The contributor is not only a producer but also a consumer too. Whitaker et al. (2015) suggested the name 'prosumers' for this new species of virtual world. What we receive and what we share is the function of commonalities in cognitive taste. The demand is broadcasted openly in virtual space (Bassi et al. 2020) with a specific timeline, adequate instructions, and possible accruing benefits. The contribution is willful, creates value (Greer & Lei 2012; Nevo & Kotlarsky 2020), and, through collaborative efforts, contributes in innovation. In crowdsourcing, the creativity of a large number of people through digital cooperation (Crecelli et al. 2022) is pooled, where a problem has been looked at with different perspectives and ideologies, and responses are provided in this context. The received information in the form of response is psycho-culturally modulated. This helps the crowdsourcer to pick and choose what suits him the best. The chances of rejection of a decision made on the basis of crowdsourcing are minimal because the inferences drawn on the basis of crowd response have the least chance of being inappropriate because the inputs are received from the source itself.

## 2.2 GLANCE AT A PRIMARY COMPONENT OF CROWDSOURCING

The World Population Review estimated that 4.9 billion people (69 percent of the total world population) actively use the Internet. As far as India is concerned, this figure is 700 million (mygov.in). And the latest worldwide trends indicate that 4 percent is the annual growth rate of Internet users. It means almost 200 million people are added each year in this bracket. The trends of a fast-expanding Internet user base indicate that crowdsourcing is likely to add an additional dimension of psycho-mobility to the data type. Psycho-mobility is a proportionate mixture of quasi-cognitive output and behavioral expression. The psycho-mobility, when expressed in terms of outcomes, represents purposeful creative ideas. The purposive creativity is when the cognitive resources are directed in a specific direction and circumscribed by the stimulus to give specific output. In the context of crowdsourcing the defining feature of the crowd is that it participates instantaneously but doesn't contribute in vacuum rather needs an impetus. That impetus can be a psychologically penetrative stimulus that drives and initiates a chain of diverse thoughts. The characteristics of a stimulus define the level and intensity of the crowd involvement and subsequent response. If the majority of the features of the stimulus synchronizes with the personality type of the contributors, the involvement of the crowd in this collective exercise is likely to be higher. The contributor's participation in crowdsourcing is the function of utility of contribution and consequently accrued tangible or intangible rewards (Ikediego et al. 2018). Psychology has a huge consultancy room in designing the opposite stimulus for optimal contribution by the targeted crowd. Why do people contribute so generously sometimes without any tangible or even intangible rewards? The answer lies in 'peace of mind'. The crowdsourcing provides a secured safety net where contributors are neither evaluated nor scrutinized. The assurance of being non-judged drives an individual to contribute even in the absence of reward. The peer evaluation and behavioral scrutiny are the two fundamental tools employed by others to make a person-specific profile for self-use. These two tools are likely to interfere with the peace of mind of the assessed.

The crowdsourcing has made significant inroads in various sectors, such as FMCG, IT, public sector (Liu 2017), marketing (Whitla 2009), automobile, public relations (Wang et al. 2020), and healthcare (Christensen & Karlsson 2018) law reforms (Aitamurto et al. 2016) and research (Bassi et al. 2020). The business corporations are leading in crowdsourcing for seeking cost-effective (Blomberg 2012; Goud et al. 2018), creative, and innovative solutions (Devece et al. 2019; Ghezzi et al. 2017). This technique helps in receiving data economically and in real time (Wazny 2017). Internationally, Dell and IBM are leading corporations in crowdsourcing (Zhu et al. 2014). However, other than industries and marketing firms, the governments across the globe are also tapping the creativity of human resources through crowdsourcing (Dutil 2015). For example, the government of India is leading in crowdsourcing through its popular Mygov web portal, established on 26 July 2014, for seeking inputs from the public on varied subjects. 'MyGov has adopted multiple engagement methodologies like discussions, tasks, polls, surveys, blogs, talks, pledges, quizzes, and on-ground activities by innovatively using internet, mobile apps, IVRS, SMS, and outbound dialing (OBD) technologies' (mygov.in). This platform has immensely contributed in producing an incredible policy document, namely National Education Policy-2020. During the formulation of

NEP-2020 of India, 'Over two lakh suggestions from 2.5 lakh gram pan-chayats, 6,600 blocks, 6,000 urban local bodies (ULBs), 676 districts were received' (*The Hindu*, 31 July 2020); the suggestions were invited in by 23 languages (*New Indian Express*, 17 Aug 2022). It's a wonderful example of crowdsourcing. Another government-led crowdsourcing example that resulted in unprecedented results is *Pariksha Pe Charcha*, an interactive program on virtual platforms. Crowdsourcing is the thematic base that has transformed the paradigms of interaction. Behavioral interaction is a bipolar process that provides opportunities for mutual learning. Learning occurs when there is modification of behavior. So, in this context, it is hypothesized that crowdsourcing is a cyclic process weighted in favor of the crowdsourcer, yet had a residual effect on the crowd in terms of behavior modification. The chapter analyzes the impact of residual effect on behavior modification and evaluates the outcomes. The ensuing changes in behavior are operationally known as behavior modification through remote behavior regulation (RBR), which is being introduced in this chapter.

**Hence, this chapter will examine the following constructs:**

- Remote behavior regulation (RBR)
- Relationship between crowdsourcing and behavior modification
- Reverse crowdsourcing (RC) and behavior modification

**And throw some conceptual light upon some of the following futuristic perspectives:**

- Improved predictive accuracy
- Improving the accuracy of artificial intelligence (AI) with big data
- Applications

## 2.3 REMOTE BEHAVIOR REGULATION

The RBR is based upon the following assumption.

**Assumption** – 'High virtual engagement results in rapid behavior modification.'

The concept of RBR is characterized by virtual engagement-led contribution by the people that is processed and converted into a finished product to be broadcasted to psychologically tempt the same crowd that contributed to its ideation. It is a psycho-marketing game where AI is pressed into service to exploit the collective cognition of people who love to be part of the virtual world. Motivation (Gould et al. 2018), knowledge (Zhu et al. 2014), and tech savviness are a few stimuli that prompt participation and contribution.

Evidence suggests that behavior is the key to human regulation. In operant conditioning, B. F. Skinner (2005) emphasized the control of an organism's behavior by a stimulus from outside the organism. A stimulus can be manipulated. This makes sense that behavior can be regulated. In conformist behavior modification techniques, the stimulus needs to be of physical nature. The conventional system, which is uneconomical in terms of money and time (Gould et al. 2018), needs the following setup to effect the desired behavioral change:

- Proper laboratory setup
- Trained professional psychologist
- Fixed location
- Mandatory lab visit

However, the Internet has over-rode the conventional setup and provided a new virtual landscape. It has thousands of windows that open up new opportunities. Crowdsourcing is one of such windows that is affecting the behavior modification silently. The word 'silent' here has a deep connotation. Interestingly, though the individual is silent physically but engaged in inner monologue, this is also referred to as an inner voice, inner speech, or silent self-talk. The monologue is an important cognitive construct that has a role in self-regulation of behavior (Alderson-Day & Fernyhough 2015).

The most complicated question before modern psychology is, What makes people remain glued to the electronic screen? The high engagement with ICT tools [touch screen mobile phone] of the virtual world is due to the simultaneous involvement of three sense modalities. The Theory of Object Engagement suggests that the more senses involved in supplying correlated relevant information, the higher the engagement ($E = (k)*num\_senses$) (Verma 2020). It is hypothesized that the high engagement with the screen affects the behavior modification through continuous homogeneous content feed. A homogenous content feed means recommendations of contents similar to the previously watched or browsed; for example, recommendations or suggestions of similar videos by YouTube. The homogenous or similar content feed cements the belief system by virtue of maintenance rehearsal. The senses are known to have unlimited hunger for pleasure seeking. In this context, the demand for more and varied contents snowballs. Each recommended feed contains a myriad information type in a wide-ranging form. It is not necessary that each information in the content feed is of some or any use to the user, still the feed goes on. However, the previous experiences and selective perception become the base for kick-starting a drive to pick up self-fitting pieces from the pool of information, further hardening the belief system. The cycle continues to make permanent changes in the cognitive domain, consequently in behavior. These hardened beliefs express themselves in the form of new behavior [modified behavior]. The modified behavior is likely to integrate with day-to-day behavioral patterns. The permanent integration and consequent behavioral expression are the indicators of behavior regulation. This has been hypothesized by the author. Interestingly, this is not what the crowdsourcer intended for, yet it occurs.

## 2.4 CROWDSOURCING AND BEHAVIOR MODIFICATION

One of the intrinsic desires of human beings is to express incognito what has been fulfilled through the modern ICT tools and engendered digital crowdsourcing. However, these tools lack capacities unique to humans, such as perceptual ability, learning from past experiences (Boulos et al. 2011), meaning-making, heuristics, evaluating pros and cons of a decision, empathetic considerations, understanding beyond the academic meaning of words i.e., reading between the lines, etc. The primary information from the crowd contains personality indicators that paint a broad picture of contributors' profiles. The author hypothesized that contributors unconsciously project themselves through their contribution. The author is of the view that the crowdsourcer, if intelligent enough and most of them are, pick up from the data what they expected from the contributor, along with the strap-on data type that is also extracted for wider gains. The strap-on data provides important clues that help in designing the behavior-regulating strategies. Here it becomes necessary and pertinent to discuss a case to vindicate the relationship between crowdsourcing and behavior modification through strap-on-data.

## 2.5 CASE OF MASKED STRATEGY

Recently (from 13 to 15 August 2022), the government of India launched the 'Har Ghar Tiranga' program. The program was launched on both physical and virtual platforms. The government wisely designed a computer application where citizens were required to pin a flag to show their commitment towards the nation. The color of nationalism inspired the general population to contribute in all possible ways to express their loyalty to the nation. The program handlers were very well aware about the deep-rooted psychological value in the 'Idea of Nationalism'. The campaign was meticulously planned and flawlessly managed. The gullible public was extensively motivated and consequently contributed in large numbers (more than 5 crore flags were pinned and 6 crore selfies were uploaded within a span of just four days) (harghartiranga.com). At the first instance, the ideas of Har Ghar Tiranga looked good with the best of intentions. However, if we look at this program from the psychological perspective, it seems to be a creative and smart data collection program intelligently designed for political gains. The author believes that the crowdsourcer in this process could assess the strong pockets where the spirit of nationalism was high (high density of pinned flag). Additionally, they could also earmark the exact geographical locations where the density of pinning virtual flags was very low [low nationalism spirit]. These figures are too significant for a political party. It helped in meeting the following objectives:

- Easy identification of areas where the followers of their ideology are fewer
- Number of people who use virtual platform regularly
- Number of people who obey such calls [compliance rate]
- Rate of transmission of call
- Media's reaction and response to it, etc.

These are some of the additional insights that prove to be very significant for a political party and government in the long run. They now have authentic data through which it can be assessed in terms of fan following where they stand their ground firmly and where they need to focus upon; a new smartly designed campaign then can be launched at the targeted locations and within specific pockets to transform the ideology, thought process, and political orientation of the general population.

Considering this case, it can be understood that masked strategies can be used in the garb of crowdsourcing to remotely regulate and consequently modify human behavior. This is to get the things done in the desired way. If the objective is negative or destructive, then behavior modification can be disastrous. Because crowdsourcing has inherent biases, such as confirmation bias, information bias, and salience bias, a great need of caution needs to be practiced to affect the behavior modification through crowdsourcing.

## 2.6 REVERSE CROWDSOURCING (RC) AND BEHAVIOR MODIFICATION

The RC is based upon the following assumption.

**Assumption:** Utility by virtue of high intrinsic value of attractiveness governs and dominates the necessity.

Behavior is an observable phenomenon affected by abstract modalities. The permanent change in behavior due to experience is learning. Experience is a personal thing that remains within the cognitive basket. The possibility and significance of learning affect behavior is not less than behavior modification affecting learning. In essence, behavior modification and learning are intricately related to each other. Crowdsourcing is exploiting this relationship. The contributors provide input, the crowdsourcer processes the input, transforms it into a workable idea or usable product, and throws it back to the source. The process is akin to input-process-output (I-P-O), suggested by Ghezzi et al. (2017). The market is full of products without which life can go on. Some of them are as follows (list is not exhaustive):

- Bath pillow
- Plastic plants
- USB vacuum cleaners for keyboards
- Q-tips (cotton swabs) for ears
- Food colors
- Toothpaste tube squeezer

For such products, demand is created by expressing its utility. These products are beyond necessity. Necessity is integral to survival while utility is transitional. Necessity is laced with needs while utility is with

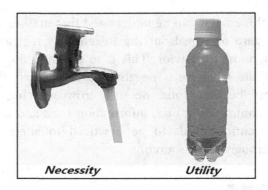

**FIGURE 2.1**
Necessity and utility.

wants (Figure 2.1). Human needs are subjugated by wants because wants seem to gratify the senses (Bhagwad Geeta, 2.62). This is the vital existential psychological difference between necessity and utility. The crowdsourcer intentionally or unintentionally exploits this humanly ineptness. Through repetitive recommendations, the utility is transformed into pseudo-necessity by presenting the product in a manner that seems to add quality to life. The utility, being transitional in nature, cannot be completely transformed into necessity. Additionally, the ease of use and accessibility creates essentiality [pseudo-necessity or transitional necessity] in life, consequently leading to buying the product. The utility seems to solve assumed problems as long as they are perceived to exist. This is what the author called RC. It is referred to as the process where a large number of people seek creative solutions through the Internet. The RC and crowdsourcing differ on certain aspects (Table 2.1).

**TABLE 2.1**

Differences between Crowdsourcing and Reverse Crowdsourcing

|   | Reverse Crowdsourcing | Crowdsourcing |
|---|---|---|
| 1 | Crowd is the consumer | Crowdsourcer is the consumer |
| 2 | Crowd seeks solutions | Crowdsourcer seeks the solution |
| 3 | Behavior modification is non-directive | Intended population type is targeted |
| 4. | Based on utility of the product | Based on necessity of crowdsourcer |

## 2.7 SOCIAL MEDIA AND CROWDSOURCING

Social media is a projective screen where contributors freely air their creative creations. Social media has extreme domination over the Interne;, for example, Facebook has, worldwide, 2.9 billion monthly users and India leads with 416.6 million (worldpopulationreview.com). The creator has to remain in constant touch with the electronic screen. The RC is dependent upon the duration of screen time. The higher the screen time, the faster the behavior modification towards problem behaviors (Guerrero et al. 2019) and other health issues such as sleep disturbances (Parent et al. 2016). One of the probable reasons for the association of screen time with behavior modification is fossilization of utility value of the stimulus. The novelty in the stimulus strengthens the desire of possession and expected pleasure in the possession. The creators are aware of this fact and constantly add value to their stimulus to circumvent the wearisomeness that is found to occur due to predictability of occurrence of responses. Unpredictability adds charm to the stimulus thereby making it attractive and interesting. RC works on the attractiveness of the utility. However, RC as a phenomenon is older than the prevalent digital crowdsourcing and has been contributing significantly in modifying behavior through remote regulation.

## 2.8 FUTURISTIC PERSPECTIVES

### 2.8.1 Improved Predictive Accuracy

Crowdsourcing has been expanding (Ghezzi et al. 2017) and is being accepted as an effective problem-solving tool across the board. Crowdsourcing is for solution, innovation, social cause, choice making, decision making, and innovating through pooling of human resources from diverse backgrounds. The collective human intelligence and AI jointly combine together to simulate the behavioral prediction. The improvement in performance of algorithms (Difallah et al. 2015) improves the predictive accuracy of AI. The predictive accuracy means the predicted value is closer to the existing value. Crowdsourcing is expected to improve the predictive accuracy with an increase in the number of willing participants. However, the major impediments in the improvement of predictive accuracy are some of the errors from the contributor side. The errors such as answering randomly or quick participation for the sake of participation, incomplete submissions, participant's bias, manipulated responses, etc. To circumvent these errors, the psycho-virtual control over the crowd is one the major requirements and expected to improve over time with development of new technology and behavior understanding. The future lies in minimizing the [human] biases, response-tracking mechanisms, bridging the gap between cognition and algorithm, self-learning controls, computational evaluations, tools that assess the integrity of responses, etc. These mechanisms are expected to improve the predictive accuracy, which aids in behavior modification through remote regulation.

### 2.8.2 Improving Accuracy of Artificial Intelligence with Big Data

Social media platforms generate tremendous amounts of data in the form of comments, likes, sharing, uploading, etc. at a high pace (Tariq et al. 2021). Big data is a new resource, and those who exploit it gain an advantage. Deciphering social media generated data for predicting human behavior (Katsikopoulos & Canellas 2022) is a very complex task. The complexity lies in the dynamism of human behavior. As already stated elsewhere, the social media platforms are projective screens where the user leaves behavioral and personality traces in digital form. In psychological terms, these traces form the big data that can form the base for utilization of AI in RBR. AI is a continuously evolving technology closing in on predictive accuracy with a rapid pace. AI and crowdsourcing are mutually associated; AI helps in crowdsourcing while crowdsourcing through its cognitive traces sharpens the AI. AI is expected to take over almost all activities reserved for human beings in the near future. Hence, in the future, crowdsourcing is likely to be replaced by 'cloudsourcing', where algorithms will communicate with algorithms and generate ideas.

## 2.9 FUTURISTIC APPLICATIONS

At present the, crowdsourcing is being extensively used by different organizations for seeking easy, quick, and aggregate solutions. The marketers search the potential customers to work with them (Prahalad and

Ramaswamy 2000), consequently using crowdsourcing to modify their behavior for making targeted purchases. Politicians achieve vote swings through crowdsourcing, intelligence strategists look for potential targets through crowdsourcing, researchers look for trends, policymakers seek opinions, etc. Crowdsourcing has future applications in academic and applied research, military, politics, policy formulation, containing corruption, law enforcement, marketing, and tourism. However, the speed at which technology is developing seems that crowdsourcing too has a short life span. The trends indicate that self-evolutionary algorithms are likely to select and connect with people with similar thought processes, ideology, and response patterns. This perspective will lead to peer sourcing (people with specific behavioral and response patterns); a similar concept 'of friendsourcing' was also proposed by Bernstein, et al. in 2010; gender sourcing; family sourcing; mob sourcing (those who are obsessed with the latest mobile handsets); and tech sourcing. In other words, AI will become efficient enough to go for target sourcing.

## 2.10 CONCLUSION

Crowdsourcing has enormous applications for almost all domains. It has the vast potential to contribute through collective innovation and creative creation. Psychology looks at crowdsourcing from a different perspective [behavioral]. The behavior is the key human expression that includes internal reflections and external responses. Since time began, humans' gratification of 'self' and more appropriately ego, has used ingenious, cruel, and a host of different means to control and regulate other human beings through direct regulation and behavior modification. The advent of the Internet has provided yet another tool for satiating the eternal greedy need of regulating others. Crowdsourcing is the by-product of Internet applications that significantly contribute to behavior modification. A sincere advice for the marketing firms is that 'Nothing can be sold unless the behavior of the potential buyer is modified'. The final idea that rests in the core of crowdsourcing is behavior modification through remote regulation.

*******

## REFERENCES

Aitamurto, T., Landemore, H., & Saldivar Galli, J. (2016). Unmasking the crowd: Participants' motivation factors, expectations, and profile in a crowdsourced law reform. *Information, Communication & Society, 20*(8), 1239–1260. 10.1080/1369118x.2016.1228993

Alderson-Day, B., & Fernyhough, C. (2015). Inner speech: Development, cognitive functions, phenomenology, and neurobiology. *Psychological Bulletin, 141*(5), 931–965. 10.1037/bul0000021

Bassi, H., Misener, L., & Johnson, A. M. (2020). Crowdsourcing for research: Perspectives from a Delphi panel. *SAGE Open, 10*(4). 10.1177/2158244020980751

Bernstein, M. S., Tan, D., Smith, G., Czerwinski, M., & Horvitz, E. (2010). Personalization via friendsourcing. *ACM Transactions on Computer-Human Interaction, 17*(2), 1–28. 10.1145/1746259.1746260

Bhagavad Gita. Gita Press Gorakhpur.

Blomberg, J. (2012). Twitter and Facebook analysis: It's not just for marketing anymore. *Social Media and Networking, 309*. Denver, CO: SAS Global Forum.

Boulos, M. N. K., Resch, B., Crowley, D. N., Breslin, J. G., Sohn, G., & Burtner, R. (2011). Crowdsourcing, citizen sensing and sensor web technologies for public and environmental health surveillance and crisis management: Trends, OGC standards and application examples. *International Journal of Health di, 10*(67). 10.1186/1476-072X-10-67

Christensen, I., & Karlsson, C. (2018). Open innovation and the effects of crowdsourcing in a pharma ecosystem. *Journal of Innovation & Knowledge.* 10.1016/j.jik.2018.03.008

Cricelli, L., Grimaldi, M., & Vermicelli, S. (2022). Crowdsourcing and open innovation: A systematic literature review, an integrated framework and a research agenda. *Review of Managerial Science, 16*, 1269–1310. 10.1007/s11846-021-00482-9

Devece, C., Palacios, D., & Ribeiro-Navarrete, B. (2019). The effectiveness of crowdsourcing in knowledge-based industries: The moderating role of transformational leadership and organisational learning. *Economic Research, 32*(1), 335–351. 10.1080/1331677x.2018.1547204

Difallah, D. E., Catasta, M., Demartini, G., Ipeirotis, P. G., & Cudr'e-Mauroux, P. (2015). The dynamics of micro-task crowdsourcing: The case of Amazon mturk. In *Proceedings of the 24th International Conference on World Wide Web* (238–247). International World Wide Web Conferences Steering Committee.

Dutil, P. (2015). Crowdsourcing as a new instrument in the government's arsenal: Explorations and considerations. *Canadian Public Administration, 58*(3), 363–383. 10.1111/capa.12134

Estelles-Arolas, E., & Gonzalez-Ladron-de-Guevara, F. (2012). Towards an integrated crowdsourcing definition. *Journal of Information Science, 38*, 189–200. 10.1177/0165551512437638

Ghezzi, A., Gabelloni, D., Martini, A., & Natalicchio, A. (2017). Crowdsourcing: A review and suggestions for future research. *International Journal of Management Reviews, 20*(2), 343–363. 10.1111/ijmr.12135

Gould, S. J. J., Cox, A. L., & Brumby, D. P. (2018). Influencing and measuring behaviour in crowdsourced activities. In M. Filimowicz, & V. Tzankova (eds.), *New Directions in Third Wave Human-Computer Interaction: Volume 2 - Methodologies*, (103–130). Springer International Publishing. 10.1007/978-3-319-73374-6_7

Greer, C. R., & Lei, D. (2012). Collaborative innovation with customers: A review of the literature and suggestions for future research. *International Journal of Management Reviews*, *14*, pp. 63–84.

Guerrero, M. D., Barnes, J. D., & Chaput, J. P. (2019). Screen time and problem behaviors in children: Exploring the mediating role of sleep duration. *International Journal of Behavioral Nutrition and Physical Activity*, *16*(105), 1–10. 10.1186/s12966-019-0862-x

Huang, Y., Vir Singh, P., & Srinivasan, K. (2014). Crowdsourcing new product ideas under consumer learning. *Management Science*, *60*(9), 2138–2159. 10.1287/mnsc.2013.1879

Ikediego, H. O., Ilkan, M., Abubakar, A. M., & Victor Bekun, F. (2018). Crowd-sourcing (who, why and what). *International Journal of Crowd Science*, *2*(1), 27–41. 10.1108/ijcs-07-2017-0005

Katsikopoulos, K. V., & Canellas, M. C. (2022). Decoding human behavior with big data? Critical, constructive input from the decision sciences. *AI Magazine*, *43*, 126–138. 10.1002/aaai.12034

Liu, H. K. (2017). Crowdsourcing government: Lessons from multiple disciplines. *Public Administration Review*, *77*(5), 656–667. 10.1111/puar.12808

Nevo, D., & Kotlarsky, J. (2020). Crowdsourcing as a strategic IS sourcing phenomenon: Critical review and insights for future research. *The Journal of Strategic Information Systems*, 101593. 10.1016/j.jsis.2020.101593

Parent, J., Sanders, W., & Forehand, R. (2016). Youth screen time and behavioral health problems: The role of sleep duration and disturbances. *Journal of Developmental & Behavioral Pediatrics*, *37*(4), 277–284. 10.1097/DBP.0000000000000272. PMID: 26890562; PMCID: PMC4851593.

Prahalad, C. K., & Ramaswamy, V. (2000). Co-opting customer competence. *Harvard Business Review*, *78*, 79–87.

Skinner, B. F. (2005). *Science and Human Behaviour*. The BF Skinner Foundation. http://www.bfskinner.org/books4sale.asp

Tariq, M. U., Babar, M., Poulin, M., Khattak, A. S., Alshehri, M.D., & Kaleem, S. (2021). Human behavior analysis using intelligent big data analytics. *Frontiers in Psychology*, *12*, 1–12. 10.3389/fpsyg.2021.686610

Verma, R. (2020, February 12). *Theory of object engagement (ToOE) and scope in management [paper presentation]*. Conclave on redefining management research in India, IIM Trichy, ICSSR, New Delhi, India.

Wang, C., Han, L., Stein, G., Day, S., Bien-Gund, C., Mathews, A., ...Tucker, J. D. (2020). Crowdsourcing in health and medical research: A systematic review. *Infectious Diseases of Poverty*, *9*(1). 10.1186/s40249-020-0622-9

Wazny, K. (2017). Crowdsourcing's ten years in: A review. *Journal of Global Health*, *7*(2). 10.7189/jogh.07.020601

Whitaker, R. M., Chorley, M., & Allen, S. M. (2015). *New Frontiers for Crowdsourcing: The Extended Mind*. 48th Hawaii International Conference on System Sciences. 10.1109/hicss.2015.197

Whitla, P. (2009). Crowdsourcing and its application in marketing activities. *Contemporary Management Research*, *5*(1), 15–28

Zhu, H., Djurjagina, K., & Leker, J. (2014). Innovative behaviour types and their influence on individual crowdsourcing performances. *International Journal of Innovation Management*, *18*(06), 1440015. 10.1142/s1363919614400155

*Internet Sources*

Retrieved on 18 August 2022 from https://worldpopulationreview.com/country-rankings/internet-users-by-country

Retrieved on 19 August 2022 from https://www.thehindu.com/news/national/rigorous-consultations-done-before-framing-new-national-education-policy-says-ramesh-pokhriyal-nishank/article32243060.ece

Retrieved on 26 August 2022 from https://www.newindianexpress.com/nation/2022/aug/17/nep-2020-centre-seeks-public-inputs-for-preparation-of-new-curriculum-2488279.html

Retrieved on 31 August 2022 from https://worldpopulationreview.com/country-rankings/facebook-users-by-country

Retrieved on 1 September 2022 from https://technotes.alconox.com/detergents/using-tap-water-alconox-cleaner/

Retrieved on 3 September 2022 from https://www.indiamart.com/proddetail/200ml-mineral-water-bottle-20300578130.html

Retrieved on 7 September 2022 from https://support.sas.com/resources/papers/proceedings12/309-2012.pdf

Retrieved on 18 September 2022 from https://hbr.org/2000/01/co-opting-customer-competence

Retrieved on 18 September 2022 https://srimadbhagavadgitahindi.blogspot.com/

# 3

# Crowdsourcing Applications in Agriculture

*Achala Shakya[1], Gaurav Tripathi[2],*
*and Devarani Devi Ningombam[3]*
[1]School of Computer Science, University of Petroleum & Energy
Studies, Dehradun, India
[2]Department of Geoinformatics, Central University of Jharkhand,
Ranchi, India
[3]Department of Computer Science and Engineering, National Institute
of Technology (NIT) Patna, Bihar, India

## 3.1 CROWDSOURCING APPLICATIONS IN THE AGRICULTURAL FIELD AND FARMING ACTIVITIES

The term *crowdsourcing* is grouping the relevant data, information, and knowledge for some specific activities by a community of non-professionals i.e., the people who are not directly associated with the professional tasks. Contributors to crowdsourcing projects paid for their contributions (Minet et al. 2017). In accordance with the above part of the stated definition, crowdsourcing refers to the externalization of routine activities for free of cost or at a minimal cost by volunteers, less paid contributors, or, from a wider perspective to more complicated collaborative actions where the knowledge of extremely competent professionals is required. Crowdsourcing, also referred to as community-based monitoring, citizen sensing (Singh et al. 2018), or participatory sensing, is used to collect data or information by volunteers after the second component (Posadas et al. 2021) and examples of crowdsourcing (Figure 3.1) include idea generation, citizen science, value creation, distributed knowledge, crowdfunding,

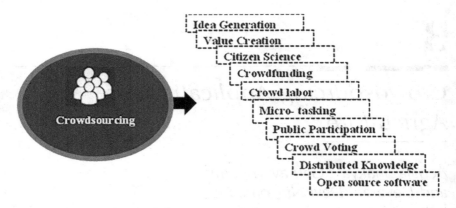

**FIGURE 3.1**
Key examples of crowdsourcing.

crowd labor, open-source software, micro-tasking, public participation, crowd voting, etc.

The more established ideas of citizen science (Singh et al. 2018) or participatory science are attributed to crowdsourcing. The growth of the Internet throughout the past ten years has been a major supporter of efforts like crowdsourcing and citizen research. The use of crowdsourcing in agriculture research includes participatory methods used in research and innovation initiatives (Minet et al. 2017). However, the concept "farm sourcing" describes crowdsourcing applications that involve knowledgeable agriculture industry stakeholders exchanging information voluntarily. In the farm sourcing strategy, information timeliness and information beyond observation are particularly crucial. It is very important to know the difference between the respective terms in farm sourcing strategy, i.e., data, information, and knowledge. Raw measurements of environmental variables, geographic details like field boundaries or a measurement point's coordinates, visual observations (images or notes), or not interpreted inputs are all examples of crowdsourced data. The information is the valuable data, i.e., processing an image for identifying the farm fields, vegetation, crops, forest, plantation, etc. Lastly, knowledge is the structured information held by contributors because of their experience and factual observations. Recent crowdsourcing applications in agricultural research and activities are provided in Table 3.1. This table categorizes the development of crowdsourcing in the agriculture or farming industry. The activities have examined to fit within this classification, but more initiatives in the future may be

**TABLE 3.1**

Crowdsourcing Literature Related to the Agricultural Sector

| Reference Number | Description | Advantage | Disadvantage/Challenge |
|---|---|---|---|
| Rahman et al. (2015) | Identification of weeds | Reduce losses caused by the delay in identifying weeds | Memory overhead |
| Singh and Saran (2015) | Utilized various crowdsourcing features for collecting the information on animal, plant, marine, as well as spatial distribution | Helpful in producing services or products | May lead to various research challenges by incorporating new software capabilities |
| Estes et al. (2016) | Land use/land cover mapping using satellite images | It maps application-programming interface. | May not accurately map the land cover |
| Marx et al. (2016) | Assessment of crop height | Offers efficient opportunities for agricultural assessment and monitoring | Data collection from regional people for the ground truth assessment |
| Yu et al. (2017) | Collection of geo-referenced agricultural land systems at small parcel level using high-resolution satellite data. | Timely acquiring land cover information | Security challenges in the application need to be addressed properly. |
| Steinke, Etten and Zelan (2017) | Farmer-generated data was tested. | Various observations resulted in statistical modeling that helped in distinguishing between different crops. | Subjective evaluations should also be considered. |
| Andrimont et al. (2018) | Crop monitoring | Effectiveness of crowdsourced imagery for identification of different crops | Extraction of desired information from images |
| Singh et al. (2018) | Species mapping | Collection of spatial and non-spatial information | Crowdsourcing data may not be accurate |
| Etten et al. (2019) | Crowdsourcing in agriculture sector | The tricot method can also be used with farmers to generate data of high quality. | To facilitate scaling, more feature extraction is required. |

*(Continued)*

**TABLE 3.1 (Continued)**

Crowdsourcing Literature Related to the Agricultural Sector

| Reference Number | Description | Advantage | Disadvantage/Challenge |
|---|---|---|---|
| Sokolov et al. (2019) | Crowdsourcing in agriculture for sustainable development | Improves the performance | Quality of the service |
| Krupowicz, Czarnecka and Magdalena (2020) | Applying citizen science for local development | Permits constructive selection of suitable social groups to involve in the planning of land procedures. | Spatial management of the rural area |
| Saran et al. (2020) | Mapping of the forest fire in real time. | Extract valid geographic coordinates and helps in capturing images of forest fire with its cause, affected species, etc. | Still citizen-centric approach for mapping of the forest fire in real-time |
| Pichon et al. (2021) | The application provides the statistics of vine water at regional level. | User-friendly application | Metrics related to seasonality of field usage and the conduct of professional users |
| Wu et al. (2021) | Crop type identification from crowdsourced road view using convolutional neural network | Yield high accuracy using decision-based fusion method | Computing performance |
| Asogba et al. (2022) | Exploring the potential and challenges linked with the conservation of African Baobab under respective climatic conditions. | High adequacy for African Baobab in West Africa | Ex-situ and in-situ conservation are necessary. |
| Saran et al. (2022) | Reviewed biodiversity information portals recognized globally. | Focused on biodiversity richness information at global level using spatial analytical tools. | Unavailability of web-based geospatial data processing applications |

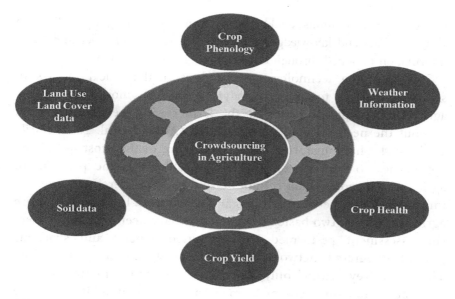

**FIGURE 3.2**
Major crowdsourcing activities in agriculture.

taken into consideration as well. Scientists, professionals, non-professionals (farmers), other beneficiaries, as well as a combination of the described groups, are direct consumers of these activities. It is also noteworthy that various crowdsourcing activities in the agricultural and farming sector have not been documented in the scientific literature. Major crowdsourcing activities in agriculture are shown in Figure 3.2.

## 3.2 CROWDSOURCING OF DATA/KNOWLEDGE FROM VARIOUS SENSOR DEVICES

The timely monitoring of agriculture at the parcel level is becoming a reality at the global level. The recent deployment of the Sentinel fleet has opened the way for new initiatives, such as the creation of farm services and the reform of agricultural policies. Ample processing capacity, trustworthy algorithm development, and methodical ground data collection are still needed to build an operational monitoring system at the parcel level (Esch et al. 2019). This study examines how crowdsourcing solutions could benefit farm monitoring by utilizing a variety of data and knowledge, including open-access reference and latent information obtained through crowdsourcing (Jin et al. 2019).

Crowdsourcing technology incorporates mathematical models in smart agriculture to quickly analyze a sizable amount of data in agricultural output and provide the farmer with useful information without the need for a skill professional (Ahmad et al. 2012; Karila et al. 2014; Shanmugapriya et al. 2019). One of the most promising approaches to address long-standing problems is the problem of agricultural products that cannot be sold because there is insufficient information flow between farmers and consumers. In order to acquire agricultural data, two basic methodologies have been frequently used: site assessment performed by committed experts and space-air ground integrated network-based sensing technologies (SAGIN). The site survey method only collects small-scale local data/information and is labor-intensive and time-consuming, making it unsuitable for crowdsourcing technology (O'Connor et al. 2015). Therefore, we consider crowdsourcing data from various sensory devices.

The term "crowdsensing," which is often referred to as "mobile crowdsensing" (MCS), refers to a strategy where a lot of individuals using mobile devices that can detect and compute share data and extract information to measure, map, analyze, or infer any processes of common interest. MCS strives to finish large-scale and complicated sensing activities with three beneficial traits: profitable, adaptability, and flexibility. Research that suggests various methods to increase the availability of MCS technology for various applications has attracted increasing interest because it is based on already-existing systems.

### 3.2.1 Agricultural Land-Use/Land-Cover Data

Agricultural parcel limits, specifically the geo-localized forms of the plots and their land-use/land-cover (LULC) attributes, serve as points or limits for agricultural data. When fields are cultivated using crop rotation, LULC attributes of the obtained agricultural fields may remain constant throughout time like indefinite grasslands and specific crops (such as rice or sugar cane), or it may shift from one growing season to the next. The data updating is often required in the latter scenario. OpenStreetMap (www.openstreetmap.org), DIY Landcover,

Collect Earth, and Geo-Wiki are a few examples of crowdsourcing projects that have demonstrated how much geographic land-use data can be effectively accumulated via crowdsourcing techniques or systems for geographical information (Bey et al. 2016; Estes et al. 2015; Fritz et al. 2012; Minet et al. 2017).

The projects named Geo-Wiki and DIY land cover created the maps related to parcel sizes of farmland and cropping area globally, respectively (Minet et al. 2017). The above-mentioned crowdsourcing projects were not able to determine the precise crop cover, including species of crops planted in the agricultural land. However, in context to OpenStreetMap several classes (i.e., tags) were created to map landscapes, such as grassland, crops, vineyard, farmland, orchard, and horticulture that lies under the widely used "land use and land cover" tags. These tags can only distinguish between grassland and cropland, moreover, exact boundaries of each parcel are lacking. Furthermore, mapping of particular types of crop is performed in OpenStreetMap underneath the crop class that is used primarily for perennial crop production, including rice, wheat, and maize as the highest utilized quantity. Therefore, OpenStreetMap has the ability to provide maps of specific crops; however, this is currently not completely susceptible because of the incompleteness and subpar updating of the data (Minet et al. 2015; Minet et al. 2017).

## 3.2.2 Weather Information

Reliable and correct weather information is crucial for the farmers as various farming activities, agricultural warning, monitoring, mentoring, and management are strongly dependent on weather. Several smartphone applications offer weather services, and most of them rely on information obtained from authorized, as well as private, weather locations (Minet et al. 2017). The desirability of crowdsourcing rainfall time-series data is reinforced by the fact that rainfall, particularly from catastrophic storms, is largely spatially uncorrelated. Favorable weather information is crucial for farmers, planners, managers, and finally operators. Flooding and waterlogging might be quite concentrated; scarcity or extreme temperature are more pervasive in an area. Farmers may obtain precise estimations that could aid adaptation, such as inundation timing or management of crop disease, in consideration for data on anticipated consequences (Muller et al. 2015).

### 3.2.3 Soil Data

Numerous types of soil data, including textural classifications, structure, microbial activity, pH, and nutrient concentration, especially mineral nitrogen subject to rapid fluctuation, may be of importance for agricultural applications. For the enhancement of current soil maps, these statistics may be of immediate importance to pedologists or farmers (Minet et al. 2017). It has been analyzed that existing crowdsourcing initiatives for soil data and soil attributes that can be gathered for enhancing the soil maps. Several centralized crowdsourcing web platforms related to soil data can benefit from the analysis of soil on a regular basis by various private agencies or laboratories that may provide results and findings of soil to the web platforms (Etten et al. 2019).

### 3.2.4 Crop Phenology

Phenology in agriculture refers to the physiological stages of crop growth from planting through harvest. Accurate crop phenology data are necessary for managing crop growth and estimating yield during the growing season. Unpredicted and extreme weather conditions, such as rain, heat, hot and cold waves are big problems to the farmers, particularly to the smallholder farmers (Manfreda et al. 2018; Torresan et al. 2017). Smallholder farmers cannot afford a high-tech mechanism or adopt expensive systems. Monitoring the relation between cyclic and seasonal natural phenomena in agriculture, phenology, using inexpensive smart devices like smartphones, is one of the main attributes, particularly in food scarcity regions in the world. In this section, we study the usefulness of monitoring crop phenology in agriculture to maximize the production rate. In particular, we demonstrate how crop phenology monitoring using smart devices, such as sensors, can quantify crop production by early detection of lodging events. Lodging events such as legion and the main contributing factors for this are excessive nitrogen levels, storm damage, soil density, disease, timing of sowing, overcrowding, and seed variety. Using sensor-based smart devices for monitoring purposes can provide visual field data and detailed information on the timing of key behavioral phases of crops and diseases that are not recorded on conventional monitoring systems like satellites.

By integrating a variety of wireless sensors, such as flow sensors for precise sowing and fertilization, intelligent agricultural gear (IAM) can boost operational efficiency of production in comparison to traditional agricultural machinery for collecting crop data. With the use of these wireless sensors, farmers may gather a wealth of useful information such as the quality of crops, fertilizers applied, and the number of crops planted, to assess the IAM's effectiveness. Farmers can specifically use the computing capabilities of smartphones to visualize the data received from wireless sensors. The gathered information will simultaneously be uploaded to the server for storage and become a historical record. Therefore, this application shows how IAM and Arka Microbial Consortiums (AMCS) are working together to sense things.

Crop phenology is divided into three phases: pre-production, in-production, and post-production. Additionally, each stage includes a number of production links, such as managing firms and preparing for production.

i. Pre-Production Phase: Farmers are forced to make hasty planting plans due to the lack of preparation time, such as crop varieties and planting area, which heavily rely on information from previous years' market sales. More significantly, the crop's eventual harvest will be impacted by the schedule at this stage. It includes genetic resources improvement, agriculture practical, and agricultural inputs.

A food system's sustainability starts long before a crop is planted or cultivated. Genetic resources are conserved and used now with the intention of improving the quality and productivity of domesticated crops in the future. Genetic resources are safeguarded and used during this pre-production stage to improve the quality and productivity of domesticated plants over time. It also covers developments in agricultural inputs like crop protection tools or fertilizer. This can contribute to increasing yields and incomes while deterring the conversion of additional land for cultivation. In order to ensure that farmers prosper in the light of the changing climate and other increasingly unexpected circumstances, it also incorporates improvement in agricultural techniques itself. Some of the well-known case studies on the pre-production phase include aiding in the more exact use of fertilizers by farmers, employing gene editing to breed better crops, etc.

ii. In-Production Phase: To maximize crop yields, farmers must dynamically manage crops grown using agricultural technology, such as irrigation and pesticide spraying, in response to changes in weather, such as rainfall, temperature, and humidity. Farmers face a variety of difficulties throughout the "production" stage; a few examples are pests and illnesses, harsh and unpredictable weather, controlling food loss, and fluctuating market conditions. By 2050, 60 percent more food is predicted to be needed; however, due to a lack of information, existing production efforts fall short of this target. The development of lowlands to increase productivity and water availability, the use of mobile phones to issue early warning systems, aiding farmers in their fight against autumn armyworm in diverse places, the beneficial effects of crop diversification, and other topics are only a few of the well-known case studies.

iii. Post-Production Phase: The "post-production" phase speaks of the actions taken to get cultivated crops from the farmer to the customer. It is also known as "supply chain." Crops can be transformed into marketable goods and then processed, packed, and stored before being delivered to customers. Post-harvest food loss is a major problem in developing countries, as there is frequently inadequate or no infrastructure, energy grids, or transportation networks. To stop these losses and increase the value of crop productivity along the way, creative supply chain programs are being implemented.

## 3.2.5 Data Related to Diseases on Plants

One of the main causes of the decreased agricultural productivity is the presence of pests and diseases on the crop. Researchers must spend a lot of time and money visiting the field to capture photographs of pests and diseases in order to learn and analyze more about them. Such a task can be carried out by farmers who have prior experience recognizing pests and diseases. Thus, researchers can focus on the examination of the data they have already obtained for longer. Additionally, a number of Android-based smartphone apps have previously been used to identify pests and diseases that affect drops. These apps can be used in conjunction with MCS technology to gather the necessary photographs of the pests and diseases on the crop.

Researchers can analyze the regularity of migratory pest's migration in this method in addition to expanding the data set of the pests and illnesses' prints.

Numerous crop biochemical and biophysical factors can be identified and measured using sensing instruments in the field or in the lab that assess crop spectroscopic parameters. They might also be employed as early warning signs of plant illnesses.

### 3.2.6 Vegetation Yield Status

Remote sensing has a number of advantages for crop monitoring and yield forecasting, which are closely related to changes in the soil, climate, and other biophysical and biochemical changes. Several remote sensing techniques, such as multi-spectral data, hyper-spectral data, radio detection and ranging (RADAR), and light detection and ranging (LiDAR) imaging, could be used for yield forecasting (Ali et al. 2021).

Smartphones' sensing capabilities have improved as a result of advances in sensing technologies. For instance, Changhong H2 is the first smartphone equipped with the small-scale molecular spectroscopy sensor that can measure the moisture and sweetness of fruits in order to determine their yield status (Shirsath et al. 2020). As a result, by examining these factors, researchers can learn more about how to identify fruits of a certain quality (Escolà et al. 2017). Meanwhile, farmers can gain an early understanding of the fruits' growth conditions, allowing them to dynamically modify their management strategies in order to maximize their productivity. In this section, we discuss various vegetarian yield status prediction where sensors are employed.

i. *A hypothetical satellite for yield prediction:* The estimation of primary productivity and the evaluation of crop acreage (Friedl et al. 2010), estimation of primary productivity, crop yield production, observation of the impact of factors affecting biodiversity related to vegetation covered, and evaluation of vegetation phonological conditions are just a few satellite data. The ability to update data over time to track changes and the huge distances that may be observed in a single image are the key advantages of satellite imaging. Satellite data from various sources were utilized to access and gauge agricultural production at the regional and local levels (Mueller et al. 2012). In order to correlate yield using linear regression models for the barley crop, used four vegetation indices: normalized difference vegetation indix NDVI, wide dynamic range vegetation index WDRVI, and green-based vegetation indices GRVI and GNDVI.

ii. *Crop yield analysis using RADAR and LiDAR:* It becomes a viable option to employ RADAR as a technique for quickly gathering distant sensing data. Regardless of the weather conditions, data about earth observation (EO) is gathered via the RADAR system (Lu 2006). Many researchers used RADAR data to calculate production aboveground and biomass (Santos et al. 2003). The saturation level depends on the wavelength portion, polarization, as well as the structural characteristics of the vegetation and the ground, which is a common issue with RADAR data.

To determine the lead density of a citrus canopy, Wei and Salyani (2005) created a laser scanning instrument. In order to find a variety of topographic features, including slop and the moisture index, Eyre et al. (2021) used LiDAR height information from southern Ontario's agricultural land. After that, crop yield information from the previous years was combined with these topography factors to predict crop output. R2 for maize was found to be 0.80, for wheat to be 0.73, for soybeans to be 0.71, and in relation to the estimation of all agricultural associations to be 0.75.

iii. *Field sensors:* Spectrometers, to collect reflectance information at greater spatial resolution, greater resolution spectral sensors, as well as various additional ground optical sensors have all been developed at different wavelengths in order to calculate agricultural yields. A form of ground-based remote sensing, called field spectroscopy (Ahamed et al. 2011), offers a wide size of the spectral bands collected over the entire electromagnetic spectrum. Spectroscopic data at the ground and leaf level in the visible and infrared ranges are supported by the assumption in the way that light interacts with the plant and the green leaf's ability to reflect light. This makes it possible to measure the chemical properties of the leaves.

## 3.3 RECOMMENDATIONS FOR DATA QUALITY CONTROL

Data quality can be defined in different forms and is very individualized. "Fitness for use" is the well-known definition of data quality. According to Redman (2001), data are fit to use if they are free of errors, readily available, accurate, timely available, complete, consistent with other sources, relevant, comprehensive, contain the right amount of detail, and are simple to read and understand. Data that can be deemed good for one scenario may not always be appropriate for another because quality is context-based.

In a wide number of areas, data quality is a prevalent area of concern. Considering the significance of agriculture to the Indian economy, it is essential that the data be relevant and of sufficient quality for use in planning and decision-making processes, among other things. Ensuring the accuracy of data utilized by experts and decision-makers to support processes like yield forecast, monitoring, and planning approaches has significant advantages. In spite of various attempts of data collection, information manufacturing systems (Ballou et al. 1998), database systems, web systems, and data mining systems, modeling different kinds of databases or information systems frequently neglects to take data quality issues into consideration. These systems generate and report data, which is then used without considering any flaws or faults. As a result, decisions made by experts are erroneous and the information collected from these data is prone to inaccuracy.

Automated processes are insufficient to handle many crucial data quality management and analysis. In order to handle these computationally challenging tasks, like crops' entity resolution, disease identification, and yield status verification, crowdsourcing is a viable method. High-quality and real-world data gathering is needed for the evaluation and verification of robust techniques. Exploratory research using crowdsourcing has already shown their potential to capture enormous amounts of high-quality data.

According to Wang and Strong (1996), quality dimensions can be thought of as qualities that enable the representations of a specific quality feature. As some of the most crucial quality aspects for information consumers, accuracy, completeness, timeliness, and consistency have been repeatedly recognized. In domains like the simulation modeling process, correctness, reliability, and usability are intriguing. Three primary elements, including the user's perception, the information itself,

**TABLE 3.2**

Classes of Data Quality Requirement with Quality Criteria and Assessment Method

| Class | | | | | |
|---|---|---|---|---|---|
| Subject Criteria | | Object Criteria | | Process Criteria | |
| Quality Criteria | Assessment Method | Quality Criteria | Assessment Method | Quality Criteria | Assessment Method |
| Assumption | Experience | Efficiency | Sampling | Correctness | Sampling |
| Interpretability | Sampling | Objectivity | Expert input | Delay | Continuous assessment |
| Materialization | Sampling | Reliability | Continuous assessment | Accessibility | Continuous assessment |
| Sensibly | Sampling | Security | Decomposition | Quantity of data | Continuous assessment |
| Gross product | Continuous assessment | Timeliness | Decomposition | Materialization | Decomposition |

and the technique used to acquire the information, are said to affect the quality of information according to Naumann and Rolker (2000). There are basically three classes of data quality criteria: subject criteria, object criteria, and process criteria. Subject criteria are those that can be determined by farmers' individual perspectives, background, and experiences. Object criteria is defined on the basis of information analysis and to process queries, process criteria is considered. The list of quality requirements is organized into classes in Table 3.2, along with suggested assessment techniques for each quality criterion.

Continuous data quality faces several difficulties, including those related to modeling, management, quality verification, analysis, storage, and presentation. According to the application scenario and the level of data quality necessary for the intended application, different approaches should be taken to address each of these issues. Thus, a crucial element is being aware of which quality traits must be assessed in a certain situation.

For data quality control, individual farmers can employ EO inputs in regulatory contexts and farm management applications such as precision farming. A regional farm inputs supplier, a machine operator, or a local watershed management agency are a few examples of the types of local, regional, and administrative aggregation levels of information that are needed by the farm service industry and regional industries to maintain the quality of data.

The reference data sets are needed for the common agricultural policy (CAP) management and monitoring, which are frequently available to the general public. Agricultural data management systems are also relying more and more on information communication technology (ICT). Additionally, through increased information exchange across the food production and processing industry, made possible by mobile connectivity, there is an unparalleled potential to provide benefits for both parties.

## 3.4 COMPARISON OF AGRICULTURAL CROWDSOURCING AT THE GLOBAL LEVEL AND INDIAN PERSPECTIVE

Crowdsourcing in agriculture can aid in gathering information and reflects more production and profit for the beneficiaries. It enables professionals to acquire a greater variety of data inputs, ultimately improves agricultural output, and sometimes encourages markets as well (FAO 2022). The use of crowdsourcing in development is fundamentally different from how it is often used in developed, developing, and underdeveloped economies around the world. "Platform" is the most significant among them. In developed countries, crowdsourcing is mainly performed using websites on computers accessed by the Internet in developing or under-developed countries mobile dominates as a platform to exchange crowdsourcing information (FAO 2020; 2021a). Based on research activities, one can say that crowdsourcing is capable enough and applicable to potential new initiatives. It is required to apply filters before selecting crowdsourcing data among available. Some of the points that can be considered before the selection of crowdsourcing data source viz. What could a person and a group's fundamental role in data collection be? Do they have adequate background knowledge to understand the purpose of data collection? Are target users literate enough to use mobile phones? And finally, are they getting paid for their active participation? We need to consider these crucial points before using crowdsourcing data (FAO 2021b). Crowdsourcing applications can benefit smallholder farmers within different agricultural development projects, which include access to essential instructions, market access to the farmer, weather data, and monitoring pest outbreaks.

Farmers in under-developed countries like India are becoming citizen scientists by adopting crowdsourcing platforms that help in generating data related to crop types, phenology, and climatic sustainability. Researchers have shown how farmers' participation in scientific studies can improve and expedite crop variety recommendations in a study spanning India, Nicaragua, and Ethiopia (Etten 2019). The research also demonstrated four ways in which analysis can enhance a variety of recommendations: by reducing climate bias, incorporating seasonal climate forecasts, risk analysis, and geographic extrapolation. The Food and Agriculture Organization of the United Nations (http://www.fao.org/faostat/en/#data/TCL) disseminates crop and livestock products data across the world and also can be used as the crowdsourcing data source. Hence, the top ten countries were selected (Table 3.3) based on higher agricultural production capacity across the world in this chapter.

**TABLE 3.3**

Crop Product (Primary and Processed) Data Set Used in Various Crowdsourcing Applications (Source: FAO 2020) (FAO-Based Top Ten Countries as per Their Agricultural Production Capacity)

| Region | Brazil | China | France | Germany | India | Japan | Mexico | Russia | Turkey | U. S. |
|---|---|---|---|---|---|---|---|---|---|---|
| **Crop Products (Primary and Processed)** | | | | | | | | | | |
| **Apple** | | | | | | | | | | |
| Area harvested (ha) | 32468 | 1911848 | 50150 | 33980 | 308000 | 35108 | 56706 | 215258 | 170903 | 119504 |
| Yield (hg/ha) | 302836 | 211842 | 323007 | 301154 | 88766 | 205197 | 125948 | 94803 | 251633 | 389166 |
| Production (tons) | 983247 | 40501041 | 1619880 | 1023320 | 2734000 | 720405 | 714203 | 2040700 | 4300486 | 4650684 |
| **Barley** | | | | | | | | | | |
| Area harvested (ha) | 104383 | 260000 | 1972270 | 1667300 | 618085 | 63600 | 294213 | 8267448 | 3092442 | 863200 |
| Yield (hg/ha) | 37089 | 34615 | 52090 | 64591 | 27828 | 34858 | 29376 | 25327 | 26840 | 41700 |
| Production (tons) | 387146 | 900000 | 10273570 | 10769200 | 1720000 | 221700 | 864293 | 20938993 | 8300000 | 3599510 |
| **Grapes** | | | | | | | | | | |
| Area harvested (ha) | 73726 | 767513 | 759060 | 100710 | 140000 | 16500 | 35485 | 72438 | 400998 | 372311 |
| Yield (hg/ha) | 194720 | 193392 | 77520 | 114144 | 223214 | 99030 | 127806 | 94137 | 104961 | 144736 |
| Production (tons) | 1435596 | 14843091 | 5884230 | 1149540 | 3125000 | 163400 | 453520 | 681908 | 4208908 | 5388679 |
| **Maize** | | | | | | | | | | |
| Area harvested (ha) | 18253766 | 41292000 | 1691130 | 419300 | 9865000 | 62 | 7156391 | 2731870 | 690553 | 33373570 |
| Yield (hg/ha) | 56955 | 63178 | 79350 | 95874 | 30573 | 26452 | 38322 | 50805 | 94127 | 107945 |
| Production (tons) | 103963620 | 260876476 | 13419140 | 4020000 | 30160000 | 164 | 27424528 | 13879210 | 6500000 | 360251560 |
| **Onion** | | | | | | | | | | |
| Area harvested (ha) | 47487 | 1085340 | 17680 | 14730 | 1434000 | 25610 | 48628 | 59908 | 70275 | 53742 |
| Yield (hg/ha) | 314953 | 218582 | 398552 | 427447 | 186457 | 493191 | 308411 | 290139 | 324440 | 710998 |
| Production (tons) | 1495618 | 23723552 | 704640 | 629630 | 26738000 | 1263061 | 1499741 | 1738165 | 2280000 | 3821044 |

(Continued)

**TABLE 3.3 (Continued)**

Crop Product (Primary and Processed) Data Set Used in Various Crowdsourcing Applications (Source: FAO 2020) (FAO-Based Top Ten Countries as per Their Agricultural Production Capacity)

| Region | Brazil | China | France | Germany | India | Japan | Mexico | Russia | Turkey | U. S. |
|---|---|---|---|---|---|---|---|---|---|---|
| | | | Crop Products (Primary and Processed) | | | | | | | |
| **Oranges** | | | | | | | | | | |
| Area harvested (ha) | 572698 | 393598 | 980 | 0 | 670000 | 2411 | 327756 | 21 | 46012 | 203840 |
| Yield (hg/ha) | 291740 | 194136 | 83265 | 0 | 147075 | 116109 | 141832 | 31905 | 289919 | 233828 |
| Production (tons) | 16707897 | 7641167 | 8160 | 0 | 9854000 | 27994 | 4648620 | 67 | 1333975 | 4766350 |
| **Rice** | | | | | | | | | | |
| Area harvested (ha) | 1677705 | 30341784 | 14810 | 0 | 45000000 | 1462000 | 47553 | 195935 | 125398 | 1208810 |
| Yield (hg/ha) | 66108 | 70402 | 51533 | 0 | 39623 | 66390 | 62107 | 58275 | 78151 | 85398 |
| Production (tons) | 11091011 | 213610729 | 76320 | 0 | 178305000 | 9706250 | 295338 | 1141819 | 980000 | 10322990 |
| **Potatoes** | | | | | | | | | | |
| Area harvested (ha) | 117253 | 4218188 | 214500 | 273500 | 2158000 | 72306 | 60855 | 1178098 | 147965 | 369930 |
| Yield (hg/ha) | 321337 | 185474 | 405217 | 428340 | 237720 | 314557 | 319433 | 166432 | 351434 | 507933 |
| Production (tons) | 3767769 | 78236596 | 8691900 | 11715100 | 51300000 | 2274435 | 1943910 | 19607361 | 5200000 | 18789970 |
| **Vegetables** | | | | | | | | | | |
| Area harvested (ha) | 233188 | 10222548 | 3760 | 2000 | 2847604 | 122198 | 96246 | 97309 | 29922 | 11650 |
| Yield (hg/ha) | 127312 | 166641 | 94468 | 114100 | 141177 | 224206 | 83587 | 204927 | 185672 | 703295 |
| Production (tons) | 2968753 | 170350037 | 35520 | 22820 | 40201745 | 2739748 | 804490 | 1994127 | 555568 | 819339 |
| **Wheat** | | | | | | | | | | |
| Area harvested (ha) | 2434703 | 23382215 | 4512420 | 2835500 | 31357000 | 212600 | 561282 | 28864312 | 6914632 | 14870740 |
| Yield (hg/ha) | 26073 | 57417 | 66803 | 78195 | 34311 | 44652 | 53212 | 29759 | 29647 | 33415 |
| Production (tons) | 6347987 | 134254710 | 30144110 | 22172100 | 107590000 | 949300 | 2986689 | 85896326 | 20500000 | 49690680 |

# REFERENCES

Ahamed, T., Tian, L., Zhang, Y. and Ting, K.C., 2011. A review of remote sensing methods for biomass feedstock production. *Biomass and Bioenergy*, 35(7), pp. 2455–2469.

Ahmad, I., Ghafoor, A., Bhatti, M.I., Akhtar, I.H. and Ibrahim, M., 2012. Satellite remote sensing and GIS based crops forecasting & estimation system in Pakistan.

Ali, A.M., Savin, I., Poddubskiy, A., Abouelghar, M., Saleh, N., Abutaleb, K., El-Shirbeny, M. and Dokukin, P., 2021. Integrated method for rice cultivation monitoring using Sentinel-2 data and Leaf Area IndexEgyptian. *Journal of Remote Sensing and Space Science*, 24(3), pp. 431–441.

d'Andrimont, R., Yordanov, M., Lemoine, G., Yoong, J., Nikel, K. and van der Velde, M. 2018. Crowdsourced street-level imagery as a potential source of in-situ data for crop monitoring, *Land*, 7, p. 127.

Assogba, D., Idohou, R., Chirwa, P. and Assogbadjo, A.E., 2022. On opportunities and challenges to conserve the African baobab under present and future climates in Benin (West Africa). *Journal of Arid Environments*, 198, pp. 104692–104712.

Ballou, D., Wang, R., Pazer, H. and Tayi, G.K., 1998. Modeling information manufacturing systems to determine information product quality. *Management of Science*, 44, pp. 462–484.

Bey, A., Sánchez-Paus Díaz, A., Maniatis, D., Marchi, G., Mollicone, D., Ricci, S., Bastin, J.F., Moore, R., Federici, S., Rezende, M. and Patriarca, C., 2016. Collect earth: Land use and land cover assessment through augmented visual interpretation. *Remote Sensing*, 8(10), pp. 807–831.

Esch, S., Reichenau, T.G., Korres, W. and Schneider, K., 2019. Soil moisture index from ERS-SAR and its application to the analysis of spatial patterns in agricultural areas. *The Analysis of Spatial Patterns in Agricultural Areas*, 12(2), p. 022206.

Escolà, A., Badia, N., Arnó, J. and Martínez-Casasnovas, J.A., 2017. Using Sentinel-2 images to implement precision agriculture techniques in large arable fields: First results of a case study. *Advances in Animal Biosciences*, 8(2), pp. 377–382.

Estes, L., McRitchie, D., Choi, J., Debats, S.R., Evans, T., Guthe, W., Luo, D., Gagazzo, G., Zempleni, R., and Caylor, K., 2015. Diylandcover: Crowdsourcing the creation of systematic, accurate landcover maps. *PeerJPrePrints*, 3, p. e1266.

Eyre, R., Lindsay, J., Laamrani, A. and Berg, A., 2021. Within-field yield prediction in cereal crops using Lidar-derived topographic attributes with geographically weighted regression models. *Remote Sensing*, 13(20).

FAO, 2020. Trade – crops and livestock products. Rome. Accessed on August 2022. Available at http://www.fao.org/faostat/en/#data/TCL

FAO, 2021a. Government expenditures in agriculture 2001–2019. Global and regional trends. FAOSTAT analytical brief series no 24. Rome. pp. 2–8. Accessed on August 2022. Available at https://www.fao.org/3/cb5128en/cb5128en.pdf

FAO, 2021b. World food and agriculture – statistical yearbook 2021. Rome. pp. 5–39. Accessed on August 2022. Available at 10.4060/cb4477en

FAO, 2022. FAOSTAT land, inputs and sustainability, land use. Rome. Accessed on August 2022. Available at http://www.fao.org/faostat/en/#data/RL

Friedl, M.A., Sulla-Menashe, D. and Tan, B., 2010. MODISCollection 5 global land cover: Algorithm refinement and characterization of new datasets. *Remote Sensing of Environment*, 114, pp. 168–182.

Fritz, S., McCallum, I., Schill, C., Perger, C., See, L., Schepaschenko, D., van der Velde, M., Kraxner, F. and Obersteiner, M., 2012. Geo-Wiki: An online platform for improving global land cover. *Environmental Modelling & Software*, 31, pp. 110–123.

Jin, Z., Azzari, G., You, C., Di Tommaso, S., Aston, S., Burke, M. and Lobell, D.B., 2019. Smallholder maize area and yield mapping at national scales with Google Earth Engine. *Remote Sensing of Environment*, 228, pp. 115–128

Karila, K., Nevalainen, O., Krooks, A., Karjalainen, M. and Kaasalainen, S., 2014. Monitoring changes in rice cultivated area from SAR and optical satellite images in ben tre and tra vinh provinces in mekong delta. *Vietnam Remote Sensing*, 6(5), pp. 4090–4108.

Krupowicz, W., Czarnecka, A. and Grus, M., 2020. Implementing crowdsourcing initiatives in land consolidation procedures in Poland. *Land Use Policy*, 99, pp. 105015–105026.

Lu, D., 2006. The potential and challenge of remote sensing-based biomass estimation. *International Journal of Remote Sensing*, 27(7), pp. 1297–1328.

Manfreda, S., McCabe, M., Miller, P., Lucas, R., Madrigal, V.P., Mallinis, G., Dor, E.B., Helman, D., Estes, L., Ciraolo, G., Müllerová, J., Tauro, F., Lima, M.I.D., Lima, J.L.M.P.D., Frances, F., Caylor, K., Kohv, M., Maltese, A., Perks, M., Ruiz-Pérez, G., Su, Z., Vico, G. and Toth, B. 2018. On the use of unmanned aerial systems for environmental monitoring. *Remote Sensing*, 10(4), p. 641.

Marx, S., Hämmerle, M., Klonner, C. and Höfle, B., 2016. 3D participatory sensing with low-cost mobile devices for crop height assessment – A comparison with terrestrial laser scanning data. *PLoS One*, 11(4), pp. 1–22.

Minet, J., Curnel, Y., Gobin, A., Goffart, J.P., Mélard, F., Tychon, B., Wellens, J. and Defourny, P., 2017. Crowdsourcing for agricultural applications: A review of uses and opportunities for a farmsourcing approach. *Computers and Electronics in Agriculture*, 142, pp. 126–138.

Minet, J., Robert, B. and Tychon, B., 2015. *The potential of OpenStreetMap for land use/land cover mapping*. FOSS4G.be, Brussels, Belgium.

Mueller, N.D., Gerber, J.S., Johnston, M., Ray, D.K., Ramankutty, N. and Foley, J.A., 2012. Closing yield gaps through nutrient and water management. *Nature*, 490(7419), pp.254–257.

Muller, C.L., Chapman, L., Johnston, S., Kidd, C., Illingworth, S., Foody, G., Overeem, A. and Leigh, R.R., 2015. Crowdsourcing for climate and atmospheric sciences: Current status and future potential. *International Journal of Climatology*, 35(11), pp. 3185–3203.

Naumann, F. and Rolker, C., 2000. Assessment Methods for Information Quality Criteria. In *IQ*, pp. 148–162. MIT.

O'Connor, B., Secades, C., Penner, J., et al., 2015. Earth observation as a tool for tracking progress towards the Aichi biodiversity targets. *Remote Sensing in Ecology and Conservation*, 1, pp. 19–28.

Pichon, L., Brunel, G., Payan, J.C., Taylor, J., Bellon-Maurel, V. and Tisseyre, B., 2021. ApeX-Vigne: Experiences in monitoring vine water status from within-field to regional scales using crowdsourcing data from a free mobile phone application. *Precision Agriculture*, 22(2), pp. 608–626.

Posadas, B.B., Hanumappa, M., Niewolny, K. and Gilbert, J.E., 2021. Design and evaluation of a crowdsourcing precision agriculture mobile application for Lambsquarters, mission LQ. *Agronomy*, 11(10), p. 1951.

Rahman, M., Blackwell, B., Banerjee, N. and Saraswat, D., 2015. Smartphone-based hierarchical crowdsourcing for weed identification. *Computers and Electronics in Agriculture*, 113, pp. 14–23.

Redman, T. C., 2001. Data quality: The field guide. Digital Pr. [u.a.].

Santos, J.R., Freitas, C.C., Araujo, L.S., Dutra, L.V., Mura, J.C. and Gama, F.F., 2003. Airborne P-band SAR allied to the aboveground biomass studies in the Brazilian tropical rainforest. *Remote Sens Environ*, 87, p. 482.

Saran, S., Chaudhary, S.K., Singh, P., Tiwari, A. and Kumar, V., 2022. A comprehensive review on biodiversity information portals. *Biodiversity and Conservation*, pp. 1–24.

Saran, S., Singh, P., Padalia, H., Singh, A., Kumar, V. and Chauhan, P., 2020. Citizen-centric tool for near real-time mapping of active forest fires. *Current Science*, 119(5), pp. 780–790.

Shanmugapriya, P., Rathika, S., Ramesh, T. and Janaki, P., 2019. Applications of remote sensing in agriculture – A review. *International Journal of Current Microbiology and Applied Sciences*, 8(01), pp. 2270–2283.

Shirsath, P.B., Sehgal, V.K. and Aggarwal, P.K., 2020. Downscaling regional crop yields to local scale using remote sensing. *Agriculture (Switzerland)*, 10(3), pp. 1–14.

Singh, P. and Saran, S., 2015a. OSGEO-India: FOSS4G 2015 – Second National Conference. Open-Source Geospatial Tools in Climate Change Research And Natural Resources Management, 8–10 June, Dehradun, India, pp. 1–4.

Singh, P. and Saran, S., 2015b. Crowdsourcing application in bioresource information retrieval. FOSS4G-India 2015, 2, pp. 1–8.

Singh, P., Saran, S., Kumar, D., Padalia, H., Srivastava, A. and Senthil Kumar, A., 2018. Species mapping using citizen science approach through IBIN portal: Use case in foothills of Himalaya. *Journal of the Indian Society of Remote Sensing*, 46(10), pp. 1725–1737.

Sokolov, K.O., Sokolova, M.I., Aliukov, S.V. and Markina, Y.V., 2019. Use of crowd-sourcing in agricultural consulting services for the sustainable development of agricultural enterprises. 40(16), pp. 1–9.

Steinke, J., van Etten, J. and Zelan, P.M. 2017. The accuracy of farmer-generated data in an agricultural citizen science methodology. *Agronomy for Sustainable Development*. 37, 32.

Torresan, C., Berton, A., Carotenuto, F., Gennaro, S.F.D., Gioli, B., Matese, A., Miglietta, F., Vagnoli, C., Zaldei, A. and Wallace, L., 2017. Forestry applications of UAVs in Europe: A review. *Int. J. Remote Sens.*, 38(8–10), pp. 2427–2447.

Van Etten, J., Beza, E., Calderer, L., Van Duijvendijk, K., Fadda, C., Fantahun, B., Kidane, Y.G., van de Gevel, J., Gupta, A., Mengistu, D.K. and Kiambi, D.A.N., 2019. First experiences with a novel farmer citizen science approach: Crowdsourcing partici-patory variety selection through on-farm triadic comparisons of technologies (tricot). *Experimental Agriculture*, 55(S1), pp. 275–296.

Van Etten, J., de Sousa, K., Aguilar, A., Barrios, M., Coto, A., Dell'Acqua, M., Fadda, C., Gebrehawaryat, Y., van de Gevel, J., Gupta, A. and Kiros, A.Y., 2019. Crop variety management for climate adaptation supported by citizen science. *Proceedings of the National Academy of Sciences*, 116(10), pp. 4194–4199.

Wang, R.Y. and Strong, D.M., 1996. Beyond accuracy: What data quality means to data consumers. *Journal of Management Information Systems*, 12(4), pp. 5–34.

Wei, J. and Salyani, M., 2005. Development of a laser scanner for measuring tree canopy characteristics: Phase 2. Foliage density measurement. *Transactions of the ASAE*, 48(4), pp. 1595–1601.

Wu, F., Wu, B., Zhang, M., Zeng, H. and Tian, F., 2021. Identification of crop type in crowdsourced road view photos with deep convolutional neural network. *Sensors*, 21(4), pp. 1165–1180.

Yu, Q., Shi, Y., Tang, H., Yang, P., Xie, A., Liu, B. and Wu, W., 2017. eFarm: A tool for better observing agricultural land systems. *Sensors*, 17(3), pp. 453–469.

# 4

# Crowdsourcing Outline for Contemporary Aided Medicinal Backup Systems

*Sonali Vyas[1], Shaurya Gupta[1], and Vinod Kumar Shukla[2]*
[1]School of Computer Science, University of Petroleum and Energy Studies (UPES), Dehradun, India
[2]Department of Engineering and Architecture, Amity University, Dubai, UAE

## 4.1 INTRODUCTION

Psychological well-being stands as a foremost communal healthiness apprehension with almost one out of seven people suffering in terms of any type of mental well-being universally (Lago et al., 2017). Though there is no perpetual therapy in terms of psychological well-being circumstances, nonetheless, long-term mental happiness is accomplished with the help of suitable administration (Abdullah et al., 2018). People need to uninterruptedly observe their indications, which in turn simplify an opportune action (Ahmadi et al., 2020). With time, there has been an upsurge in the number of lessons exploiting technical expertise in order to enable programmed indication (Barnett et al., 2018). Varied models designed and developed for the purpose of data acquisition are in the developing phase for patients and wellness experts, which will be upgrading the digital healing conveyance of people. Taking an example, a platform called Beiwe was established and is being verified for predicting the reversion or relapse phase in schizophrenic patients with the help of individual cardinal equipment. Contemporary digital healthiness architectures principally have an emphasis on recognition besides imagining (Saha et al., 2017). The "care delivery" constituents in existing architectures miss the carefulness factor. Currently, there is an urgent prerequisite concerning the digital well-being design regarding suitable means of linking people to suitable platforms wherein any variation in psychological health can be perceived. Peer sustenance is well-defined as "provision of expressive assessment, besides informational aid formed by social network associates who hold experimental information regarding conduct or behavior of objective populace" (Shalaby et al., 2020). Nowadays, according to study carried by authors Huber et al. (2018), Prescott et al. (2020) and Cheng et al. (2020) crowdsourcing has been useful in aiding medicinal and healthcare domain. Nowadays, there is substantial evidence, like peer sustenance, that is quite operative in plummeting indications besides hospitalization (Huber et al., 2018) inclusive of numerous well-being circumstances, straddling from cancer (Prescott et al., 2020), to clusters of individuals fronting communal variations like new mums (Cheng et al., 2020; Sharma et al., 2020). With time, peer sustenance has increased, though not much technical expertise has exploited much provisions. Scheming software architecture of any peer sustenance method is non-trivial because of the following reasons:

- As there is no state-of-the-art effort methodically bestowing requirements, the need for the purpose of extraction lengthily besides classifying exceptional requirements is obligatory.
- Furthermore, there is a need to design a suitable software design in support of expansion of peer sustenance structures, meeting caused necessities.

The chapter is prepared as follows: Section 4.2 presents work related to software framework for crowdsourcing in the area of mental health. Section 4.3 discusses the challenges in providing early mental health support and necessities gathered through co-design actions conducted with people with first-hand experience of suicidal ideation and mental health specialists. Section 4.4 states a proposed peer-sourcing design methodology to support predictive skills in mental health. Finally, in Sections 4.5 and 4.6, we have discussed our proposed methodology and conclusion of work, respectively.

## 4.2 LITERATURE REVIEW

Nowadays, there are ample challenges in providing distant psychological well-being sustenance, with the help of technology. The authors have discovered that in a five- to ten-minute cell phone discussion with a trainer, apart from web-centered interference, users presented a lot of enhanced withholding towards their recovery (Mohr et al., 2013). Though many prototypes assure enlightening customer appointments, there are still a number of blockades involving provisioning fees besides complications concerning programming amongst parties (Gidugu et al., 2015). Peer sustenance exercise considering psychological well-being reassures allocation of data besides practices leading to managing of repossession engrossed accomplishments (O'Leary et al., 2018), apart from that it has been successfully implemented in making the lives of individuals healthy and happier (Lloyd et al., 2014). Additionally, communal psychological well-being amenities are increasingly acknowledged worldwide for improving quality of life (Tolley et al., 2020). In developed countries, a number of amenities are administered by an ample number of professionals (Du Plessis et al., 2020). With time, there has been a mounting curiosity of individuals in gaining knowledge and undergoing some sort of short-term course for imparting psychotherapy counseling (Ibrahim et al., 2020). Peer sustenance pays back the psychotherapy counselor and the patient also (Schlichthorst et al., 2020). Furthermore, it advances the community, besides work-related operatives of peer enthusiasts (Fortuna et al., 2020). It can be conveyed in a face-to-face mode that gives a human touch (Gillard, 2019). A peer-to-peer web-centered intellectual reassessment platform has expressly produced additional custom action besides superior customer or consumer understanding (Anderson et al., 2020).

## 4.3 MENTAL HEALTH SUPPORTIVE ARCHITECTURE

There are quite a number of software developments considering psychological well-being, but very few of them showcase their minutiae regarding designs in addition as in what way they assist a psychological healthiness sphere. Whereas numerous software designs described beneath focuses more on physical and remote monitoring of patients. These healthcare systems emphases are on varied verticals like:

1. **Individual Well-Being Structures:** These kinds of systems deliver individual well-being administration via observation besides broadcasting, characteristically by means of personal gadgets like smartphones and medicinal devices. Considering an instance of

design premeditated precisely for psychological well-being stands as an inescapable design in terms of anxiety observed in individuals' well-being structure (Verma et al., 2021). The authors (Staner et al., 2022) have discoursed an outline in terms of design in terms of smartphones, besides wearable devices, in terms of observing anxiety of people by means of cohesive experimental resolution sustenance structures. It is quite appropriate for protracted anxiety nursing throughout customary commotion because of submissive nursing. Some of the well-being encompasses a service-oriented architecture by means of incident-determined architectural fundamentals (Altaf et al., 2022).

2. **Medical Resolution Sustenance Structures:** Any medical decision sustenance system supports well-being authorities in taking resolution-oriented responsibilities by extending opportune, supplementary info associated to particular diseased individuals. The four foremost categories of such a system includes the following (Beri et al., 2022).
   - Impartial
   - Incorporated into any sort of well-being information system or any kind of automated well-being record
   - Custom centered
   - Service-oriented

In cases of obstructive pulmonary diseases, the service oriented design of grid plays a critical role in terms of identification of such kind of disease at an early stage (Elhanan et al., 2022). A disseminated clinical decision support system is discussed with an assortment of amenities considering software-oriented architecture besides integrating automated fitness accounts. Additional instances of clinical decision support system involve improved medicinal record in the case of elderly people's brains (Bull et al., 2016), which is formed with help of Software as a Service and varied software architectures and it helps in managing individuals suffering from aged intellect illnesses, like dementia.

## 4.4 CROWDSOURCING SYSTEMS

The concept of crowdsourcing was initially devised by Jeff Howe and Mark Robinson (Liu et al., 2020) in order to designate how companies used the Internet in outsourcing of any kind to a crowd. The foundation idea of it involves influencing the control of crowd in comprehensively resolving a complex assignment (Hassan et al., 2017; Mao et al., 2017). In past times, crowdsourcing-centered systems were extensively used in countless domains, like inhabitant knowledge science, semantic netting, besides crowdfunding (Dhinakaran et al., 2021; Niu et al., 2019; Sarı et al., 2019). In order of sustenance of numerous crowdsourcing-centered uses, countless software substructures including middleware, plus program design agendas are anticipated. Amazon Mechanical Turk (MTurk) (Paulheim et al., 2017) stands as a crowdsourcing dais, making lives very easy for people besides industries in outsourcing anthropological intellect responsibilities to dispersed personnel who all can achieve tasks of such kinds effectively. MTurk delivers Application Programming Interfaces in terms of crowdsourcing. The authors (Bernardino et al., 2020; Lublóy et al., 2020) have projected program design contexts with development besides runtime sustenance in terms of mobile crowd-sensing applications, used in location-centered municipals detecting information like traffic positioning and airborne quality. The authors in Bessière et al. (2020) projected an amenity policy that enabled anthropological substance lessons including assessment conveyances and managing with the help of crowdsourcing. Epicollect (Cicchiello et al., 2022) permits the formation of crowdsourcing errands in respect to ecology. Software substructures or outlines delivering decent sustenance for its objective solicitation provinces. Nevertheless, they can't fulfill the peer tracing psychological well-being sustenance development because of underlying causes:

- The software structures pertaining to crowdsourcing at times can't trace health dimensions of individuals as crowdsourcing structures generally relies on a central architecture wherein suppliers are very well associated with controllers, but incases of distributed computing the overall structure does not perform to its full potential (Fadzil et al., 2021). Apart from that the peer sourcing and crowdsourcing does not function well in unison as they lack in terms of synchronous communication (Bernardino et al., 2022; Bessière et al., 2020).
- Secondly, facility suppliers in terms of crowdsourcing structures are frequently similar in standings of proficiency, besides dependability in implementation of pertinent responsibilities. Peers in peer-obtaining structures comprise of numerous participants with assorted

**TABLE 4.1**

Peer Sourcing versus Crowdsourcing

| Peer Sourcing | Crowdsourcing |
| --- | --- |
| Distributed | Centralized |
| Diverse | Consistent |
| Candidate deficient | Adequate candidates |
| High task insistence | Lesser task insistence |

characteristics. Taking an instance, peers in our psychological healthiness sustenance circumstances may be companion nobles including folks from helpers besides families; specialized peers include psychological healthcare specialists, besides peer sourcing managers like National Health Service (NHS) sustenance groups (Bernardino et al., 2022).

- Third, crowd-sourcing platforms frequently own an enormous system facilitating applicant provision suppliers with little insistence necessities, whereas peer sourcing frequently grieves from inadequacy of facility suppliers temporarily with sophisticated pressing prerequisites. Lastly, synchronous communications in between supplicant plus sponsor are mandatory in peer sourcing, though this is not at all required in crowdsourcing (Bessière et al., 2020). In conclusion, crowdsourcing styles may not be openly embraced to peer-sourcing applications because of the differences in Table 4.1.

## 4.5 NEIGHBOR-BACKED MEDICINAL CRISIS STRUCTURE

Considering a real-time scenario, a fellow citizen or neighbor near any kind of medicinal crisis would be the quickest responder, though it is quite difficult for an ambulance facility or caregiver in terms of initiating a prompt action in support of a patient countering the medicinal crisis (Estrada et al., 2022; Nguyen et al., 2021). According to past incidents, there lies an urgent need to assimilate neighbors besides households for intensification procedure that in turn reduces the reaction period besides patient causations. A NAMES outline involving four phases is being showcased in Figure 4.1.

Crucial rudiments among each and every phase are being showcased in Figure 4.2.

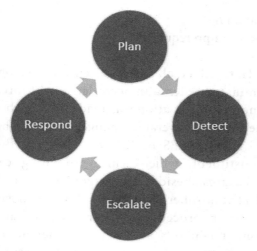

**FIGURE 4.1**
Phases of NAMES process.

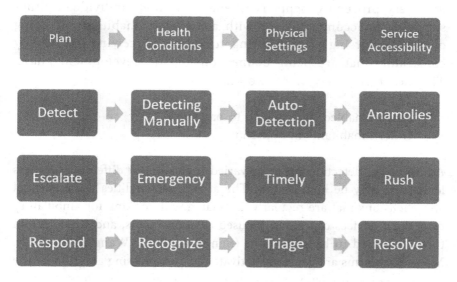

**FIGURE 4.2**
Crucial rudiments among NAMES phases.

Medicinal circumstances and corporeal atmosphere besides admittance to amenities are scrutinized. Therapeutic circumstances of a distinct person varies in terms of:

- Type of carefulness
- Crisis procedure prerequisite

The authors (Hameed et al. 2022) discussed the observation regarding discriminating edema in accordance with breathing rate of individuals. Another observation was made by Addobea et al. (2022) which examined the discoverable changes with the help of triaxial accelerometer. The NAMES outline escalates the therapeutic circumstances constituent, which will be defining care strategies, acceleration measures, besides triage guidelines. Deliberations in terms of physical atmosphere will finally allow the development for a suitable appreciation procedure. A corporeal situation comprises patient location, inhabitants at home, and neighbor compactness in terms of proximity. Lastly, admittance to amenities comprises consideration of which remedial services that are accessible in supporting patients at every moment (Sasireka et al., 2022). The discovery procedure happens whenever a single individual, either surviving unaccompanied or with additional inhabitants, is being observed. Nursing or monitoring comprises perceiving irregularity constraints that are being defined during the development phase. The monitoring may be of two kinds:

- Sensor enabled robotic help to patients
- Other inhabitants in household

Additionally, detection prompts varied indicators of different sternness levels that may be high or low. The at-risk personalities use medicinal apprehensions that are regularly associated with looking for ambulatory care. Such devices can either be used as adornments, and which are in turn connected to base locations (Ren et al., 2022; Wang et al., 2022). Medicinal alarms are generally activated by just pressing a button by the patient to raise any kind of crisis, which subsequently initiates the action of communication of the medical emergency team with the patient on the loud-speaker mode at the base division to check whether the inhabitant is fine or not. If there is no response received, an ambulance will be remitted straightforward (Liu et al., 2022).

Instead, the incongruity constraints are sensed by medicinal devices that may activate a high medicinal disaster. A low crisis gesture happens whenever a specific individual necessitates instant assistance but doesn't

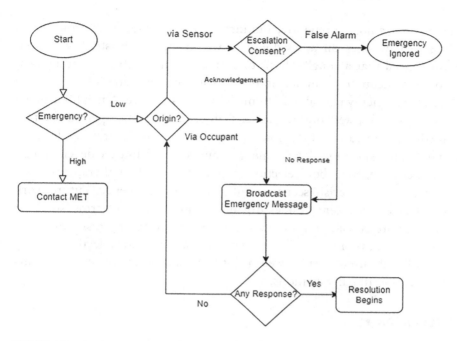

**FIGURE 4.3**
The intensification procedure.

need substantial medicinal interference (Braun et al., 2022). The intensification procedure is being deliberated in Figure 4.3.

The intensification procedure retains truthfulness of high sternness medicinal traumas, though it broadcasts low sternness difficulties to fellow neighbors and for that a waiting controller is used; finally, if no answer is realized, then the system permits populaces in rebroadcasting or intensifying it to a very high sternness sign (Moro et al., 2022). Crisis signs may be constituted in use of omnipresent info structures including mobile applications, text messages, etc. The foremost neighbor will respond, besides acknowledging other neighbors also at the same time so that they can also assist if interested (Lee et al., 2022). If the neighbor still needs, it can activate a strictness crisis signal at that very moment.

## 4.6 CONCLUSION AND FUTURE SCOPE

The contemporary exercises generally consist of observing in terms of user services besides enabling an interference whenever unforeseen variations amongst repetitive outlines are documented apart from that it completely relies on accessibility of well-being specialists. It has been inferenced that a suitable basis of sustenance necessities regarding customer's inclinations in terms of engagement, inclusive of carefulness besides explicitly partiality in terms of peer sustenance. A neighbor-aided medicinal disaster outline lessens disaster response period besides medicinal operative cost. Apart from that, a crowdsource model augments intensification development in any kind of disaster development. Furthermore, neighbor selection besides the level of therapeutic info being used in a crisis scenario still stands as a challenge. Future work involves employment besides organizing an instance of crowdsourcing architecture considering practical influences like timing restraints, peer choice besides confidentiality protection in addition to collection of reply from facility users besides well-being experts in terms of improvements besides additional valuations.

## REFERENCES

Abdullah, S., & Choudhury, T. (2018). Sensing technologies for monitoring serious mental illnesses. *IEEE MultiMedia*, 25(1), 61–75.

Addobea, A. A., Li, Q., Amankona, I. O., & Hou, J. (2022). A batch processing technique for wearable health crowd-sensing in the Internet of Things. *Cryptography*, 6(3), 33.

Ahmadi, A., Farahbakhsh, K., Moatamedy, A., Khodaei, M., & Safi, M. H. (2020). The effectiveness of family psychological training on prevention of recurrence of symptoms in patients with schizophrenia spectrum disorders. *Iranian Journal of Psychiatric Nursing*, 8(3), 93–103.

Altaf, M. A., Shahid, R., Ren, M. X., Naz, S., Altaf, M. M., Khan, L. U., & Ahmad, P. (2022). Melatonin improves drought stress tolerance of tomato by modulating plant growth, root architecture, photosynthesis, and antioxidant defense system. *Antioxidants*, 11(2), 309.

Anderson, G. S., Di Nota, P. M., Groll, D., & Carleton, R. N. (2020). Peer support and crisis-focused psychological interventions designed to mitigate post-traumatic stress injuries among public safety and frontline healthcare personnel: a systematic review. *International Journal of Environmental Research and Public Health*, 17(20), 7645.

Barnett, I., Torous, J., Staples, P., Sandoval, L., Keshavan, M., & Onnela, J. P. (2018). Relapse prediction in schizophrenia through digital phenotyping: a pilot study. *Neuropsychopharmacology*, 43(8), 1660–1666.

Beri, R., Dubey, M. K., Gehlot, A., Singh, R., Abd-Elnaby, M., & Singh, A. (2022). A novel fog-computing-assisted architecture of E-healthcare system for pregnant women. *The Journal of Supercomputing*, 78(6), 7591–7615.

Bernardino, S., & Santos, J. F. (2020). Crowdfunding: an exploratory study on knowledge, benefits and barriers perceived by young potential entrepreneurs. *Journal of Risk and Financial Management*, 13(4), 81.

Bernardino, S., Santos, J. F., & Silva, R. (2022). Does gender really matter in crowd-funding campaigns? An exploratory study. *International Journal of E-Entrepreneurship and Innovation (IJEEI)*, 12(1), 1–21.

Bessière, V., Stéphany, E., & Wirtz, P. (2020). Crowdfunding, business angels, and venture capital: an exploratory study of the concept of the funding trajectory. *Venture Capital*, 22(2), 135–160.

Braun, V., & Clarke, V. (2022). Conceptual and design thinking for thematic analysis. *Qualitative Psychology*, 9(1), 3.

Bull, C. N., Asfiandy, D., Gledson, A., Mellor, J., Couth, S., Stringer, G., & Sawyer, P. H. (2016). Combining data mining and text mining for detection of early stage dementia: the SAMS framework.

Cheng, P., Xia, G., Pang, P., Wu, B., Jiang, W., Li, Y. T., & Bi, X. (2020). COVID-19 epidemic peer support and crisis intervention via social media. *Community Mental Health Journal*, 56(5), 786–792.

Cicchiello, A. F. F., & Kazemikhasragh, A. (2022). Tackling gender bias in equity crowdfunding: an exploratory study of investment behavior of Latin American investors. *European Business Review*.

Dhinakaran, K., Nedunchelian, R., & Balasundaram, A. (2021). Crowdsourcing: descriptive study on algorithms and frameworks for prediction. *Archives of Computational Methods in Engineering*, 1–18.

Du Plessis, C., Whitaker, L., & Hurley, J. (2020). Peer support workers in substance abuse treatment services: a systematic review of the literature. *Journal of Substance Use*, 25(3), 225–230.

Elhanan, S., Benslimane, S. M., Khalfi, M. F., & Fechfouch, M. (2022). QASIS: a QoC aware stress identification system using machine learning approach. *International Journal of High Performance Systems Architecture*, 11(1), 12–25.

Estrada, R., Valeriano, I., & Torres, D. (2022). Multi-task versus consecutive task allocation with tasks clustering for mobile crowd sensing systems. *Procedia Computer Science*, 198, 67–76.

Fadzil, F. M. (2021). Theatre makers' experience with crowdfunding: an exploratory study (Doctoral dissertation, University of Warwick).

Fortuna, K. L., Naslund, J. A., LaCroix, J. M., Bianco, C. L., Brooks, J. M., Zisman-Ilani, Y., & Deegan, P. (2020). Digital peer support mental health interventions for people with a lived experience of a serious mental illness: systematic review. *JMIR mental health*, 7(4), e16460.

Gidugu, V., Rogers, E. S., Harrington, S., Maru, M., Johnson, G., Cohee, J., & Hinkel, J. (2015). Individual peer support: a qualitative study of mechanisms of its effectiveness. *Community Mental Health Journal*, 51(4), 445–452.

Gillard, S. (2019). Peer support in mental health services: where is the research taking us, and do we want to go there? *Journal of Mental Health*, 28(4), 341–344.

Hameed, M., Yang, F., Ghafoor, M. I., Jaskani, F. H., Islam, U., Fayaz, M., & Mehmood, G. (2022). IOTA-based mobile crowd sensing: detection of fake sensing using logit-boosted machine learning algorithms. *Wireless Communications and Mobile Computing*, 2022.

Hassan, N. H., & Rahim, F. A. (2017). The rise of crowdsourcing using social media platforms: security and privacy issues. *Pertanika Journal of Science & Technology*, 25(110).

Huber, J., Muck, T., Maatz, P., Keck, B., Enders, P., Maatouk, I., & Ihrig, A. (2018). Face-to-face vs. online peer support groups for prostate cancer: a cross-sectional comparison study. *Journal of Cancer Survivorship*, 12(1), 1–9.

Ibrahim, N., Thompson, D., Nixdorf, R., Kalha, J., Mpango, R., Moran, G., & Slade, M. (2020). A systematic review of influences on implementation of peer support work for adults with mental health problems. *Social Psychiatry and Psychiatric Epidemiology*, 55(3), 285–293.

Lago, L., Glantz, M. D., Kessler, R. C., Sampson, N. A., Al-Hamzawi, A., Florescu, S., & Degenhardt, L. (2017). Substance dependence among those without symptoms of substance abuse in the world mental health survey. *International Journal of Methods in Psychiatric Research*, 26(3), e1557.

Lee, C., Thomas, M., Kassam, A., Whittle, S. L., Buchbinder, R., Tugwell, P., & Hazlewood, G. S. (2022). Crowdsourcing trainees in a living systematic review provided valuable experiential learning opportunities: a mixed-methods study. *Journal of Clinical Epidemiology*.

Liu, E., Iwelunmor, J., Gabagaya, G., Anyasi, H., Leyton, A., Goraleski, K. A., & Tucker, J. D. (2020). 'When she rises, we all rise': a crowdsourcing challenge to increase women's participation in an infectious diseases research fellowship. *BMC infectious diseases*, 20(1), 1–7.

Liu, Z. J., Panfilova, E., Mikhaylov, A., & Kurilova, A. (2022). COVID-19 crisis impact on the stability between parties in crowdfunding and crowdsourcing. *Wireless Personal Communications*, 122(1), 915–930.

Lloyd-Evans, B., Mayo-Wilson, E., Harrison, B., Istead, H., Brown, E., Pilling, S., & Kendall, T. (2014). A systematic review and meta-analysis of randomized controlled trials of peer support for people with severe mental illness. *BMC Psychiatry*, 14(1), 1–12.

Lublóy, Á. (2020). Medical crowdfunding in a healthcare system with universal coverage: an exploratory study. *BMC Public Health*, 20(1), 1–20.

Mao, K., Capra, L., Harman, M., & Jia, Y. (2017). A survey of the use of crowdsourcing in software engineering. *Journal of Systems and Software*, 126, 57–84.

Mohr, D. C., Duffecy, J., Ho, J., Kwasny, M., Cai, X., Burns, M. N., & Begale, M. (2013). A randomized controlled trial evaluating a manualized tele coaching protocol for improving adherence to a web-based intervention for the treatment of depression. *PLoS ONE*, 8(8), e70086.

Moro, C., Phelps, C., & Birt, J. (2022). Improving serious games by crowdsourcing feedback from the STEAM online gaming community. *The Internet and Higher Education*, 55, 100874.

Nguyen, T. N., & Zeadally, S. (2021). Mobile crowd-sensing applications: data redundancies, challenges, and solutions. *ACM Transactions on Internet Technology (TOIT)*, 22(2), 1–15.

Niu, H., & Silva, E. (2019, September). *Crowdsourced Data Mining for Urban Activity: A Review of Data Sources, Applications and Methods*. ASCE.

O'Leary, K., Schueller, S. M., Wobbrock, J. O., & Pratt, W. (2018, April). "Suddenly, we got to become therapists for each other" designing peer support chats for mental health. In *Proceedings of the 2018 CHI Conference on Human Factors in Computing Systems* (pp. 1–14).

Paulheim, H. (2017). Knowledge graph refinement: a survey of approaches and evaluation methods. *Semantic Web*, 8(3), 489–508.

Prescott, J., Rathbone, A. L., & Brown, G. (2020). Online peer to peer support: qualitative analysis of UK and US open mental health Facebook groups. *Digital Health*, 6, 2055207620979209.

Ren, Y., Liu, W., Liu, A., Wang, T., & Li, A. (2022). A privacy-protected intelligent crowdsourcing application of IoT based on the reinforcement learning. *Future Generation Computer Systems*, 127, 56–69.

Saha, H. N., Auddy, S., Pal, S., Kumar, S., Pandey, S., Singh, R., & Saha, S. (2017, August). Health monitoring using the internet of things (IoT). In 2017 8th Annual Industrial Automation and Electromechanical Engineering Conference (IEMECON) (pp. 69–73). IEEE.

Sarı, A., Tosun, A., & Alptekin, G. I. (2019). A systematic literature review on crowd-sourcing in software engineering. *Journal of Systems and Software*, 153, 200–219.

Sasireka, V., & Ramachandran, S. (2022). Optimization based multi-objective framework in mobile social networks for crowd sensing. *Wireless Personal Communications*, 1–22.

Schlichthorst, M., Ozols, I., Reifels, L., & Morgan, A. (2020). Lived experience peer support programs for suicide prevention: a systematic scoping review. *International Journal of Mental Health Systems*, 14(1), 1–12.

Shalaby, R. A. H., & Agyapong, V. I. (2020). Peer support in mental health: literature review. *JMIR Mental Health*, 7(6), e15572.

Sharma, A., Choudhury, M., Althoff, T., & Sharma, A. (2020, May). Engagement patterns of peer-to-peer interactions on mental health platforms. In Proceedings of the International AAAI Conference on Web and Social Media (Vol. 14, pp. 614–625).

Staner, L. (2022). Sleep and anxiety disorders. *Dialogues in Clinical Neuroscience*.

Tolley, J. A., Michel, M. A., Williams, A. E., & Renschler, J. S. (2020). Peer support in the treatment of chronic pain in adolescents: a review of the literature and available resources. *Children*, 7(9), 129.

Verma, S. K., Sahu, P. K., Kumar, K., Pal, G., Gond, S. K., Kharwar, R. N., & White, J. F. (2021). Endophyte roles in nutrient acquisition, root system architecture development and oxidative stress tolerance. *Journal of Applied Microbiology*, 131(5), 2161–2177.

Wang, W., Wang, Y., Huang, Y., Mu, C., Sun, Z., Tong, X., & Cai, Z. (2022). Privacy protection federated learning system based on blockchain and edge computing in mobile crowdsourcing. *Computer Networks*, 109206.

# 5

## Crowdsourcing-Based Recommendations in Travel and Tourism Market: A Review

*Sujoy Chatterjee[1] and Thipendra P. Singh[2]*
[1]Department of C.S.E, Amity University, Kolkata, India
[2]School of Computer Science Engineering & Technology, Bennett University, Greater Noida, NCR, India

### 5.1 INTRODUCTION

There is mounting evidence that social media's interconnection and people's impulsive volunteering have given businesses and governments new ways to interact with their constituents, advertise their services, and provide those services. The purpose of this study is to present various current techniques to utilize the power of crowd for tourism data. Here, it is to examine the government usage of Facebook (FB) as an open forum for public participation, involvement, and promotion of travel experiences in light of the current changing environment [1–4]. It has been observed that FB is utilized to crowdsource travel knowledge and experiences for public tourism organizations [5]. A spectrum of research is already performed to understand the behavior of crowd. This case study research, which includes a quantitative and qualitative evaluation of the Tourism Australia FB page [5], offers a thorough knowledge of citizen participation. Now this type of experience, if processed efficiently, can be a huge resource to society for solving different decision-making problems for the travel and tourism industry.

In another study, Brown and Chalmers [6] explored the several problems that travelers can run into when traveling on a specific day. According to the researchers, tourists want to understand what to do, how

DOI: 10.1201/9781003346326-5

to go about it, where to do it, and when to do it. The reason is there is no idea of what to accomplish or where to go. In the process of making a choice right away, the amount of locations to visit must be considered when making this choice, as well as duration of each attraction.

Even if a tourist has pre-planned his vacation, thus, according to Brown and Chalmers [6], the tourist will frequently find himself on the ground having to make decisions about what to see. This is the case when choosing on the fly which sections of a huge museum to see, even when we are aware that we will be visiting this museum before our trip. Online communities and social networks are gradually taking center stage in the tourism marketing industry. Information shared in these networks has a growing impact on consumer behavior.

Social media users can share ideas, opinions, experiences, suggestions, and disclaimers since they are a community of people connected by various factors, such as geographic positioning, centers of interest, and needs that may be neighboring or similar. This enables using social networks and online communities as resources for information, shopping, and education.

According to a state-of-the-art research paper [7], the re-engineering of business processes brought on by the technological revolution would unavoidably have an impact on tourism. This is due to the intended usage of information technologies in the tourism industry. Tourists are becoming more demanding to make the itinerary of their tour easier. It could be useful to have a map of tourist attractions because bringing tourists to remote areas could jeopardize attempts to reduce travel times.

## 5.2 TOURISM-BASED RECOMMENDER SYSTEM USING CROWDSOURCING

The study question focuses on the variability of tourism resources in terms of their nature (various kinds), longevity, and quantity. Ephemeral resources, like seasonal deals, are dynamic and new resources are continually being created. The system depends on inputs from stakeholders (end users and enterprises) to enable the ongoing development, updating, and improvement of the tourist information database. This crowdsourcing of tourism-related data, which makes use of the current social network trend of data sharing, depends on publisher trust and reputation models for content validation.

In recent years, big data has been cited as a new problem for tourism by Chareyron et al. [8]. The World Travel and Tourism Council (WTTC) and Future Foundation (2014) discusses the consequences of adopting big data in the travel sector, including the benefits and drawbacks. In order to increase the precision of suggestions, here, authors plan to employ big data to merge multiple data sources for user profile. Similar to previous work, a number of studies are available that performs big data analytics on a knowledge infrastructure framework gathered from heterogeneous social networks in order to address the needs of tourists. The first application analyzes and detects typical tourist behavior in heterogeneous social networks [9].

## 5.2.1 Different Variants

As mentioned in the previous paragraph, the various approaches of leveraging crowdsourced data for recommendations are very promising. Among them, the few examples are personalized context-aware resource recommendations, improved big data filtering algorithms for user (tourist and tourism business) profiling, and trust and reputation to evaluate crowd-sourced data regarding tourism resources. According to our knowledge, this new method for mobile tourist applications combines information crowdsourcing (confirmed by Trust and Reputation), profiling (supported by big data algorithms), and recommendations (aided by Trust and Reputation). The detailed descriptions of a few models are discussed below.

## 5.2.2 Tourism Recommendation Using Crowdsourcing

Using heterogeneous crowdsourced information automatically in tourism recommendation systems that fully utilize data mining techniques has received scant attention in the literature. A discussion is made based on the prior work [10], which merely relies on the crowdsourced data available and does not require extra engagement from the tourists (questionnaire/ forms). In order to identify undiscovered travel destinations, authors have investigated both crowdsourced tourism data and recommendation techniques using data mining techniques. This study expands on that idea by evaluating a sizable amount of heterogeneous crowd-sourced data via visitor reviews in order to enhance traveler recollection and destination/ location details.

## 5.3 DIFFERENT STEPS OF PROPOSED APPROACHES

### 5.3.1 Different Steps of the Recommendation Algorithm

- Input: Hotel Data H = *Hotel h, location l*, User Data: U = (User u, Hotel h, Review ru)
- Data preprocessing tokenizes textual reviews and eliminates nonsensical terms (special characters, stop words, and numerical parameters) from both individual user and aggregated location reviews.
- Topic modeling is performed via linear discriminant analysis (LDA)
- Finding semantic similarity to understand. Ontologies are used to calculate semantic relatedness and calculate the separation between phrases or concepts. WordNet is one of the most well-known databases that has been used frequently to calculate semantic relatedness.
- Evaluation Metrics: The Precision Recall and F-Measure categorization metrics were used to evaluate the results.

### 5.3.2 Leveraging Crowdsourcing to Improve the Amenities and Services Provided by Hotels

In order to address client expectations, the hospitality industry looks for answers primarily from customers, but also contributions from experts and social media sources [10,11]. Therefore, the involvement of users and other stakeholders, as well as the information they can offer through techniques through crowdsourcing and their involvement in social networks, is valuable in designing and adapting all types of hotel hospitality to meet the needs of customers. The reason is it aids hotel managers in improving the quality of products and services with ongoing feedback. In hotels, for example, crowdsourcing can be used to enhance maintenance by lowering the likelihood of defects, specifically by making maintenance issues visible to guests, by co-producing the identification of issues by involving its stakeholders in its processes, or by allowing them to contribute ideas and solutions.

## 5.4 CROSS-CULTURAL RECOMMENDATION USING CROWDSOURCING

A recent work [12] introduces the OurPlaces cross-cultural crowdsourcing platform, which allows users from many cultures to share their geographical experiences. Here, (i) authors created a three-layered architecture made up of the places (locations that people have visited); (ii) the cognition, or how people have experienced these locations, is then recognized; and (iii) ultimately, a recommendation system is developed based on user feedback from those who have gone to these locations. Notably, cognition is portrayed as the integration of two comparable cultural regions (e.g., Versailles and Gyeongbokgung in France and Korea, respectively). In this work, the authors used a simulation with a data set gathered from TripAdvisor and the OurPlaces platform to build a cross-cultural tourist recommendation system as a case study. Four categories were used to distinguish the tourism locations, i.e., hotels, restaurants, shopping malls, and attractions. Moreover, feedback from individuals from various nationalities (taken to be equivalent to cultures) was used to develop a platform-based cognition layer and measure the similarities across tourist destinations.

The steps of finding similar users can be identified by the Information representation based on previous user activity: Users' priorities for choosing similar tourist destinations must be examined and modeled (user cognition pattern).

Humans' cognitive patterns are often created through a three-layer design. The key in choosing a pair of related tourist destinations is the definition of similarities between individuals' cognitive processes. Based on the cognitive similarity between people, authors classify and find the k-nearest neighbors of active users. Here, these three layers are: (a) Place Layer: Among the relevant places based on the calculated similarity between the retrieved features, of the pertinent locations. (b) Cognition Layer: Comparing people' cognitive similarity based on their shared interest in a tourist destination. (c) User Layer: Based on explicit data taken from the cognitive network, a user-relating network is created.

## 5.5 CROWDSOURCING-BASED STREAMING DATA PROCESSING FOR BETTER TRAVEL

Personalized travel suggestions are created via entity profiling, which involves building and maintaining entity models. It is feasible to create models of the stakeholders based on the corresponding digital footprints recorded in crowdsourcing platforms for tourism using data collected from the crowd. Resources (item) can be profiled based on inherent qualities, crowdsourced data, and semantic enrichment. Most tourist (user) profiles are based on data collected from the general public, which fall within the categories of feature-based or entity-based [13,14].

The majority of user (tourist) profiles are created using crowdsourced information, which falls into two categories: entity-based and feature-based. Feature-based profiles rely on inherent qualities, such as category, location, topic, etc., entity-based profiles are directly linked to tourism resources. There are more types of profiles identified in the literature based on the content of crowdsourced data. On the other hand, depending on the content of profile, it can be processed into different ways, as follows:

- Textual Reviews: Textual reviews are used to construct profile-based reviews. The descriptions and comments in these reviews are typically of a high caliber. In place of being seen as static in this sense, a collection of reviews creates a continuing stream, which gives rise to opinion stream mining [15].
- Context-based: Profiles make use of context data, which includes contextually aware information data as well as personal and social context data. By utilizing accessible context data, Gomes et al. [16] (2010) suggest a context-aware system incorporating streaming data learning for enhancing the performance of current drift detection techniques.
- Quality-based: Profiles make use of context data, which includes contextually aware information data as well as personal and social context data. By utilizing accessible context data, Gomes et al. [16] suggested a context-aware system with data stream learning to enhance the performance of current drift detection techniques. To detect traffic in almost real time, Akbar et al. [17] investigate context-aware stream processing.
- Rating-based: By integrating data from wiki streams of publisher-page-reviews, profiles employ ratings to indicate opinions about the quality of publishers and pages. Nilashi et al. provide a stream-based multiple-criteria approach leveraging ensemble approaches [18].

## 5.6 CROWDSOURCING-BASED WALKING ROUTES

Discovering scenic roads and tourist sites in new places is always a challenge and a goal for travelers. Since travel-related information is becoming more extensive, detailed, and sophisticated, first-time travelers must handle and mine massive amounts of data to improve their trip planning. Users nowadays post geo-tagged photographs to social media photo-sharing services, which grow more well-liked and widely used by tourists to communicate their vacation experiences [19]. These user-generated "digital footprints" can be handled, mined, and interpreted to rebuild user travel paths and retrieve their activity and knowledge. This work illustrates how to efficiently compute walking tourism itineraries by mining user trajectories using the Flickr geotagged crowdsourced photo library.

By modeling the tourism context, this methodology mines discovering scenic roads and tourist sites in new places, and it is always a challenge and a goal for travelers. Since travel-related information is becoming more extensive, detailed, and sophisticated, first-time travelers must handle and mine massive amounts of data to improve their trip planning.

By relying on non-local users' experiences, the authors reduce the risk of relying on the local community's numerous general photographers' experiences from across the world who do not formally contribute to tourist data. These rely on the understanding that local photographers typically take pictures across the city, whereas tourism-oriented photographers display certain activities related to tourist attractions, beautiful, and scenic locations [20]. In order to do this, the authors examined the metadata associated with the geotagged images in the Flickr database, automatically reconstructing trip routes and taking a variety of spatio-temporal adaptive key descriptors into account to categorize tourism photographers. The following phase of their plan is to investigate popular cells that are intersected by their paths using a cell-grid technique. The three main steps are explained here in the following order:

- Geotagged Photos and Metadata
- Defining the Tourism User
- POI Identification

## 5.7 CONCLUSION

Recently, crowdsourcing-based feedback provides various promising avenues to solve different real-life complex problems. More importantly, technology has completely transformed both travel and the tourism sector. In particular, it not only helps travelers at every stage of their journey, including planning, booking, experiencing, and sharing, but it has also turned previously business-oriented platforms for the travel industry into crowdsourcing platforms, like Expedia, where knowledge about travel accumulates as travelers leave their digital footprints. These online tracks are extremely important to both businesses and visitors.

As a further study direction, numerous algorithmic and technological challenges in the domain of crowdsourced data stream recommendations for tourism are discussed. The algorithmic design takes into account additional concept drift identification, crowd dependability, distributed processing, model learning, preference evolution, and transparency. As seen, various study areas are starting to be investigated, although much work remains. The data reliability, velocity, and volume, as well as the operation close to real time, impose extremely demanding criteria for supporting technology.

## REFERENCES

1. Brabham, D.C.: Detecting stable clusters using principal component analysis. *Methods Mol. Biol.* 224(10) (2013)
2. Howe, J.: The rise of crowdsourcing. *Wired Magazine* 14(6), 1–4 (2006)
3. Hovy, D., Kirkpatrick, T.B., Vaswani, A., Hovy, E.: Learning whom to trust with MACE. In: Proceedings of the NAACL-HLT. pp. 1120–1130. Atlanta, Georgia (2013)
4. Raykar, V.C., Yu, S.: Eliminating spammers and ranking annotators for crowdsourced labeling tasks. *Journal of Machine Learning Research* 13, 491–518 (2011)
5. Alam, S.L., MacKrell, D., Rizvi, S.M.U.: Crowdsourcing travel experience: a case study of user participation on the tourism Australia Facebook page. In: MCIS 2012 Proceedings. No. 32 (2012)
6. Brown, B., Chalmers, M.: Tourism and mobile technology. In: Kuutti, K., Karsten, E.H., Fitzpatrick, G., Dourish, P., Schmidt, K. (eds.) *ECSCW 2003*. pp. 335–354. Springer Netherlands, Dordrecht (2003)
7. Buhalis, D.: Strategic use of information technologies in the tourism industry. *Tourism Management* 19(5), 409–421 (1998)
8. Chareyron, G., Da-Rugna, J., Raimbault, T.: Big data: a new challenge for tourism. (10 2014)
9. Zhou, X., Wang, M., Li, D.: From stay to play – a travel planning tool based on crowdsourcing user-generated contents. *Applied Geography* 78, 1–11 (2017), https://www.sciencedirect.com/science/article/pii/S0143622816306051
10. Leal, F., Malheiro, B., Burguillo, J.: Trust and reputation modelling for tourism recommendations supported by crowdsourcing. pp. 829–838 (03 2018)
11. Leal, F., Malheiro, B., Burguillo, J.: Analysis and prediction of hotel ratings from crowdsourced data. Wiley interdisciplinary reviews: data mining and knowledge discovery. 9 (03 2019)

12. Luong Vuong, N., Jung, J., Hwang, M.: Ourplaces: cross-cultural crowdsourcing platform for location recommendation services. *International Journal of GeoInformation* 9, p. 711 (11 2020)

13. Leal, F., Malheiro, B., Burguillo, J.: Recommendation of tourism resources supported by crowdsourcing. (02 2016)

14. Leal, F., Malheiro, B., Burguillo, J.: Semantic profiling and destination recommendation based on crowd-sourced tourist reviews. In: Proceedings of the International Symposium on Distributed Computing and Artificial Intelligence (06 2017)

15. Leal, F., Veloso, B., Malheiro, B., Burguillo, J.: Crowdsourced data stream mining for tourism recommendation. pp. 260–269 (04 2021)

16. Gomes, J., Menasalvas, E., Sousa, P.: Calds: context-aware learning from https://www.overleaf.com/project/634fb2126262ed12e24753b5 data streams. In: Proceedings of the First International Workshop on Novel Data Stream Pattern Mining Techniques. pp. 16–24 (06 2010)

17. Akbar, A., Carrez, F., Moessner, K., Sancho, J., Rico, J.: Context-aware stream processing for distributed IoT applications. In: Proceedings of 2015 IEEE 2nd World Forum on Internet of Things (WF-IoT). pp. 663–668 (02 2015)

18. Nilashi, M., Jannach, D., bin Ibrahim, O., Ithnin, N.: Clustering and regression based multi-criteria collaborative filtering with incremental updates. *Information Sciences* 293, 235–250 (2015)

19. Mor, M., Dalyot, S.: Enriching walking routes with tourism attractions retrieved from crowdsourced user generated data. *ISPRS Annals of Photogrammetry, Remote Sensing and Spatial Information Sciences* V-4-2020, 95–102 (08 2020)

20. K´adar, B.: Measuring tourist activities in cities using geotagged photography. *Tourism Geographies* 16(1), 88–104 (2014)

# 6

# A Comparison of Capability Measurement between Various Incident Handling and Reporting Schemas

*Gyana Ranjana Panigrahi[1], Nalini Kanta Barpanda[1], Prabira Kumar Sethy[1], and Debabrata Samantaray[2]*

[1]Department of Electronics, SUIIT, Sambalpur University, Burla, Odisha, India
[2]School of Forensic Sciences, Centurion University of Technology and Management (CUTM), Bhubaneswar, Odisha, India

## 6.1 INTRODUCTION

Recently, it appears that the number of hosts with a high level of intricacy has progressively increased, bearing various possible susceptibilities that put the entire scheme in jeopardy (F. Skopik and Roman 2016). It is with an increasing number of potential threats for host connection in progression. Various threats can range from small stand-alone malware to various complex appearances, with an impact not only on critical applications but also on various physical components that can be decisively rumbled through classy embattled bouts (Serketzis, Katos, Ilioudis, Baltatzis and Pangalos 2019; Elmellas 2016; Leszczyna and Wróbel 2019). Also, it results in financial loss and data forfeiture. Various research has been successfully carried out to make significant research and development in information and data menace (Sahrom, Rahayu, Ariffin and Yusof 2018). It announces the information of damage happenings through a cyber incident that has already happened. Thus, these approaches make it possible to enhance the degree of risk detection and the immediate reporting capability of partaker knowledge (Noor, Anwar, Malik and Saleem 2019).

DOI: 10.1201/9781003346326-6

To diminish different forms of cyber-affairs, one of the essential cyber-hazardous technologies in the enterprise has to develop (Ahluwalia and Marriott 2005; Line and Bernsmed 2014; Vlietland and van Vliet 2014). The iterative process and learning capabilities of organized event management are defined by critical processes and events that threaten privacy, accessibility, and the veracity of data (Ruefle et al. 2014). In order to work together and cooperate in collective cyber responses, it is necessary to develop common methods of exchange of information on cyber threats. Automated cyberbullying information exchange systems allow cyber-reaction teams to exchange information about cyber-attacks (Mitropoulos and Douligeris 2006). The key part of intelligence distribution in risk management is how to utilize the predefined data schemas of security information and event management efficiently to fulfill the built-in requirements in the form of future deployments (Wu and Chen 2016). Detection of security breaches is necessary to notify the organization before the incident happens (Eling and Wirfs 2019; Tosh, Sengupta, Kamhoua and Kwiat 2018; Line and Jaatun 2014). If you look at Figure 6.1, it shows statistics about breaching and epidemic sources from various data breach responses time reported by IBM, which shows where we should be focusing our attention in the future.

The important study is that according to the severity of an incident, the organization can mitigate the impact of the conflict by containing it and ultimately recovering from it (Baskerville, Spagnoletti and Kim 2014; Buchler, Rajivan, Marusich, Lightner and Gonzalez 2018; Mahmoud and Hamdan 2019). The most important aspect of dealing with the events is coordination and exchange of information, where different organizations share information about danger, attack, and vulnerability so that the knowledge of each organization can benefit others. Based on heuristics and signatures, the stabilized approach to traditional security protection does not fit the dynamic nature of the new generation of threats considered to be polite, flexible, and complex (Steinberger, Kuhnert, Sperotto, and Pras 2016).

Incident handling and reporting is a scheme that is considered two essential edges of cyber-defense. Therefore, these two principles must be used in the process of incident detection. Hence, proposing integrating a process of future notification before the incident happens is a challenging problem in cybersecurity (Asgarli and Burger 2016). However, it improvises incident detection and reporting performance through the upgrade, update, and deployment in a cyclic process. From time to time, many scholars have done

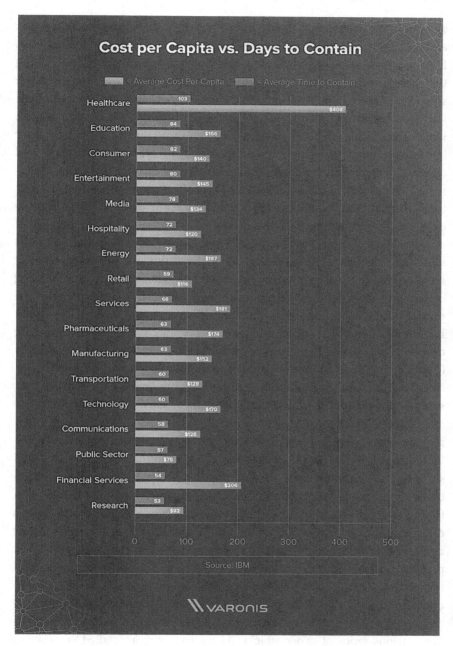

**FIGURE 6.1**
Breach sector (where breaches happen).

a lot of work in this field. Some have focused on incident detection work, and some others are focused on reporting work. However, at the very least, focus on both sides. Why? Because the problem lies in fitting and finding the exact security schema according to its ability to recover from negative situations. Unification is the only solution that gives us a chance to do both jobs simultaneously. Hence, we are supposed to propose a generic model, which gives a chance to integrate both schemes into one model, which is our key motivation. The initial step is to create an evaluation standard and criteria by grouping the entire model into three distinct modes of assessment. This will help measure the level of proficiency in presenting resilient tools (Caron 2021) and making significant contributions. To effectively evaluate the performance of the model, it is crucial to establish a set of standards and criteria. This can be achieved by categorizing the entire model into three distinct modes of assessment. By doing so, we can accurately measure the level of proficiency in presenting resilient tools and making meaningful contributions. Last but not least, here, we again emphasize the primary data collection from different IT companies using a five-point Likert scale about the security tools to measure the capabilities in controlling cyber-attacks, which helps us create the assessment standard accordingly (Nespoli, Papamartzivanos, Marmol and Kambourakis 2017). Here, we focused on facts and issues related to the literature review on impact measurement of risk management using machine-assisted cyber tools and safety infringement of information and breach and risk areas at different firms. A structural overview has been presented regarding information-sharing systems using different resilient tools for cyber-insurance by motivating and showing the requirements, highlighting legal aspects and authorization bodies, and surveying technological and organizational implementation (Orlando and Yautsiukhin 2017). A detailed analysis of the theoretical basis of an evolutionary game and an analysis of the economic consequences of cybersecurity information sharing has been done and the consequences of participating in search in the game using CYBEX have been presented (Tounsi and Rais 2018). To build a self-indicting model, it is necessary to compare multiple security formats using their terms and definitions to measure the degree of impact and capabilities of new resilient tools to ensure various types of cyber-attacks. There has been a detailed analysis on what grade of overlap can deliver additional benefits through a security format exchange, and future notification using the nature of existence from standard sets of libraries. We have to identify the key entities in this context to underpin the creation of an auto-notifying model for networked incidents. Afterward, the focus on incident detection schemas and the assessment structure to be processed for detection of various threats, which ultimately helps us to develop a key model (Panigrahi, Barpanda and Panda 2021; Wang 2019). It was examined and studied thoroughly on cyber-defense usability in major technical systems by comparing different scientific approaches to analyze the current market and summarize their findings as a solution for our work. Because there are now more than a million users, there is a pressing need to investigate the implications of this trend. Some studies estimate that there might be more than 14.4 billion unique Internet-enabled gadgets in use today. It is extremely challenging to analyze the impact of risk using classic isolated instruments for protecting against the modern risk environment for the protection of sensitive data, especially when trying to fulfill the needs of small office home offices (SOHOs), multinational companies (MNCs), and their infrastructures. For the past several days, cybercriminals from across the world have been targeting the eastern region of India, namely Odisha State, in an effort to halt the country's digital advancement and demonstrate their dominance. It suffers from unforeseen vulnerability to a wide range of assaults, including sophisticated hacking. Computer network defenses must be implemented immediately. Every product, database, and electronic communication must incorporate it into its design. We can all do our share to safeguard the future of cyberspace if governments, businesses, and universities work together and people all over the world work together to educate people about the risks they face online and take proactive measures to address them. As a result, it leads to a root of incomplete knowledge; so, there may be a chance of improving the present situation by overall danger findings, which aids in bridging the issues between sufferers and establishments in a different approach. Many new technologies and systems are being made possible by the development of smart contracts and blockchain contracts, which will allow for the trustworthy and auditable tracking, exchanging, and supplying of commodities, data, and services. One category of device that has been getting a lot of focus in recent years is crowdsensing systems. Crowd-sensing systems utilize consumer devices for the deployment of large-scale sensor networks, such as mobile phones and IoT devices. We highlight some of the most significant privacy and security concerns related to the implementation of payment systems and blockchain in crowd-sensing systems wherein the impact of risk using classic isolated instruments for protecting against the modern risk environment for the protection of sensitive data, especially when trying to fulfill the needs of SOHOs, MNCs, and their infrastructures.

Major security risks with these systems are discussed, and potential remedies are also investigated (Perez and Zeadally 2022). For many years, businesses have turned to blockchain-based crowdsourcing solutions to combat internal threats and free-riding/false reporting (Jiang and Tian 2022). An essential and foundational area of study in the field of IIoT is the reliability and efficiency of mobile crowdsourcing. Real-time and reliable data transmission is crucial for IIoT. Since IIoT is used in mission-critical situations, collecting and storing data reliably is both essential and difficult. It is common practice for MCs to compensate participants for providing data samples or computation results as a means of encouraging them to carry out their assigned activities (Chen and Kantarci 2021; Zhang and Liu 2022). Since highly specialized expertise is required to categorize network traces, the process of labeling a comprehensive network traffic sample is both difficult and expensive. Therefore, most existing traffic labeling systems rely on the auto-generation of artificial network traces, which conceals many of the crucial elements required for clear discrimination between normal and malicious activity (Ma and Zhu 2022; Guerra and Veas 2022; Malandrino and Cimellaro 2022). Maintaining anonymity of users' whereabouts is crucial to expanding MCS's user base. As a result, there has been a lot of research done over the past few years on how to keep people's location secret during mobile crowdsourcing projects (Chen and Xu 2022; Ibrahim and Pietro 2022; Chen and Kantarci 2021). A conceptual framework, supported by research hypotheses, surveys the literature on the relationship between social media, different types of social entrepreneurship, and the success of these businesses (Balt and Papadopoulos 2022; Ray and Kumar 2021). An increasing number of people are paying attention to artificial intelligence (AI)-enabled protection mechanisms as a result of heightened concern for protecting sensitive data in cutting-edge software (Hu and Wu 2022; Hu and Qi 2022; Zeddin and Barbot 2021).

## 6.2 A STRUCTURAL DATA-ASSEMBLY MODEL FOR INCIDENT DETECTION

The process of incident detection begins only after the completion of raw data from various sources, like records using the evaluated system, routing logs, etc. Later, it requires normalizing the data obtained to allow them for further detection and processing. It is only possible through a structured mark-up format to represent events as active supervisors. Once a standard data set is created, it may take further analysis to identify potential pointers to security-related events. In this way, we don't look at these pointers in the same way as future signs of possible events as precursors, possible agreements of new nodes as signs of compensation, detailed data of attackers as signs of an attack, and more safekeeping data as signs of interest. Later, particular event administrations have been recognized and merged by comparing the former with recent indicators. After identifying a known attack plan, the template can be linked by scheming, which is responsible for the event occurrences. Predictions can be used to develop a shared knowledge of threats and associated factors, in addition to the key elements of an event-detecting procedure. It, in turn, helps us by avoiding misinterpretation in the event-finding process and provides a technique for quicker incident recognition, which is our ultimate objective for the proposal.

## 6.2.1 Resilient Incident Reporting Formats (Schemas)

The semantics that have been used to cover the arrangements can be planned by sharing the system's raw data and transferring it through structured event data. As a minimum requirement, we have focused on different methods for representing an event incident and its detection using a structural data assembling model for the automation process. Another thing we show you is how each format that has a specific order looks. IODEF, STIX, X-ARF, and VERIS are examples of such systems. This shows how important the traditional formats are. Since these have been published the most recently, it shows how important they are. Table 6.1 shows a summary of all the forms.

### 6.2.1.1 STIX

The Structured Threat Information eXpression is a global threat-sharing system across the network. The use of the persuasive XML format

**TABLE 6.1**

Summary of Resilient Security Tools and Its Schema

| Format | STIX. 1-XML | STIX. 2-JSON | IODEF.1-XML | IODEF.2-XML | VERIS -JSON | XARF -JSON |
|--------|-------------|--------------|-------------|-------------|-------------|------------|
| Schema |             |              |             |             |             |            |

combined with a XML plan authentication offers comprehensive broadcasting competencies. STIX-2 is a powerful method for the cyber-threatened intelligence-sharing system. Using the JSON deployment process provides data transfer with a little redundancy.

### 6.2.1.2 IODEF

The Incident Object Description Exchange Format (IODEF) event information is a method for offensive bot chat. Using the XML presentation and the XML format for validating data represents an essential structure for the occurrence of an event. Twenty-seven percent of these threats share information using IODEF, which is practically necessary for information platforms. The IODEF-2 event is a method of exchanging event information because it represents a series of extensions to the original model that change the IODEF approach to focus solely on the attack.

### 6.2.1.3 VERIS

The Vocabulary for Event Recording and Incident Sharing (VERIS) is the risk management context for the representation of data security and its events. As per the foundation of SANS, this is used by 23 percent of corporations working as a bearing technology for threat exchange, which itself is of great significance from its category.

### 6.2.1.4 X-ARF

The Extended Abuse Reporting Format (X-ARF) is a human-decipherable format for exchanging hazardous information to create an exchange mechanism using e-mail only. It is one of the most manageable formats that combine event descriptions with the capabilities of embedded encryption. It uses the JSON format to verify YAML data structures and content for data playback, using MIME extensions for transport.

## 6.3 STANDARDS FOR ASSESSING THE FORMS OF INCIDENT DISCLOSURE

To meet the specific needs of incident reporting templates, we use criteria from academic literature and modify them as necessary. Our third conclusion is that we feel that more criteria are required for a full study.

## 6.3.1 Parameters for Seismic Performance Evaluation

Structural definitions define all possible representations, which is why this is crucial. Each of them can handle a wide range of formats and application scenarios. As a consequence, criteria drawn from hierarchical definitions and corporate representations make sense. The quantitative analysis of the presentation may be able to confirm qualitative assertions regarding the coverage of reporting formats made during the presentation. This work covers the size, capacity, and granularity of data structures. This strategy appears to be appropriate for acquiring a broad view of the formats under consideration. As a result, this criterion serves as the foundation for our inquiry. Qualitative components, on the other hand, should, in our opinion, be considered as well. This might be due to the different structures and approaches to lower-level items used by the various reporting formats. As a result, each of the research parts will have its ongoing coverage specified. Additionally, using quantitative techniques provides an overall picture of the format's structural depth and granularity, which is useful in determining how well the format works in practice.

## 6.3.2 Assessing the Overall Quality of a Product

Exchange standards have been analyzed and have offered numerous criteria for comparing these formats in terms of semantics. Structured formats like XML, which assure machine-decipherable and unambiguous semantics, are one component of semantic usability that must be considered. It is fair to differentiate between readability and semantics, even if the formats examined in this study are all based on structured formats (Mahmoud and Hamdan 2019).

### 6.3.2.1 Machine-Readability

This is a fundamental premise that must be established to allow incident sharing automatically. Even though the format is based on a predetermined linguistic structure, it is required to assess the format's structural scope. This is because free-text fields that allow for unstructured content can cut down on how much information can be read by machines.

### 6.3.2.2 Human-Readability

When it comes to automated threat sharing, it is a condition that is of little importance. When conducting complete research, it is crucial to keep in mind that many use cases require user involvement. Therefore, this is an important consideration. This is especially true if there aren't any tools for evaluating an event reporting format, which means that a human study will have to be done.

### 6.3.2.3 Explicit Semantics

Ambiguity in transmitted data structures can have a detrimental impact on machine readability and data interpretation. Framework proposed some additional criteria for comparing security event exchange mechanisms (Steinberger, Kuhnert, Sperotto, and Pras 2016). These can also be used to evaluate incident reporting forms. Interoperability relates to the capability to transmit information from one place to another without losing the substance or meaning of the material being transmitted. Because transmitting tries to attack, by definition, entails the participation of several players, each of whom may accept a different format standard, this is particularly critical. Thus, poor interoperability may pose problems when exchanging incident information, and it may even prevent such sharing in specific cases.

### 6.3.2.4 Fungibility

It addresses the capability of supplementing the supplied exchange formats with data that is not contained in their original specifications. If you're talking about automatic threat sharing, this isn't a big deal. As part of a thorough investigation, it is necessary to bear in mind that many use cases demand user engagement; therefore, this is a significant factor. That's especially true when the event reporting format doesn't provide any evaluation instruments.

### 6.3.2.5 Ductility

It denotes the ability to express various episodes and their relationships. If the exchange procedure just covers isolated incidents, it implies that aggregating incident information also provides more information regarding incident coherences, which can help enhance the issue being handled in the long run.

### 6.3.2.6 Real-Time Usage

It refers to technologies and institutions that facilitate the use of a certain incident-sharing format. As with interoperability, the practical application may be used to determine how well reporting formats can be used in practice. Interoperability standards can be reduced if the likelihood that the trading partner will use the same format is high enough to warrant it. Other criteria are the use of capabilities to describe development kits (Tounsi and Rais 2018). We feel that it is appropriate and will adapt this criterion to our needs.

### 6.3.2.7 Peripheral Dependences

All organizations involved in an incident-sharing system will benefit from having a common knowledge base. This eliminates the possibility of misunderstood or ambiguous data structures being conveyed.

### 6.3.2.8 Indicators for Additional Assessment

Additional criteria are needed to examine reporting formats in their entirety, in addition to those based on the framework given and the basic criteria offered as per the level of each criterion's fulfillment given in Figure 6.2. Whether a format is chosen and how it is used can be heavily influenced by licensing restrictions. License agreements may be to blame for this, as they set forth regulations for how the format may be used. For example, such legislation may restrict the ability to customize the format's content, reducing the format's structural flexibility. The amount of time it takes to maintain a reporting format is also an important issue. Attacks and the IT systems they affect are always evolving, so incident representation must keep pace. As a result, continuing format development assures that current dangers may be represented indefinitely. The regularity with which format updates are provided can be used to gauge maintenance efforts. Documentation has a significant influence on the progress and use of a format. Structures that are clearly described guarantee a syntactically and semantically

**Degree of fulfilment for each criterion**

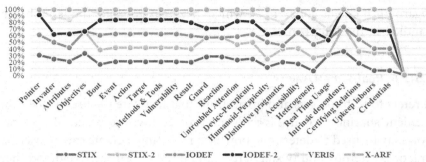

FIGURE 6.2
Level of each criterion's fulfillment.

TABLE 6.2

List of Test Sets

| Parameters for Seismic Performance Evaluation | Assessing the Overall Quality of a Product | Indicators for Additional Assessment |
|---|---|---|
| Pointer | Device-Perspicuity | Certifying Relations |
| Invader | Humanoid-Perspicuity | Upkeep labors |
| Bout | Distinctive-Pragmatics | Credentials |
| Guard | Accessibility | |
| Untroubled Attention | Heterogeneity | Extensibility |
| Real-Time Usage | Intrinsic dependency | Aggregability |

proper exchange between sharing parties and simplify deployments using Table 6.2, a list of test sets.

## 6.4 SUMMARY OF THE ANALYSIS

Table 6.3 is the summary for an overall view of the analysis results, summarizing the findings of the assessed criteria, shown as rows, while the studied formats are shown as columns. The study's findings are represented as four-quarters of a scale value, indicating the level of fulfillment for each criterion.

**TABLE 6.3**

Test Set Summarization

| Test Sets | STI X | STI X-2 | IOD EF | IOD EF-2 | VER IS | X ARF |
|---|---|---|---|---|---|---|
| Pointer | 1 | 1 | 0 | 1 | 0.25 | 0 |
| Invader | 1 | 1 | 0 | 0.5 | 1 | 0.5 |
| Attributes | 1 | 1 | 0 | 1 | 1 | 0.75 |
| Objectives | 1 | 1 | 0 | 0 | 1 | 0 |
| Bout | 0.75 | 1 | 1 | 1 | 0.5 | 0.25 |
| Event | 1 | 1 | 1 | 1 | 0.5 | 0.25 |
| Action | 1 | 1 | 1 | 1 | 0.5 | 0.25 |
| Target | 1 | 1 | 1 | 1 | 0.5 | 0.25 |
| Methods and Tools | 1 | 1 | 1 | 1 | 0.5 | 0.25 |
| Vulnerability | 1 | 1 | 1 | 1 | 0.5 | 0.25 |
| Result | 1 | 1 | 1 | 1 | 0.75 | 0.25 |
| Guard | 1 | 1 | 0 | 0.5 | 1 | 0 |
| Reaction | 1 | 1 | 0 | 0.5 | 1 | 0 |
| Untroubled Attention | 1 | 1 | 0.5 | 1 | 0.5 | 0.25 |
| Device Perspicuity | 1 | 1 | 0.5 | 0.75 | 0.5 | 0.25 |
| Humanoid Perspicuity | 0.25 | 0.25 | 0.5 | 0.25 | 0.5 | 0.25 |
| Distinctive pragmatics | 1 | 1 | 0.25 | 1 | 0.75 | 1 |
| Accessibility | 0.75 | 1 | 1 | 1 | 0.5 | 0 |
| Heterogeneity | 0.25 | 0.75 | 0.75 | 0.75 | 0.75 | 0.5 |
| Real-Time Usage | 1 | 0 | 0.75 | 0 | 0.5 | 1 |
| Intrinsic Dependency | 1 | 1 | 0 | 0.75 | 0 | 0 |
| Certifying Relations | 1 | 1 | 1 | 1 | 0.5 | 1 |
| Upkeep Efforts | 0.25 | 1 | 0.25 | 1 | 0.75 | 0.5 |
| Credentials | 0.25 | 1 | 0.25 | 1 | 0.75 | 0.5 |

The summary underlines STIX. Its versions both provide a complete data model with few uncertainties, a few expansion features, and excellent machine understandability. As a result, they are ideally suited for the automatic sharing of event data. Because of the complexity and limited human readability, a system-automated approach can only help manual analysis a little. They are also very practicable due to high accessibility, unlimited subscription conditions, ongoing development, and usage of STIX and maybe STIX2. Considering the impact and aggregating threat information also helps in threat analysis. It's also possible to communicate info on "quasi-attacks" using IODEF. After then, domain specialists enhance the automatic analysis of the event data. Free-text fields, ambiguity, and the possibility for expansion necessitate human interpretation. RFCs are the only source of format documentation. As a further benefit, IODEF offers high practicality, variable subscription periods, and regular maintenance operations. This is compounded by the fact that there is no external reference point for additional danger evaluations. A more complete method of threat exchange of information is provided by IODEF2, in contrast. Semi-structured data must be processed both automatically and manually, like its predecessor. Furthermore, IODEF2 is likely to have significant practical usefulness in the future. In addition to providing external references and incident aggregation, IODEF2 is rather well suited to enabling future analyses of threat data. With the VERIS technique, the assailant, defenders, and impact information are the primary focus points. Semi-structured assault information is given far less attention. This makes it ideal for conveying information about an event's impact and requires both automated and manual evaluation. Even though VERIS provides limited interoperability under rigorous licensing restrictions to enable some use cases, a significant concentration of practicability is nevertheless possible. A large part of this success may be attributed to the thorough documentation and ongoing support, and also to the inclusion of risk mitigation use cases that the other formats do not allow for. These full formats, on the other hand, use X-ARF's design approach. It does not allow the presentation of indications or defensive information and simply provides basic information about the attacker as well as the attacks that have been carried out. In terms of human readability, the X-ARF format is the best of the formats studied, making it suitable for threat sharing and subsequent manual evaluations. Accordingly, even if there is little documentation and the format's implementation is cost-effective, it has a high level of practical relevance. Combined with the format's open licensing restrictions, this shows just how practical it is.

## 6.5 ASSESSMENT STANDARDS

We summarize the tools' capabilities in Table 6.4 to fit the outcome "n" into our proposed model, as given later in Figure 6.6. Here it summarizes a graphical analysis between recommended formats and attributes for the capability identification of various forms using a full scale with an error margin rate of ±20%. Evaluation standards and criteria overview have been categorized into operational, global, and additional assessment standards and performance measures according to the schema of their attributes and signatures.

**TABLE 6.4**

Assessment Standards Summary

| Detection and Reporting Stage (Operational Standards) | Analyze and Resolve Stage (Overall Standards) | Respond to Post-Incident Stage (Supplementary Standards) |
|---|---|---|
| Pointer | Machine-Readability | Certifying Relations |
| Invader | Human-Readability | Upkeep labors |
| Bout | Explicit Semantics | Credentials |
| Guard | Fungibility | Aggregability |
| Untroubled Attention | Ductility | Peripheral Dependences |

The column operational assessment standard exhibits the impact calculation of proposed formats through model base entities, which can be improved by giving continual attention to the core components in the form of first-phase initial detection and reporting measures as provided in the graph of Figure 6.3. The column global evaluation standard shows the impact calculation of proposed formats, which is a direct derivative of related schema and used signature through analyzing and resolving measures, as given in the graph of Figure 6.4.

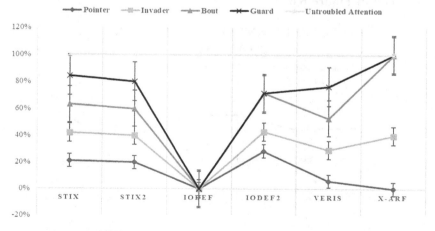

**FIGURE 6.3**
Detection and reporting capabilities.

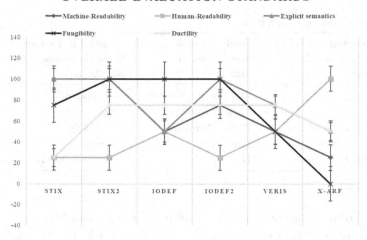

**FIGURE 6.4**
Analyze and resolve capabilities.

Conclusively, the column supplementary assessment standard shows the impact calculation of the proposed formats of the extra measures proposed within the work to respond to post-incident phase measures by notifying in the form of future alarms as given in the graph of Figure 6.5. These standards formulate the basis for the qualified inspection to present a generic model, which has been displayed in flow chart in Figure 6.6.

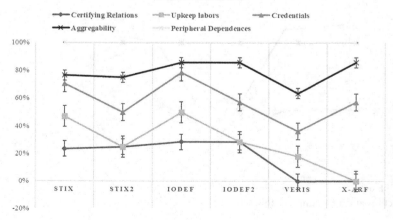

**FIGURE 6.5**
Respond to post-incident capabilities.

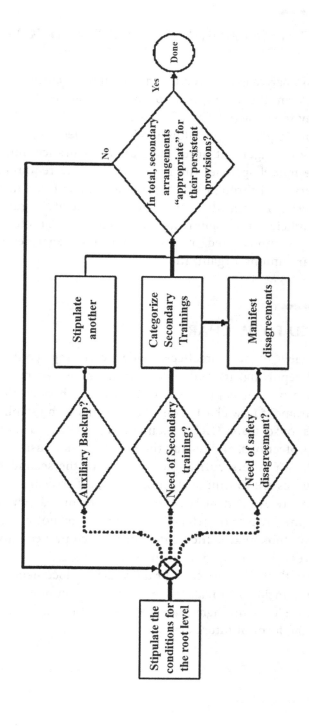

**FIGURE 6.6**

The proposed generic model for incident gathering and future alarming.

## 6.6 INCIDENT GATHERING AND FUTURE NOTIFICATION MODEL

When an event is analyzed and given priority, then the incident reaction team should inform the appropriate people so that all the people involved can play their roles.

Here, it exhibits a generic workflow model using feeding-back lessons for security management procedures on an assurance modeling framework. The model specifies the root-level security requirements that can be determined through sub-requirements, identified through supporting experiences, and developed through security arguments, which are self-sufficient for supporting requirements to handle future cyber-incidences demonstrated by Figure 6.6. The exact reporting requirements vary among organizations.

## 6.7 PROPOSED FLOW CHART

To obtain a review of best practices, evidence seizing, continuous upgrading, and reporting, it needs five critical phases for managing the cyber-defense system, as presented in Figure 6.7, through the risk intensity measurement flow chart. This phase begins with establishing an incident response team (IRT), maintaining security awareness, implementing protections, and testing the plan so that a business may be prepared when a cybersecurity issue occurs. In the second stage, information sources are continuously monitored, cybersecurity events are detected, and relevant data is collected and recorded. There are three phases in the process of determining whether or not a network security incident took place. Incidents must be contained, investigated, and addressed to a solution in the fourth phase.

Aside from that, the fifth phase calls for tasks such as documenting and understanding the incident to make improvements to an organization's security and procedures through evidence preservation and improvement efforts in the form of future alerts.

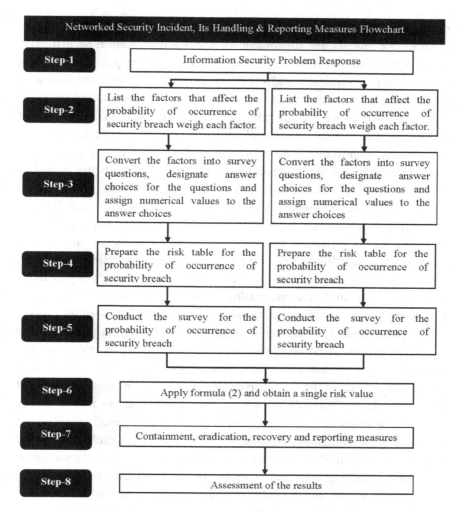

FIGURE 6.7
Risk intensity measurement flow chart.

## 6.8 RISK EVALUATION AND DISCUSSION

There are two kinds of risk assessment methodologies. Risk is represented mathematically and statistically in quantitative risk analysis methodologies. Risk is assessed using adjectives rather than numbers in qualitative risk analysis approaches. Risk analysis methodologies that rely heavily on quantitative metrics are unsuitable for today's information security risk assessment. Today's information systems, in contrast to previous decades, have a complex structure and extensive usage. As a result, sophisticated mathematical techniques used to predict risk in complex situations complicate the procedure. Calculations conducted during the risk assessment procedure are likewise rather sophisticated. In today's complex risk circumstances, quantitative methodologies may not be able to simulate them well enough. Qualitative approaches to risk analysis are better suited to today's information technology risk environment, which is more complicated than ever. Consistency in outcomes is a significant drawback of qualitative risk analysis methodologies. Rather than using tools like mathematics and statistics, this method depends heavily on the views of the people conducting the risk analysis. Qualitative risk assessments may lead to erroneous conclusions if used incorrectly. These examples demonstrate both quantitative and qualitative ways of risk analysis. Managers and staff should be able to participate fully in the risk analysis process thanks to modern computer technologies. It may take a long time and the aid of an expert to conduct risk analysis using modern statistical and mathematical methods in today's technological era. The use of only qualitative metrics in the risk analysis process is also a mistake. This might have subjective effects. Risk analysis approaches that do not meet the demands of firms may not be effective. If a security breach does occur, the risk may be evaluated as the chance of such an event multiplied by the severity of the consequences of the breach. A security risk assessment is done by conducting a thorough investigation and then implementing a plan of action. Surveys are being conducted using two alternative and independent techniques for each of the risk variables in the calculation. It is detailed by the clearly defined procedures that produce risk and how the survey will be prepared, carried out, and assessed through the flow chart in Figure 6.8. A formula is a numerical representation of these stages. Following risk analysis, certain corporate managers may be obliged to calculate the annual loss expectancy (ALE). The model does not compute single loss expectancy (SLE) or adjusted loss expectancy (ALE) during the risk calculation. "Risk" is not a monetary unit. A discrete number in the range of 1 to 25 is used instead. This can be done by risk analysts when they present survey data to the top of the company's hierarchy. The model makes it easy to convert a risk assessment to ALE values using the model. There are examples of how the case study result may be converted under

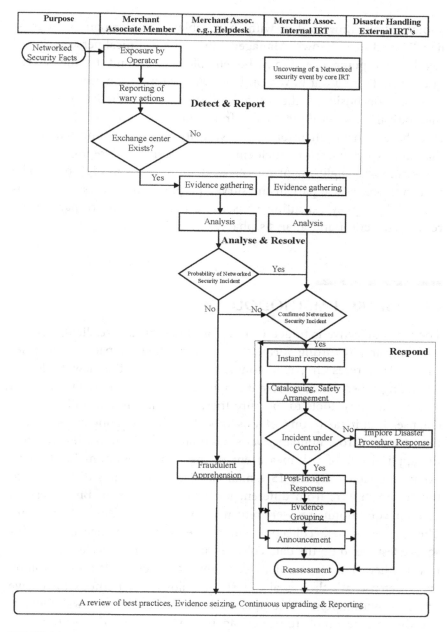

**FIGURE 6.8**
Proposed flow chart.

the section on "Verification, comparison, and application results." The model's objective is to quantify the danger that security-related issues pose. Use what people think about the subject to do this. To find out what people think, surveys are used to ask people. A survey is made up of questions and choices about how to deal with the problem of information security, like "How do you know?" Managers, directors, technical personnel, and regular computer users may be eligible to respond to the survey questions. To find out how a problem with information security affects a system or business, the survey asks people to fill out a form. A methodical study is done by the framework to figure out how much risk there is from an information security issue. As indicated in the diagram, a cybersecurity incident, its treatment, and reporting measures comprise eight major phases, as demonstrated in Figure 6.7. The first four phases are part of the survey preparation process, the fifth is part of the survey execution phase, and the final two are part of the results collection and analysis phase.

## 6.9 RESEARCH METHODOLOGY

The main objective is to get a survey on different new resilient incident handling and reporting formats to measure their impact on cybersecurity. This research paper concentrates on how the new tools are impacting cyber-defense. Here it emphasizes the primary data collection to take the latest tools to measure the capabilities in controlling cyber-defense. Empirical testing of this model by investigating network administrators across Bhubaneswar's multinational IT companies confirms the applicability of risk measurement theory in cross-domain IT management systems. Of the 15 e-mail-based questionnaires distributed to the administrators from different large IT companies in Bhubaneswar, 12 usable questionnaires were returned, for a response rate of 80 percent. The nature of data collection emphasizes the acceptance of the chi-square test based on the data collected under the Likert scale. The aim is to test whether there is a significant impact of new tools on controlling cyber-defense. It's their goal to test the following hypothesis for twelve different multinational IT companies that are near Bhubaneswar, Odisha, and that use new tools to protect against cyberattacks. Due to time and financial constraints, this research has been restricted to Odisha. It is the reason why 12 companies have been included in the sample survey. It has worked well with Minitab® 20.3. We used the chi-square method to find out how important the resilient tools are from the information we found.

### 6.9.1 Hypothesis

H0: There is no significant impact of new tools in controlling cyberecurity.
H1: There is a significant impact of new tools in controlling cybersecurity.

### 6.9.2 Sample Size and Data Collection

It's important to make this work clearer and more understandable so that it fits into our framework. We also want to get a statistical analysis scheme on incident management so that we can prove it through science and math by following some standard theories. This can be achieved by differentiating between the traditional and core tools from two sets of different clusters, like one from MNCs (90 companies) and the other from the small corporate (12 companies) sector by analyzing their culture of behavior in their respective fields of work. So, it's very important and recommended that you get data from two of these sectors to figure out the sample size of 73 from Figure 6.9. A confidence level of 95 percent, by taking the confidence

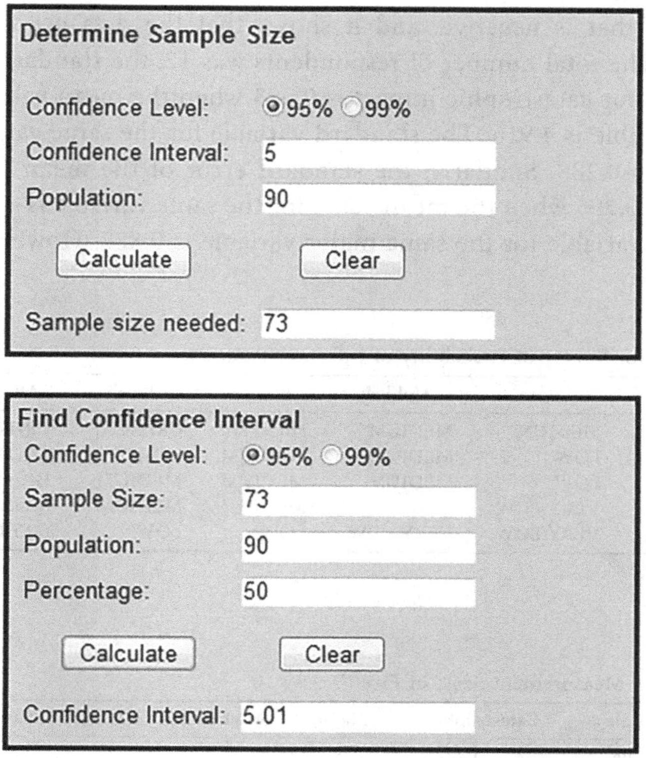

**FIGURE 6.9**
Determining sample size and confidence interval.

interval out of scale 5, is highly acceptable to collect the valued data from a population of 90, resulting in a confidence interval of 5.01 to evaluate with core companies by taking the same data from the sample size of 12 bigger companies. All the data has been collected by mailing the questionnaire prepared by us to their corresponding mail ID on a scale of five between both companies to deduce the final acceptance by rejecting the other using the chi-square test.

## 6.10 DESCRIPTIVE STATISTICS OF CATASTROPHIC, MAJOR, MODERATE, MINOR, AND INSIGNIFICANT

It may be observed from the above tabulation by referring to Tables 6.5, 6.6, and 6.7 and Figures 6.10, 6.11, 6.12, 6.13, and 6.14 that the catastrophic and moderate effects of the tools exhibit a negative skewness that is negative, and it shows that the data are negatively skewed. The total number of respondents was 12; the standard error of the mean for catastrophic impact is 0.083 when the mean value for the same variable is 4.916. The standard variable for the same catastrophic variable is 0.288. Similarly, the standard error of the mean for major impact is 0.256 when the mean value for the same variable is 4.667. The standard variable for the same major variable is 0.888. However, when

**TABLE 6.5**

Risk Table for Survey of Probability of Infection Parameter

| Impact | Rare | Unlikely | Possible | Likely | Almost Certain |
|---|---|---|---|---|---|
| Catastrophic | MEDIUM | MEDIUM | HIGH | CRITICAL | CRITICAL |
| Major | LOW | MEDIUM | MEDIUM | HIGH | CRITICAL |
| Moderate | LOW | MEDIUM | MEDIUM | MEDIUM | HIGH |
| Minor | VERY LOW | LOW | MEDIUM | MEDIUM | MEDIUM |
| Insignificant | VERY LOW | VERY LOW | LOW | LOW | MEDIUM |

**TABLE 6.6**

Quantitative Measurement Scale of Five

| Qualitative Scale | Catastrophic | Major | Moderate | Minor | Insignificant |
|---|---|---|---|---|---|
| Qualitative Scale | 1 | 2 | 3 | 4 | 5 |

**TABLE 6.7**

Descriptive Statistics of Catastrophic, Major, Moderate, Minor, Insignificant

| Variable | N | Percent | Mean | SE Mean | StDev | Minimum | Median | Maximum | Skewness |
|---|---|---|---|---|---|---|---|---|---|
| Catastrophic | 12 | 100 | 4.916 | 0.083 | 0.288 | 4 | 5 | 5 | −3.46 |
| Major | 12 | 100 | 4.667 | 0.256 | 0.888 | 2 | 5 | 5 | −2.95 |
| Moderate | 12 | 100 | 4 | 0.123 | 0.426 | 3 | 4 | 5 | 0 |
| Minor | 12 | 100 | 3.5 | 0.23 | 0.798 | 2 | 4 | 4 | −1.29 |
| Insignificant | 12 | 100 | 2.333 | 0.284 | 0.985 | 1 | 3 | 3 | −0.81 |

the moderate impact is accessed, the mean for the moderate impact is 0.123 when the mean value for the same variable is 4.000. The standard variable for the same controlled variable is 0.426. The minor impact has been accessed through the standard error of the mean for small impact, which is 0.230 when the mean value for the same variable is 3.500. The standard deviation for the same minor variable is 0.798. When the questions were asked about the impact of tools on cyber-security, some of the information received was grouped under the insignificant impact. The insignificant impact has been accessed and

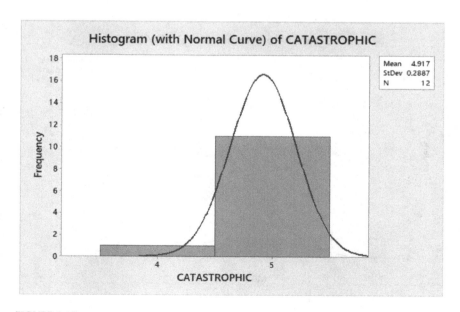

**FIGURE 6.10**

The catastrophic impact has negatively skewed with −3.46, evidently observed from the above plot.

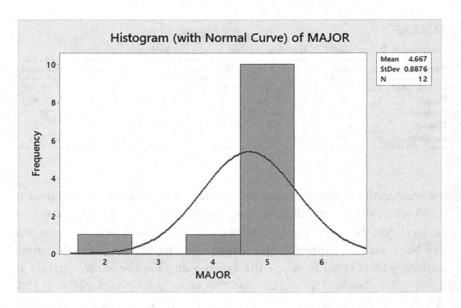

**FIGURE 6.11**
The significant impact has negatively skewed with −2.96, evidently observed from the above plot.

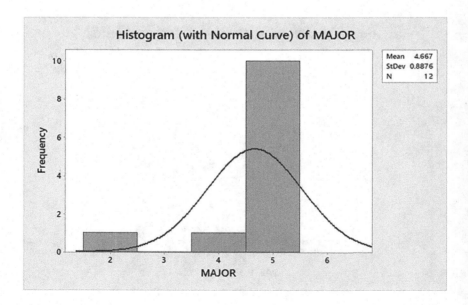

**FIGURE 6.12**
The insignificant impact has negatively skewed with −0.81, evidently observed from the above plot.

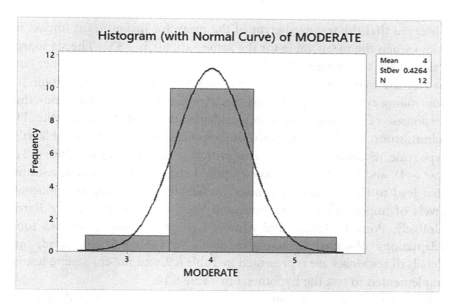

**FIGURE 6.13**
The moderate impact has positively skewed with 0.00, evidently observed from the above plot.

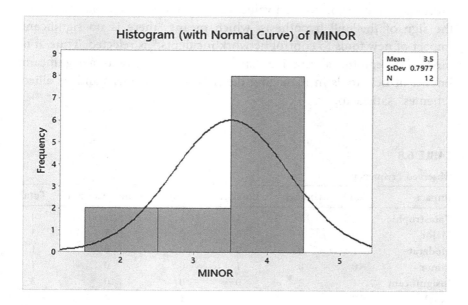

**FIGURE 6.14**
The minor impact has negatively skewed with −1.29, evidently observed from the above plot.

observed that the standard error of the mean for insignificant impact is 0.284 when the mean value for the same variable is 2.333. The standard variable for the same insignificant variable is 0.985. The researcher has to test the hypothesis, "There is no significant impact of new tools in controlling cybersecurity." To test this hypothesis, the researcher took the responses of 12 responsible respondents, distributed among the IT administrative staff, and obtained the responses using a five-point Likert's type scale, where the used ranges are critical (=1), high (=2), medium (=3), low (=4), and very low (=5). We enquired about five common questions that lead to the catastrophic, major, moderate, minor, and insignificant levels of impact after using tools, and they were grouped under Rare, Unlikely, Possible, Likely, and Almost Certain derived for various tool adaptations' observed frequency, as given in Table 6.8. Afterward, the details of responses are represented in Table 6.9, and the chi-square test is implemented to test the hypothesis in Table 6.10.

From the above test, it is noted that the tabulated value at 16 degrees of freedom at 5 percent level of implication is 26.296, which is lower/smaller than the calculated value, i.e., the calculated value is higher/more than the tabulated value (28.58 > 26.296). Next, the assessed value is more than that of the charted value, i.e., 28.58 > 26.296, which indicates the sign of the null hypothesis, which means "there is no significant impact of new tools to control network incidents," is rejected. Thus, it is now to accept the alternative explanation, i.e., "there is a significant impact of new tools in managing the networked incident and its allied schemes" satisfactorily.

**TABLE 6.8**

Observed Frequency

| Impact | Rare | Unlikely | Possible | Likely | Almost Certain | Total |
|---|---|---|---|---|---|---|
| Catastrophic | 0 | 1 | 1 | 1 | 1 | 4 |
| Major | 0 | 0 | 0 | 0 | 3 | 3 |
| Moderate | 1 | 0 | 0 | 0 | 0 | 1 |
| Minor | 0 | 0 | 1 | 0 | 0 | 1 |
| Insignificant | 1 | 2 | 0 | 0 | 0 | 3 |
| Total | 2 | 3 | 2 | 1 | 4 | 12 |

**TABLE 6.9**

Expected Frequency

| Impact | Rare | Unlikely | Possible | Likely | Almost Certain | Total |
|---|---|---|---|---|---|---|
| Catastrophic | 0.67 | 1 | 1.33 | 0.33 | 0.67 | 4 |
| Major | 0.5 | 0.75 | 1 | 0.25 | 0.5 | 3 |
| Moderate | 0.17 | 0.25 | 0.33 | 0.08 | 0.17 | 1 |
| Minor | 0.17 | 0.25 | 0.33 | 0.08 | 0.17 | 1 |
| Insignificant | 0.5 | 0.75 | 1 | 0.25 | 0.5 | 3 |
| Total | 2 | 3 | 4 | 1 | 2 | 12 |

**TABLE 6.10**

Chi-Square Test

| Time | Calculated Value | df | Tabulated Value | Decision |
|---|---|---|---|---|
| Chi-square ($\chi^2$) | 28.58 | 16 | 26.296 | REJECT |

## 6.11 SCOPE AND LIMITATIONS

The limitation in this research is that the sample size taken from the sectors like different multinational IT corporations is small, i.e., 12, which was the limit in the sample formation, financial support, and geographical reachability. If the sample size had been bigger, then the result might not have been the same, as it is right now. Thus, this itself leaves the scope for others to test it with a higher sample size for incident management accurately and reliably.

## 6.12 CONCLUSION

Matching the daunting security vulnerabilities through incident handling and its immediate reporting measures is in practice to signify the degree of capabilities for various resilient tools. After steady comparison analysis, resilient tools divulge their state of skills, shortcomings, and additional evidence. However, the increasing number of identified attacks necessitates the development of faster and more efficient defenses. New tools describing their degree of ability to fit themselves appropriately must survive in the cyber world as a cyber trooper. Based on these findings, our current deployments can emphasize process automation through different research approaches presented as an incident reporting and handling measure to notify future incidents successfully. It also provides a comparative examination of the reporting forms. This study yields a computed chi-square value of 28.58, which is more than the tabulated value of 26.296, indicating that new tools have a considerable influence on properly handling cybersecurity incidents.

## ACKNOWLEDGMENTS

I am very much indebted to the esteemed guide and institution for giving me such a real-time environment to do my research work successfully.

## REFERENCES

Ahluwalia, J., & Marriott, L. (2005). Critical incident reporting systems. *WB Saunders Seminars in Fetal and Neonatal Medicine, 10* (1), 31–37.

Asgarli, E., & Burger, E. (2016). Semantic ontologies for cyber threat sharing standards. *IEEE Xplore*, 516–522.

Balt, I. A. M., & Papadopoulos, T. (March 2022). Social media platforms and social enterprise: Bibliometric analysis and systematic review. *International Journal of Information Management, 184*, 102510.

Baskerville, R., Spagnoletti, P., & Kim, J. (2014). Incident-centered information security: Managing a strategic balance between prevention and response. *Information and Management, 51* (1), 138–151.

Buchler, N., Rajivan, P., Marusich, L. R., Lightner, L., & Gonzalez, C. (2018). Sociometric and observational assessment of teaming and leadership in a cybersecurity defense competition. *Computers and Security, 73*, 114–136.

Cardini, A., Borlera, S. L., Malandrino, F., & Cimellaro, G. P. (February 2022). Seismic vulnerability and resilience assessment of urban telecommunication networks. *Sustainable Cities and Society, 77*, 103540.

Caron, F. (2021). Obtaining reasonable assurance of cyber resilience. *Managerial Auditing Journal, 36* (2), 193–217.

Chen, Z., Fiandrino, C., & Kantarci, B. (May 2021). On blockchain integration into mobile crowdsensing via smart embedded devices: A comprehensive survey. *Journal of Systems Architecture, 115*, 102011.

Eling, M., & Wirfs, J. (2019). What are the actual costs of cyber risk events? *European Journal of Operational Research, 272* (3), 1109–1119.

Elmellas, J. (2016). Knowledge is power: The evolution of threat intelligence. *Computer Fraud and Security, 2016* (7), 5–9.

Guerra, J. L., Catania, C., & Veas, E. (September 2022). Datasets are not enough: Challenges in labeling network traffic. *Information Sciences, 120,* 102810.

Hove, C., Tarnes, M., Line, M. B., & Bernsmed, K. (2014). *Information security incident management: Identified practice in large organizations.* IEEE XPLORE. (In 2014 Eighth International Conference on IT Security Incident Management & IT Forensics).

Inedjaren, Y., Maachaoui, M., Zeddini, B., & Barbot, J. P. (August 2021). Blockchain-based distributed management system for trust in VANET. *Vehicular Communications, 30,* 100350.

Leszczyna, R., Wallis, T., & Wróbel, M. R. (2019). Developing novel solutions to realise the european energy – information sharing and analysis centre. *Decision Support Systems, 122,* 113067.

Li, Y., Feng, Y., Hao, R., Liu, D., Fang, C., Chen, Z., & Xu, B. (February 2022). Classifying crowdsourced mobile test reports with image features: An empirical study. *Journal of Systems and Software, 184,* 111121.

Line, M. B., Tøndel, I. A., & Jaatun, M. G. (May 2014). *Information security incident management: Planning for failure.* IEEE XPLORE.

Liu, Q., Wang, G., Hu, J., & Wu, J. (August 2022). Preface of special issue on artificial intelligence: The security & privacy opportunities and challenges for emerging applications. *Future Generation Computer Systems, 133,* 169–170.

Mahmoud, M. S., & Hamdan, M. M. (2019). Improved control of cyber-physical systems subject to cyber and physical attacks. *Cyber-Physical Systems, 5* (3), 173–190.

Mitropoulos, S., Patsos, D., & Douligeris, C. (2006). On incident handling and response: A state of-the-art approach. *Computers and Security, 25* (5), 351–370.

Nespoli, P., Papamartzivanos, D., Marmol, F. G., & Kambourakis, G. (2017). Optimal countermeasures selection against cyber-attacks: A comprehensive survey on reaction frameworks. *IEEE Communications Surveys and Tutorials, 20* (2), 1361–1396.

Noor, U, Anwar, Z., Malik, A. W., Khan, S., & Saleem, S. (2019). A machine learning framework for investigating data breaches based on semantic analysis of adversary's attack patterns in threat intelligence repositories. *Future Generation Computer Systems, 95* (7), 467–487.

Oligeri, O., Sciancalepore, S., Ibrahim, O. A, & Pietro, R. D. (October 2022). GPS spoofing detection via crowdsourced information for connected vehicles. *Computer Networks, 216,* 109230.

Orlando, A., Marotta, A., Nanni, S., Martinelli, F., & Yautsiukhin, A. (2017). Cyber-insurance survey. *Computer Science Review, 24* (35–61).

Panigrahi, G. R., Barpanda, N. K., & Panda, M. (2021). Machine automation making cyber-policy violator more resilient: A proportionate study. In *Handbook of Research on Automated Feature Engineering and Advanced Applications in Data Science,* 329–345.

Perez, A.J., & Zeadally, S. (February 2022). Secure and privacy-preserving crowdsensing using smart contracts: Issues and solutions. *Computer Science Review, 43,* 1–11.

Ray, P. P., & Kumar, N. (March 2021). SDN/NFV architectures for edge-cloud oriented IoT: A systematic review. *Computer Communications, 169,* 129–153.

Ruefle, R., Dorofee, A., Mundie, D., Householder, A. D., Murray, M., & Perl, S. J. (2014). Computer security incident response team development and evolution. *IEEE Security and Privacy, 12* (5), 16–26.

Sahrom, Md., Rahayu, S. S., Ariffin, A. & Yusof, R. (2018). Cyber threat intelligence: Issue and challenges. *Indonesian Journal of Electrical Engineering and Computer Science, 10* (1), 371–379.

Serketzis, N., Katos, V., Ilioudis, C., Baltatzis, D., & Pangalos, G. J. (2019). Actionable threat intelligence for digital forensics readiness. *Information and Computer Security, 27* (2), 273–291.

Skopik, F., Settanni, G., & Roman, F. (2016). A problem shared is a problem halved: A survey on the dimensions of collective cyber defense through security information sharing. *Computers and Security, 60,* 154–176.

Steinberger, J., Kuhnert, B., Sperotto, A., Baier, H., & Pras, A. (2016). Collaborative DDoS defense using flow-based security event information. In *NOMS IEEE/IFIP Network Operations and Management Symposium,* 516–522.

Tong, W., Dong, X., Shen, Y., Zhang, Y., Jiang, X., & Tian, W. (June 2022). CHChain: Secure and parallel crowdsourcing driven by hybrid blockchain. *Future Generation Computer Systems, 131,* 279–291.

Tosh, D., Sengupta S., Kamhoua, C. A., & Kwiat, K. (2018). Establishing evolutionary game models for cybersecurity information exchange (Cybex). *Journal of Computer and System Sciences, 98,* 27–52.

Tounsi, W., & Rais, H. (2018). A survey on technical threat intelligence in the age of sophisticated cyber-attacks. *Computers and Security, 72,* 212–233.

Vlietland, J., & van Vliet, H. (2014). Improving it incident handling performance with information visibility. *Journal of Software: Evolution and Process, 26* (12), 1106–1127.

Wang, S., Hu, Y., & Qi, G. (November 2022). Blockchain and deep learning based trust management for internet of vehicles. *Simulation Modelling Practice and Theory, 120,* 102627.

Wang, S. S. (2019). Integrated framework for information security investment and cyber insurance. *Pacific-Basin Finance Journal, 57,* 101–173.

Wu, K., Li, Y., Chen, F., & Chen, L. (March 2016). A method for describing industrial control system network attack using object Petri net. *Transactions on Electrical and Electronic Engineering, 11,* 129–256.

Zhang, R., Li, Z., Xiong, N. N., Zhang, S., & Liu, A. (September 2022). TDTA: A truth detection based task assignment scheme for mobile crowdsourced industrial Internet of Things. *Information Sciences, 610,* 246–265.

Zhou, B., Ma, W., Li, Q, El-Sheimy, N., Mao, Q., Li. Y., Gu, F., Huang, L., & Zhu, J. (July 2022). Crowdsourcing based indoor mapping using smartphones: A survey. *ISPRS Journal of Photogrammetry and Remote Sensing, 177,* 131–146.

# 7

# Performance Evaluation of Support Vector Machine Kernel Functions on Students' Educational Data Set

Sulaiman O. Abdulsalam[1], Rafiu A. Ganiyu[2],
Elijah O. Omidiora[2], Stephen O. Olabiyisi[2],
and Micheal O. Arowolo[3]

[1]Department of Computer Science, Kwara State University, Malete, Nigeria
[2]Department of Computer Science and Engineering, Ladoke Akintola University of Technology, Ogbomoso, Nigeria
[3]Department of Electrical Engineering and Computer Science, University of Missouri, Columbia, Missouri, United States of America

## 7.1 INTRODUCTION

Data mining, when applied to academic domain brings innovative methodologies, techniques, and technologies to the development of the student learning. In order to acquire an improved understanding of the undergraduates' educational process, the most recent advancement offers helpful tools for analyzing and interpreting large data sets employing knowledge discovery techniques. Today's academic institutions function in a challenging and competitive world. Academic institutions experience many problems, such as assessing and comparing, ensuring excellent education, devising methods for measuring student progress, and envisioning the future. These establishments must enhance student preventative strategies in order to address difficulties students face throughout their schooling (Albreiki et al., 2021).

DOI: 10.1201/9781003346326-7

Education is one of society's most important pillars. It controls students' character and intellect. The present educational scheme may not be adequate to meet society's changing and dynamic needs. One of the most significant features of the new educational paradigm is the skill to forecast student performance in advance. Because students are the primary stakeholders in educational systems, academic institutions can meet the changing needs of society by evaluating student data and emerging various predictions based on it. Furthermore, the outcomes of predictions can be useful in developing approaches to advance educational quality. A higher-quality education aids in the development of skilled and distinctive students. This lets you analyze academic information. Utilizing machine learning techniques, student achievement classifiers analyze information of students. Many academic achievement classifiers exist. Both the research and treatment communities have considered students achievement predictive models. Academic achievement predictions scientists suggest semesters, GPA, CGPA, and pass/fail courses (Zaffar et al., 2022).

In EDM (educational data mining), the goal of developing computer models for academics is not simply to obtain optimal precision of prediction, but additionally to aid instructional authorities in evaluating academic achievement. Learners are a society's most important asset, and the primary objective of every academic institution is to provide them with a higher educational attainment. Moreover, great education contributes to the development of talented and unique students. Models for predicting student achievement facilitate the examination of data collected, utilizing numerous data mining techniques. The creation of models for predicting student achievement has required considerable time and effort. There are two methods for developing standardized testing prediction models. The first technique is supervised, but the second is unsupervised. Classification is a form of supervised learning methodology. The parameter out of which we want to infer whether or not a student passed or failed was provided explicitly as the input vector in the clearly indicate. Therefore, we decided to use the classification approach in a model that predicts students' grades (Guo et al., 2015).

Evaluating students' work helps teachers and other educators draw useful conclusions and make necessary adjustments so that they can better serve students and the evolving needs of society. When trying to improve forecast accuracy and create actionable plans for raising students' academic performance, the attributes chosen for use in making those predictions are crucial. The literature suggests that present methods have pros and cons when it comes to determining ideal attributes for machine learning models utilized to predict student performance (Zaffar et al., 2022).

The performance of four Support Vector Machine (SVM) kernel functions, polynomial function (PF), linear function (LF), radial basis function (RBF), and sigmoid function (SF), are investigated using the grid search method, with the objective of determining the best kernel function, using students' educational data set obtained from the Department of Computer Science in Nigerian universities in the north-central region from 2009 to 2014.

## 7.2 RELATED WORKS

Students' performance prediction model using Iterative Dichotomiser 3 (ID3) and C4.5 classification algorithms in a Nigerian University was developed. The data set used contained students' academic records such as gender, SSCE grade, age, post/Unified Tertiary Matriculation Examination (UMTE) scores, and the first-year student grade. From the result of their work, ID3 algorithm outperforms the C4.5 with respect to identification of significant attributes that contributed greatly to the determination of students' academic performance (Afeni 2019).

An artificial neural network (ANN) is utilized to analyze and forecast students' CGPAs based on their socioeconomic level and entrance exam scores for undergraduate education at a Chinese institution. Through the use of confusion matrix, error histogram, regression analysis, and mean square error, ANN performance was examined. ANN attained an accuracy of 84.8 percent and an Area under the curve (AUC) of 0.86. Despite this, ANN performed badly in identifying undergraduates due to their gender and produced a high rate of false negatives as a result of a high imbalanced ratio data sample (Lau et al., 2019).

A log-data segmentation approach was suggested for determining student disengagement in introductory programming programs by identifying individuals who really remain focused with programming lectures. During a 90-minute examination of 39 beginning-level computer program learners, the research employed a way to predict undergraduate withdrawals utilizing the virtual terminal connection input sequence, outliers classification, and an unsupervised machine learning methodology (Oeda & Hashimoto, 2017).

A classification model for predicting critical courses that affects student's performance using ID3 decision tree initiation algorithm was developed (Altujjar et al., 2016). The researcher model was built using 100 records of feminine students in the King Saud University, Information Technology Department. Their result divulged those dependable predictions are attained due to the performance of scholars in the second year progresses and also discovered significant courses that help as pointers of scholar academic performance.

Employing a Waikato Environment for Knowledge Analysis (WEKA) information mining application, a comprehensive review of classification models, Nave Bayes (NB), a Bayesian network, Instance-based learning with parameter k (IBk) approach, a slow predictor, and Classification and Regression Tree (CART), a tree-based technique, was conducted using the true positive rate, false positive rate, and productivity accuracy. They utilized the educational data of 385 individuals with seven parameters (sex, age, entrance method, city of residence, denomination, 200-level CGPA, and final examination) from the Computer Science Department and Technology at LAUTECH. In contrast to NB and CART, which had performance levels of 64 percent and 62 percent, separately, IBk was capable of making predictions for all stages of education with a highest accuracy of 86 percent. Furthermore, the outcomes of the performance analysis revealed that Naïve Bayes, Instant Based, as well as CART had comparable results. They discovered that IBk provided the performance accuracy (PA) with the smallest normality test and also performed the greatest with increased true positive rating (TPR) intensity (Ayinde et al., 2015).

The influence of the quality for predicting the academic performance of first college freshmen premised on their degree relatives and previous educational attainment was suggested. They examined the data of 1,500 computer science majors at Babcock Nigerian University between 2001 and 2010. In developing a prediction model, ten learning algorithms (five classification tree methods: Random Forest, J48, Decision tree [dt], REPTree, and decision tree trunk, and five supervised learning procedures: OneR, JRip, PART, ZeroR, and Classification model) and a multilayered perceptual were utilized. Utilizing the tenfold cross-validation (10-FCV) and retention approaches, the accuracy, confusion matrix, and computational efficiency of the produced models were measured. It was discovered that the Random tree method outperformed other strategies employed in their research (Kuyoro et al., 2013).

An improved SVM feature selection algorithm is widely employed for the large-scale email dataset. Particle swarm optimization (PSO) procedure was employed for finding the optimal parameters values and also for obtaining optimal feature subset. The result of this learning revealed that the improved SVM procedure generated a classification accuracy while the standalone SVM produced an accuracy of 68 percent in 6.33 seconds for e-mail data set of 1,000. In addition, with the use of 3,000 e-mail data set, the optimized SVM and standalone SVM yielded classification accuracy and computation time of 91 percent, 0.60 second and 47 percent, and 60 seconds, respectively. Likewise, using 6,000 e-mail data set, 93 percent, 0.20 second and 18 percent, 92 seconds were achieved for augmented SVM method and standalone SVM individually. The researchers argued that the experimental results acquired establish that for each rise in data set dimensions, there is constantly a lessening in the classification of SVM classifier with a significant rise in computational time. This study concluded that the optimized SVM technique outperformed the standalone SVM with respect to classification accuracy and time consumption in the face of huge e-mail data set (Oludare et al., 2014).

An optimization of RBF kernel parameters to attain maximum accuracy value in nonlinear multiclass SVM classifier for the recognition of images of Indonesian Batik data set with geometric decorative patterns. The researcher applied grid search method with cross-validation (CV) process to optimize a range of values of parameters C (Cost) and $\gamma$ (Gamma) of SVM-RBF kernel. Additionally, the discrete wavelet transform (DWT) algorithm was used for feature extraction and the extracted feature data set was employed for training and testing sets. The experimental result produced a maximum accuracy value for the Batik data set when using the constraints C = 27 and $\gamma = 2-15$. The researcher concluded that the obtained optimal values and reduced variety of constraint principles can be utilized as a reference for numerary image recognition with qualities keeping geometric enhancing patterns with SVM-RBF kernel classification (Budiman, 2019).

Afeni et al. (2019) developed a students' performance prediction model using ID3 and C4.5 classification procedures at a Nigerian university. The data set used contained students' academic records such as gender, SSCE grade, age, post/UMTE scores, and the first-year student grade. From the result of their work, ID3 algorithm outperforms the C4.5 with respect to identification of significant attributes that contributed greatly to the determination of students' academic performance.

Lau et al. (2019) utilized the ANN to analyze and evaluate the individuals' cumulative grade point average based on their social economic level and entry-standardized test scores for undergraduate studies at a Chinese institution. Through using a prediction model, multiple regressions, inaccuracy distribution, and root-mean-square average, the functionality of ANN was examined. ANN achieved an accuracy rate of 85 percent and an AUC of 0.90. Nevertheless, the performance of ANN was poor in categorizing scholars with respect to their gender and achieved a high false negative rate result due to a high imbalance ratio data sample.

In light of assessing standardized testing data, Oeda and Hashimoto (2017) suggested utilizing a file segmentation technique to predict learner dropouts in introductory training. This approach might be necessary for universal screening, especially for individuals who struggle with computational training. During such a 90-minute examination of 39 beginning programmers, the researchers used UNIX command input records to develop a technique for anticipating learner attrition by applying feature extraction to clustering records with an unsupervised learning approach.

Altujjar et al. (2016) developed a classification model for envisaging critical courses that affects student's performance using ID3 decision tree induction algorithm. The researcher model was built using 100 records of feminine students in the King Saud University, Information Technology Department. Their result divulged that dependable predictions are attained due to the performance of scholars in the second year progresses and also discovered important developments that serve as pointers of student academic performance.

Ayinde et al. (2015) performed a comparative analysis of three classifiers, Naïve Bayes, a Bayesian network, IBk procedure, a lazy classifier, and CART, a decision tree procedure in terms of true positive rate, false positive rate, and performance accuracy in mining students' educational data using WEKA data mining software. They used 385 students' academic records, with seven attributes each (gender, age, admission mode, state of origin, religion, 200 level CGPA, and students' final grade), of the Computer Science and Engineering, Department at LAUTECH. Their results revealed that IBk was able to expect for all the classes of grades with an overall performance rate of 86 percent, unlike NB and CART with a performance rate of 64 percent and 62 percent, respectively. The average TPR for NB, IBk, and CART was 55.4 percent, 79.4 percent, and 59 percent, consecutively; the average FPR was 58 percent, 42 percent, and 66 percent; and the average PA score was 59 percent, 82 percent, and 69 percent. They concluded that IBk gave the PA with the lowermost insignificant hypothesis and also performs best with increasing value of TPR.

The best method for predicting the hypothetical success of first-year postsecondary students based on their family history and past academic achievements was discovered by Kuyoro et al. (2013). They analyzed information from 1,500 CS majors at Nigeria's Babcock University from 2001 to 2010. Ten classification methods (five classification tree methods: Random Forest, J48, Random tree, REPTree, and Decision root, and five supervised learning algorithms: OneR, JRip, PART, ZeroR, and Decision tree) and a multilayered perceptual were utilized in generating classification techniques. The resulting models were verified both 10-FCV and retention methods to estimate of average accuracy, confusion matrices and computational efficiency. Results exhibited that the Random tree method achieved improved than the others tested.

Oyedele et al. (2010) predicted students' performance with the K-means clustering procedure integrated with the deterministic model based on the data set of a private institution in Nigeria. A total number of 79 students that offered nine courses each in a semester was sampled and a scheme for examining students' outcomes-based clustering analysis and utilized statistical processes to position their scores' information conferring to the degree of performance was demonstrated.

Ayinde et al. (2013) applied Naïve Bayes and Decision Stump procedures in predicting the scholars' concluding year mark at Ladoke Akintola University of Technology, Ogbomoso, Nigeria. A total of 473 students comparing 10 attributes namely, gender, age, admission mode, faith, pre-degree grade, scholar enrolment number, origin, 200-level CGPA, 500-level GPA, and students' final grades were used. The outcomes of their study divulged that the Naïve Bayes with an average precision of 77 percent performed better than the decision stump algorithm with an average precision of 57 percent.

Akinola et al. (2012) utilized the ANN to advance a data mining model for performance of computer science students' prediction in computer programming development taken at the 200 level using their pre-qualification ordinary level results and their results obtained in 100-level mathematics and physics courses. Two hundred records of scholars in the Computer Science Department, University of Ibadan, were used for the study and it was discovered that a previous background knowledge of mathematics and physics were vital in instruction for a scholar excelling in computer programming.

Minaei-Bidgoli's (2003) research attempted a method to predict students' final evaluation by classifying them based on extracted features from recorded information in a teaching web-based system. An ensemble of classifiers was designed, implemented, and evaluated on an online programmed data set at Michigan State University (USA), relating to 2002 data. Conclusions from a methodological viewpoint show that the use of multiple classifiers resulted in a major upsurge in classification accuracy (as research in ensemble methods confirms) and that this method could be extremely helpful in recognizing scholars at risk early on, particularly in large classes, and allowing the teacher to deliver timely advising.

Barker et al. (2004) studied the problem in a perspective of classifying student graduation performance from numerous demographic, academic, and attitudinal variables. They used neural networks and SVM algorithms over data from the first-year advising center of the University of Oklahoma (USA), composed via a review assumed to all inbound freshmen. An overall conclusion of this study is the lack of area information about the data set and that underprivileged outcomes (one-third of the students were misclassified) are not the fault of the algorithm. Delivering a pessimistic view, the authors realized that it may be difficult to capture appropriate and suitable information about student completion.

Herzog (2005) research was more specific as it measured the influence of high college training, first-year academic performance, multi-institute enrollment, and economic aid sustenance on second-year determination. A methodology was developed using multinomial logistic regression. The recognized scholar data system included data on scholar demographics, academics, economic support, and student on-campus jobs data, as well as the institution's payroll system. The findings show the importance of looking at risk issues from both a dropout and a transfer-out viewpoint, while taking into account the possibility that a scholar might be enrolled at added institution at the same time. When evaluating freshmen retention, the findings show that first-year mathematics knowledge, math strength of the acknowledged major, concurrent enrollment at extra higher education institutions, and second-year economic aid suggestions are all important factors to consider. Furthermore, middle-income undergraduates with more unmet needs are more probable to drop out, while educationally well-prepared freshers with unmet needs are more probable to move.

Herzog (2006), in further research, took another perspective on predicting retaining and graduation time using decision trees, neural networks, and logistic regression. Like previous research, data from the institutional student information system was used, together with parent income data, and a system to identify transfer-out students. The analysis revealed that when analyzing the generalization ability of numerous data mining procedures to regression models, the complexities of the data set utilized and the primary objective may greatly guide the selection of an evaluation method. Decision tree algorithm and neural networks can help analysts discover which qualities improve prediction performance when interacting with huge amounts of information.

Romero et al. (2008) compared various data mining approaches for classifying scholars based on their Moodle "e-learning system" use information and concluding characters in their individual programs. The methodology relied on a particular mining tool to make data mining technique setup and execution simpler for instructors. The data included students' usage log in a web-based program of seven Moodle programs in the University of Córdoba (Spain) and the final marks obtained. The algorithms used were neural networks and genetic and decision trees. When preprocessing tasks (discretization and rebalancing data) were applied, some algorithms improved their classification efficiency, while others did not. A classification algorithm intended for pedagogical usage must be exact and straightforward for instructors to be beneficial for strategic planning.

Dekker et al. (2009) research aimed to predict which electrical engineering scholars would drop out after their initial semester and to define success factors unique to that program. Over the years 2000 to 2009, data was collected on 648 Eindhoven University of Technology freshman students (Netherlands). A Bayesian classifier, logistical algorithm, principal classifier, and decision tree model were examined. The OneR predictor also functioned as a measure and estimator of variable predictiveness. Decision trees have valuable insights with accuracies between 75 and 80 percent, according to experimental results. Conclusions delve into showing ways of further improvement in prediction without having to collect additional data about the students.

Zhang et al. (2010) wanted to recognize potential difficulties as primary as conceivable and to trail with involvement decisions to improve student retention. For that purpose, a system was built, including data mining techniques, using Naïve Bayes, SVM, and decision trees algorithms. This system monitored and analyzed student academic behavior with the aim to provide a basis for efficient intervention strategies. The data used was from the university system of the Thames Valley University (UK). The main conclusions were that Naïve Bayes attained the maximum prediction accuracy outperforming decision trees and SVM.

Socio-demographic factors (such as gender, age, ethnicity, employment position, educational attainment, and disability) and the learning environment were investigated by Kovacic's (2010) research. From 2006 to 2009, 450 scholars at the Open Polytechnic of Wellington (New Zealand) were included in the data set. The strategy involved a combination of cross-tabulation analysis (situational tables), feature selection, and prediction using four distinct kinds of decision trees. The most important criteria between successful and unsuccessful students were found to be students' race and their participation in a particular program. After making some methodological considerations, we found that the CART model achieved the highest accuracy (60.5 percent total) in our classification task.

Kabakchieva (2012) aims to illustrate the promising importance of data mining systems for school administrators in order to enable academic institutions run increasingly profitable enrollment campaigns and recruit the brightest students. The determination of this study was to advance data-mining algorithms that might predict a student's future abstract performance based on their unique set of pre-university, collegiate, and post-collegiate experiences. Many different algorithms, including the neural networks, OneR rule learning, decision trees, and k-nearest neighbor (k-NN) classifiers, were put to the test. The data set used in this research is comprised of three years' worth of admissions data from the University of National and Financial System in Sofia. Specifically, the outcomes exhibited that the neural network model had the precise results, followed by the prediction model and the k-NN model. Attributes of data pertaining to students' university entrance scores and the number of unsuccessful attempts on that first university studies are two of the most significant criteria in the classification stage.

Decision tree algorithms, ANNs, naive classification algorithms, instance-based learning, regression models, and SVMs were among the supervised machine learning algorithms developed by Kotsiantis et al. (2004) to expect scholar success at the Hellenic Open University based on key demographic variable measure and assignment marks. The percentage of correct predictions wide-ranging from 58 percent (when a neural network was utilized) to 65 percent (when only demographic variables were included) (when using SVMs). The Naïve Bayes classifier proved to be the greatest effective method for expecting student success when additional data were included in addition to demographics.

Students' risk levels were determined using a combination of neural networks, decision trees, and linear discriminant analysis by Vandamme et al. (2007). The academic success of first-year scholars at French colleges in the kingdom of Belgium was found to be significantly correlated with a variety of demographic and personal factors. Students' academic success was best predicted by their level of education, the number of hours they spent on mathematics, their financial stability, and their age, but not by their gender, their parents' education or career, or whether or not they were married. But none of the three techniques used to foretell moot success actually worked. Overall, the classification accuracy of decision trees was 40.63 percent, that of neural networks was 51.88 percent, and that of discriminant analysis was 57.35 percent.

Secondary student grades were estimated in two groups by Cortez and Silva (2008) using a variety of factors including prior academic performance, demographics, social information, and other school-related information. To get there, we used a variety of machine learning systems like neural networks, random forests, decision trees, and SVMs. When taking into account prior grades, they proved to be rather accurate in predicting future performance. In certain situations, they incorporated socioeconomic factors into their models in addition to demographic factors (such as a student's age, their parents' occupation, and their level of education). There were several factors that Open Polytechnic students simply couldn't get to (for example, previous student grades).

Predictive model Chi-square automatic interaction detector (CHAID) with a seven-class response variable was developed by Ramaswami and Bhaskaran 2010) to evaluate students' performance in Indian higher secondary institutions. The model relied on highly impacting predictive factors obtained through feature selection. The CHAID prediction model was built using data from several different Tamilnadu universities and 772 student records. Therefore, the CHAID prediction model was used to generate a set of rules, and the system's efficacy was evaluated.

The Course Registration Planning Model (CRPM) was first proposed by Pathom et al. (2008), and its development was proposed by a classifier algorithm. The four classifiers that were considered for this task were the Bayesian network, C4.5, the decision forest, and the NB tree.

Undergraduate enrollments, including GPAs and grades, were used to generate the data.

Lykourentzou et al. (2009) used three algorithms of machine learning and individual information to identify e-learning withdrawals. The Municipal Tech College of Athens' Collaborative Communication Institute sponsors the e-learning crew (Greece). Feed-forward neural pathways, SVMs, and deterministic ensembles fuzzified ARTMAP were in use. On the whole, the strategy's consistency, responsivity, and specificity were significantly comparable to those shown in the field.

The phrases "stop out," "maintained," and "transferable" were defined by Sujitparapitaya (2006). The determination of this case study was to recognize the most important factors that freshmen consider while making their final decision. Based on the model, incoming freshmen can choose between staying at their current school, transferring to a different post-secondary institution, or dropping out altogether. The data used came from the National Student Clearinghouse, which is widely recognized as an authoritative repository for academic credentialing and student performance statistics across American universities. The algorithms deployed included logistic regression, neural networks, and C5.0 (decision tree). In terms of predicting first-year retention, the C5.0 rule induction model looks to do slightly better than the other two. The findings are noteworthy because they show that changes in campus, scholar, and parental values are just as important as changes in basic norms and rewards for effective retention programs that increase student learning.

## 7.3 METHODOLOGY

### 7.3.1 Data Acquisition and Description

The experimental set of data used in this research is a multi-class student educational data set obtained from the Department of Computer Science in a university in north-central region of Nigeria. The data set is made up of records of 153 graduated students with variables sex, age, and their 64 respective courses offered as the predictor variables and their obtained final year grades as the class label. The descriptions of predictor variables (sex, age, and students' scores in different courses offered) and class label (final grade obtained at graduation) used in the data sets, the final grade obtained at graduation had five distinct values: (First, Second Upper, Second Lower, Third Classes, and Pass).

The students' educational data set was first separated into two portions of 80:20 ratios. Eighty percent of the data went through 10-FCV, while the remaining 20 percent served as the validation set and was put through its paces in the testing phase. In other words, out of a total of 153 samples, 122 were used to train/build the four SVM models (with a linear, polynomial, radial basis, and sigmoidal SVM Kernel function), and the outstanding 31 examples were used as a validation test set to determine how well the developed hybrid rule extraction method from SVM performed.

## 7.3.2 Support Vector Machine (SVM)

The SVM is an educational method that is founded on the statistical learning model (Vapnik, 1995). SVM has gained popularity as a potent data mining technology that can be used to address the challenge of knowledge extraction (Burges-Christopher, 1998). By making use of kernel functions, SVM is able to change input qualities from lower to higher dimensions. A wide variety of applications have been utilized, such as the forecasting of financial time series (Kim, 2003), marketing (Ben-David & Lindenbaum, 1997), face recognition (Chowdhury et al., 2011), cervical cancer diagnosis, and the classification of gene expression data (Das et al., 2020).

For classification techniques, SVM aims to discover an ideal hyperplane that maximizes the margin that accurately distinguishes data points as much as feasible and divides class labels to the greatest extent practicable, while minimizing the likelihood of mishandling training data set and unlabeled testing set. The purpose is to discover a hyperplane that maximizes the boundary that meaningfulness information points and separates them as much as feasible (Vapnik, 1998). Other training instances can't define binary class bounds. Support vectors are training spots near the optimal separation hyperplane. SVM projects nonlinearly recoverable information to a higher dimensional space and then looks for the linear boundary. SVMs can tackle linear and nonlinear sorting issues, but their bid to multi-class challenges is restricted because of its one-to-one methodology. This offers SVMs a competitive advantage (Sampon et al., 2011). Numerous individuals present a multiclass challenge as many problems involve binary classification (one-to-all difficulties) (Luts et al., 2010).

Provided a training set of instance-label pair $(x_i, y_i)$, $i = 1, 2, \ldots, m$ where $x_i \in R^n$ and $y_i \in \{+1, -1\}$, SVM identifies an ideal extrication hyperplane with the determined boundary by resolving the subsequent optimization task:

$$\underset{w,b}{\text{Min}} \quad \frac{1}{2} w^T w \tag{7.1}$$

Subject to: $y_i(\langle w \cdot x_i \rangle + b) - 1 \geq 0$

where $x_i$ is an actual-valued n-dimensional input trajectory and $y_i$ is a tag that defines the class of $x_i$. An untying hyperplane is achieved through an impertinent vector $\mathbf{w}$ and a partiality b.

It is well understood that the burden point of the Lagrange role is found to resolve this quadratic equation optimization issue:

$$L_P(w, b, \alpha) = \frac{1}{2} w^T \cdot w - \sum_{i=1}^{m} (\alpha_i y_i (\langle w. x_i \rangle + b) - 1) \tag{7.2}$$

where the $\alpha_i$ denotes Lagrange multipliers, hence $\alpha_i \geq 0$. The exploration for an optimum burden opinion is essential since the $Lp$ necessitate is diminished with reverence to the primal variables w and b and exploited with reverence to the non-negative double variable $\alpha_i$. By distinguishing with reverence to $w$ and $b$, and familiarizing the Karush Kuhn–Tucker (KKT) approval for the optimal inhibited function, then $Lp$ is distorted to the double Lagrangian $L_D(\alpha)$:

$$\underset{\alpha}{\max} \, L_D(\alpha) = \sum_{i=1}^{m} \alpha_i - \frac{1}{2} \sum_{i=1}^{m} \alpha_i \alpha_j y_i y_j \langle x_i. x_j \rangle \tag{7.3}$$

Subject to: $\alpha_i \geq 0 \, i = 1, \ldots, m \, and \, \sum_{i=1}^{m} \alpha_i y_i = 0$

Finding the best hyperplane, a twofold Lagrange $L_D(\alpha)$ necessitates exploiting with reverence to non-negative $\alpha_i$. The answer $\alpha_i$ for the twofold optimization issue describes the constraints $w^*$ and $b^*$ of the ideal hyperplane. Hence, the ideal hyperplane result function $f(x) = sgn(\langle w^*. x \rangle + b^*)$ can be described as

$$f(x) = sgn\left( \sum_{i=1}^{m} y_i \alpha_i^* \langle x_i, x \rangle + b^* \right) \tag{7.4}$$

Small subclass of the Lagrange multipliers α_i is typically superior than zero in a normal classification task. These vectors are the most geometrically similar to the ideal hyperplane. The relevant training vectors having non-zero $\alpha_i$ are termed support vectors, as the best verdict hyperplane $f(x, \alpha^*, b^*)$ depends on them entirely.

These notions also apply to non-separable cases (linear comprehensive SVM). In terms of these new inequality constraints, the task of discovering the hyperplane with the fewest training mistakes (i.e., minimizing constriction error) is expressed as follows:

$$\min_{w,b,\xi} \frac{1}{2}w^T w + C \sum_{i=1}^{m} \xi_i \qquad (7.5)$$

Subject to: $y_i(\langle w. x_i \rangle + b) + \xi_i - 1 \geq 0 \quad \xi_i \geq 0$

where C is the non-negative relaxed variables and is a penalized variable on the training error. By analyzing all possible hyperplanes, SVM finds the one that results in the fewest blunders during training (that is, to retain the limit error as minor as conceivable).

This optimization model can be solved using the Lagrangian approach, which is corresponding to the method used to resolve the optimization technique in the independent assortment. The Lagrangian with two independent variables must be optimized:

$$\max_{\alpha} L_D(\alpha) = \sum_{i=1}^{m} \alpha_i - \frac{1}{2} \sum_{i=1}^{m} \alpha_i \alpha_j y_i y_j \langle x_i. x_j \rangle \qquad (7.6)$$

Subject to: $0 \leq \alpha_i \leq C \ i = 1, \ldots, m$ and $\sum_{i=1}^{m} \alpha_i y_i = 0$

Finding an optimum hyperplane, a twofold Lagrange $L_D(\alpha)$ needs to be exploited with reverence to non-negative $\alpha_i$ under the constraint $\sum_{i=1}^{m} \alpha_i y_i = 0$ and $\leq_0 \alpha_i \leq C$. The consequence constraint C, which is the higher bound on $\alpha_i$, is resolute by the user. Lastly, the procedure of best hyperplane result function is the same as (7.4).

The nonlinear SVM plans the training models from the input space into a higher-dimensional feature planetary via a plotting purpose $\phi$. In the twofold Lagrange (7.6), the internal products are swapped by the kernel function (7.7), and the nonlinear SVM dual Lagrange $L_D(\alpha)$ (7.8) is related with the linear global instance.

$$(\Phi(x_i)\cdot\Phi(x_j)) := k(x_i, x_j) \tag{7.7}$$

$$L_D(\alpha) = \sum_{i=1}^{m} \alpha_i - \frac{1}{2} \sum_{i=1}^{m} \alpha_i \alpha_j y_i y_j k \langle x_i \cdot x_j \rangle \tag{7.8}$$

Subject to: $0 \le \alpha_i \le C$ $i = 1, \ldots, m$ and $\sum_{i=1}^{m} \alpha_i y_i = 0$.

The decision function is obtained in the following form after the measures defined in the linear generalized case:

$$
\begin{aligned}
f(x) &= sgn\left(\sum_{i=1}^{m} y_i \alpha_i^* \langle \Phi(x), \Phi(x_i) \rangle + b^*\right) \\
&= sgn\left(\sum_{i=1}^{m} y_i \alpha_i^* \langle x_i, x \rangle + b^*\right)
\end{aligned}
\tag{7.9}
$$

By selectively plotting their involvements into high-dimensional feature spaces, SVM is able to efficiently execute nonlinear classification thanks to the kernel trick. The essential roles that a system should serve have been proposed in abundance. The computational efficiency of SVM can be enhanced by replacing its fundamental functions with those optimized for specific data attributes.

### 7.3.2.1 SVM Kernel Functions

To keep the computational complexity acceptable, SVM systems define dot products in terms of a kernel function so that they may be easily calculated in terms of the parameters in the innovative feature space $k(x,y)$ (Teukolsky et al., 2007). To generalize the optimal hyperplane with the biggest margin between two sets, an SVM uses a nonlinear kernel function to translate information from an input space to a potentially high-dimensional feature space (Chapelle et al., 2002). Kernels aid in the definition of a set of features that may be utilized to do a classification operation with ease. To improve classification precision, it is important to adjust the appropriate kernel parameters in the relevant kernel functions. There are two merits to using the kernel function. To begin with, it can be used in conjunction with linear classifiers to generate nonlinear decision boundaries. Furthermore, it allows classifiers to be applied to data that initially lacks a clear representation in a fixed-dimensional vector space (Huang et al., 2014). Generally accepted SVM kernel functions include the four possible forms:

Linear kernel function:

$$K(x_i, y_j) = x_i^t \cdot y_j \qquad (7.10)$$

Polynomial kernel function:

$$K(x_i, y_j) = (\gamma x_i^t x_j + r)^m, \quad \gamma > 0 \qquad (7.11)$$

Radial basis/Gaussian kernel function:

$$K(x_i, y_j) = \exp(-\gamma \ \|x_i - y_j\|^2), \ p \ \gamma > 0 \qquad (7.12)$$

Sigmoid kernel function:

$$K(x_i, y_i) = Tanh(\gamma x_i^t \cdot y_j + r), \qquad (7.13)$$

The kernel function is used to introduce nonlinearity and deal with arbitrary data structures. In most cases, successful classification results require fine-tuning not only the kernel function's parameters but also the other SVM parameters.

Choosing the right kernel and adjusting the right kernel parameters, as well as narrowing down the collection of functions to use, are essential steps toward regaining SVM's classification accuracy (Akay, 2009). Therefore, it begs the question, "Which SVM kernel delivers the best classification accuracy among various kernels?" Exploring the several SVM kernels to find the one with the best classification accuracy for a specific task is the only way to get an answer to this topic (Omidiora et al., 2014; Ovidiu, 2007). Finding the optimal kernel function and its appropriate kernel's parameters based on the students' educational data set, this study experiments with the four common SVM kernel functions, with linear, polynomial, radial basis, and sigmoid purposes.

### 7.3.2.2 Factors that Influence SVM Model Prediction Accuracy

The penalty factor $C$ and the kernel parameters are constraints that have the greatest impact on SVM prediction accuracy. The penalty factor $C$ calculates the penalty for data with greater deviations than precision $\varepsilon$. They have an effect on classification accuracy and the capacity of the SVM model to generalize. There is, however, no universal formula for enhancing the two parameters. The grid search method is the most commonly used technique (Chen et al., 2004; Friedrichs & Igel, 2005), where the pair ($C$, and other kernel parameters) are checked, and the CV accuracy of the best one is selected. As a result, the grid search method employs a CV procedure to increase SVM prediction accuracy. The grid search method was used to determine the appropriate kernel's parameter and best kernel function among the four SVM kernel functions investigated in this study.

### 7.3.2.3 Applications of SVM Models

Pattern recognition and image processing are two examples of applications where SVM has been used (Romon & Christodoulou, 2006). SVM has been used in control engineering in recent years. SVM, on the other hand, has yet to be widely used in educational science (Huang, 2011). Kotsiantis et al. (2003) conducted a study using SVM to predict the attrition rate of first-year scholars. The data was gathered through four written assignments, one-on-one advising sessions with instructors, and comprehensive tests. Scholars at peril of falling out of college were classified using the collected data and additional variables (such as gender, age, and parent work). The results demonstrated that Support Vector Machines (SVM) outperformed neural networks after the third training stage, which incorporated data from both the second stage and the initially recorded requirements. Individual ordinal data were used in this learning by Kotsiantis et al. (2003). Moreover, no education has yet been shown on the prediction accuracy and understandability of SVM in informative investigations employing students' educational data set.

### 7.3.2.4 SVM Kernel Parameters Optimization Using a Grid Search Method

To specify the best hyperplane with the biggest boundary amongst the two classes, SVMs begin by constructing a nonlinear kernel function to translate information from the input space into a presumably high-dimensional feature space (Chapelle et al., 2002). When using a kernel, defining a set of features that facilitates categorization is simplified. Optimizing the kernel parameters in the kernel functions can boost classification precision. First, the kernel function aids in the creation of nonlinear corresponding points inside the framework of linear classifier techniques, which is a great benefit. Second, it lets people classify information that doesn't seem to fit neatly into any predetermined vector space. From what I've read (Huang et al., 2014), polynomial kernel functions, linear kernel functions, radial basis/Gaussian kernel functions, and sigmoid kernel functions are the most often used SVM kernel functions.

To confirm that the existing results are reliable and comprehensive for making predictions regarding original data, a k-fold CV is used to randomly split the data set into training and independent testing sets. Individual k subgroups perform as its own holdout testing set for the training model using the remaining k-1 subcategories. Tenfold CV was employed for the analysis in this study. CV helps since it lessens the impact of data dependence and boosts the credibility of the results.

In this research, we used a grid exploration to invent the optimal kernel function for the SVM and its optimal parameters. Finding the optimal values for C, the penalty cost, and the other kernel parameters of the SVM may be done quickly and easily using the grid search technique. The original grid search was a comprehensive scan of a small region of the full hyper-parameter space. The hyper-parameters can be set by specifying a minimum value, maximum value, and the desired number of steps. Utilizing a CV technique as a performance measured, grid search optimizes the SVM parameters (C, degree, and coefficient (r)). The objective is to optimize the classifier's hyper-parameters so that it can reliably predict future outcomes.

When using $k$-fold CV to select $C$ and, the educational data set for students is first partitioned into $k$ subgroups (in this research, $k$ is set to 10). The remaining k-1 training subsets are used for analysis, while one is used as testing input. Then, for each value of $C$, and other parameters, the corresponding CV error for the SVM classifier is computed. A number of hyper-parameter clusters are compared, and the one with the best CV accurateness (smallest CV error) is picked for full-data set SVM training. The linear kernel has a single, crucial optimization parameter called $C$; the RBF kernel has two, called $C$; and the sigmoid kernel has three, called $C$, and coefficient ($r$); and the polynomial kernel has four, called $C$, degree, and coefficient ($r$). Figure 3.3 depicts a flowchart for optimizing the parameters of SVM kernels using a grid search. Parameter optimization using SVMs does not rely on hard-and-fast sets of parameter values. When there are more parameters to choose from, the

**FIGURE 7.1**
Framework of the study.

grid search strategy has a better chance of locating the optimal combination parameter. Thus, we employed the ranges [$C$ and] = 0.0001 to 10,000, [degree] = 1 to 5, and [$r$] = 1 to 10 in this investigation. The research design is depicted in Figure 7.1.

## 7.4 RESULTS AND DISCUSSION

The grid search method was used to optimize SVM parameters ($C$, $\gamma$, degree, and coefficient ($r$)) using CV. Various combinations of hyperparameters rate were entered and the one with the top CV precision (or the lowest CV error) was designated. The range of values used in parameter tuning of each of the four SVM kernel functions (LF, RBF, PF, and SF) considered in this research is shown in Table 4.2. In addition, Table 4.3 revealed the optimal parameter values of each of the four SVM kernel functions after parameter optimization.

The results obtained in the parameter optimization experimentation on the performance of each of the four SVM kernel functions in terms of classification accuracy, sensitivity, specificity, number of support vectors, and computation time are shown in Tables 4.4 and 4.5. As shown in Tables 4.4 and 4.5, the evaluation results of LF, RBF, PF, and SF yielded classification accuracies of 79.31, 86.21, 82.76, and 34.5 percent, respectively. Also, LF, RBF, PF, and SF recorded sensitivities of 71.12, 75.56, 65.56, and 22.20 percent, respectively. Moreover, LF, RBF, PF, and SF produced specificities of 94.44, 96.34, 95.36, and 74.06 percent, respectively. Likewise, the number of support vectors generated for LF, RBF, PF, and SF were 78, 80, 82, and 121, respectively. Furthermore, LF, RBF, and PF utilized the same computation time of 0.03 seconds, while SF executed for 0.06 seconds.

The findings from the results divulged that the RBF kernel was the best in terms of classification accuracy, sensitivity, and specificity. In addition, the RBF kernel has the same computation time as that of LF and PF. Likewise, RBF generated 80 support vectors, which is the closest to that of the LF kernel that produced the least number of support vectors (78).

From the result of parameter optimization, it can be deduced that the RBF kernel outperformed the three other SVM kernel functions and that SF performed least in terms of performance evaluation metrics and the data set used in this study.

Additionally, Tables 7.1, 7.2, 7.3, and 7.4 depict the comparative analysis of each of the four SVM kernel functions in terms of classification accuracy, sensitivity, specificity, number of support vectors, and computation time, respectively.

This study provides a machine learning technique for tuning SVM kernel functions using a data set acquired from the education domain and also focuses on accurate prediction of learners at peril of dropping out. With an 86 percent advantage, RBF-SVM outperforms the three kernel functions.

**TABLE 7.1**

Range of Values Used in Setting the Parameters for the SVM Kernel Functions

| Parameters | Values |
| --- | --- |
| **Cost (C):** | 0.00001, 0.0001, $\cdots$, 0.1, 1, 10, 100, $\cdots$, 10000 |
| **Gamma ($\gamma$)** | 0.00001, 0.0001, $\cdots$, 0.1, 1, 10, 100, $\cdots$, 10000 |
| **Coefficient (r):** | 1, 2, 3, 4, 5, 6, 7, 8, 9, 10 |
| **Degree (°)** | 1, 2, 3, 4, 5 |

**TABLE 7.2**

Optimal Parameter Values of SVM Kernel Functions after Optimization

| SVM Kernel Function | Optimal Parameter Values |
| --- | --- |
| Linear | Cost C: 10 |
| Radial Basis | Cost C: 100 |
| | Gamma ($\gamma$): 0.0001 |
| Polynomial | Cost C: 1 |
| | Gamma ($\gamma$): 0.001 |
| | Degree (°): 1 |
| | Coefficient (r): 1 |
| Sigmoid | Cost C: 100 |
| | Gamma ($\gamma$): 0.0001 |
| | Coefficient (r): 1 |

**TABLE 7.3**

Computation Time for Tuning SVM Kernel Functions

| SVM Kernel Function | Computation Time (Seconds) |
|---|---|
| Linear | 0.03 |
| Radial Basis | 0.03 |
| Polynomial | 0.03 |
| Sigmoid | 0.06 |

**TABLE 7.4**

Accuracy, Sensitivity, Specificity, and Amount of Support Vectors of SVM Kernel Functions

| SVM Kernel Function | Metrics | | | |
|---|---|---|---|---|
| | Accuracy (Percent) | Sensitivity (Percent) | Specificity (Percent) | Number of Support Vectors |
| Linear | 79.31 | 71.12 | 94.44 | 78 |
| Radial Basis | **86.21** | **75.56** | **96.34** | 80 |
| Polynomial | 82.76 | 65.56 | 95.36 | 82 |
| Sigmoid | 34.5 | 22.20 | 74.06 | 121 |

## 7.5 CONCLUSION

Education institutions should be able to predict their students' academic performance. It is a necessity for educators in any domain of study to provide adequate teaching resources which propel a better learning environment. SVM kernel functions fine-tuning employing grid search approach were carried out in this work. The classification accuracies of LF, RBF, PF, and SF were 79.31, 86.21, 82.76, and 34.5 percent, respectively, based on the evaluation results. In addition, the sensitivities of LF, RBF, PF, and SF were 71.12, 75.56, 65.56, and 22.20 percent, respectively. Furthermore, the specificities for LF, RBF, PF, and SF were 94.44, 96.34, 95.36, and 74.06 percent, respectively. Based on the performance measures and data set used in this study, the results demonstrated that the RBF kernel is more efficient than the three other kernel functions. In the future, this research suggests using a hybridized optimization strategy.

# REFERENCES

Afeni, B.O., Oloyede, I.A., & Okurinboye, D. (2019). Students' Performance Prediction Using Classsification Algorithms, *Journal of Advances in Mathematics and Computer Science*, 30(2), 1–9. 10.9734/JAMCS/2019/45438

Akay, M.F. (2009). Support Vector Machines Combined with Feature Selection for Breast Cancer Diagnosis, *Expert Systems with Applications, Elsevier*, 36, 3240–3247.

Akinola, O.S., Akinkunmi, B.O., & Alo, T.S. (2012). A Data Mining Model for Predicting Computer Proficiency of Computer Science Undergraduate Students, *African Journal of Computing and ICT*, 5(1), 43–52.

Albreiki, B., Zaki, N., & Alashwal, H. (2021). A Systematic Literature Review of Student' Performance Prediction Using Machine Learning Techniques, *Education Sciences*, 11(9), 552. 10.3390/educsci11090552

Altujjar, Y., Altamimi, W., Al-Turaiki, I., & Al-Razgan, M. (2016). Predicting Critical Courses Affecting Students Performance: A Case Study, *Procedia Computer Science*, 82, 65–71. 10.1016/j.procs.2016.04.010

Ayinde, A.Q., Adetunji, A.B., Odeniyi, O.A., & Bello, M. (2013). Performance Evaluation of Naïve Bayes and Decision Stumps Algorithms in Mining Students' Educational Data, *International Journal of Computer Science Issues*, 10(4), 147–151.

Ayinde, A.Q., Omidiora, E.O., & Adetunji, A.B. (2015). Comparative Analysis of Selected Classifiers in Mining Students', *Educational Data, Communication on Applied Electronics, Foundation of Computer Science*, New York, USA, 1(5), 5–8.

Barker, K., Trafalis, T., & Rhoads, T. (2004). Learning from Student Data, *In 2004 System and Information Engineering Design Symposium.*

Ben-David, S. & Lindenbaum, Y. (1997). Learning Distributions by Their Density Levels: A Paradigm for Learning without a Teacher, *Journal of Computer and System Sciences*, 55, 171–182.

Budiman, F. (2019). SVM-RBF Parameters Testing Optimization Using Cross Validation and Grid Search to Improve Multiclass Classification, *Scientific Visualization*, 11(1), 80–90.

Burges-Christopher, J.C. (1998). A Tutorial on Support Vector Machines for Pattern Recognition, *Data Mining and Knowledge Discovery*, 2(2), 121–167.

Chapelle, O., Vapnik, V., Bousquet, O., & Mukherjee, S. (2002). Choosing Multiple Parameters for Support Vector Machines, *Machine Learning*, 46, 131–159.

Chen, P.W., Wang, J.Y., & Lee, H.M. (2004). Model Selection of SVMs Using GA Approach, *Proceedings of the International Joint Conference on Neural Networks*, Budapest, Hungary, 2035–2040.

Chowdhury, S., Sing, J.K, Basu, D.K, & Nasipuri, M. (2011). Face Recognition by Generalized Two-Dimensional FLD Method and Multi-Class Support Vector Machines, *Applied Soft Computing*, 11(7), 4282–4292.

Cortez, P., & Silva, A. (2008). Using Data Mining to Predict Secondary School Student Performance, *In Proceedings of 5th Annual Future Business Technology Conference*, Porto, Portugal, 5–12.

Das, P., Roychowdhury, A., Das, S., Roychowdhury, S., & Tripathy S. (2020). sigFeature: Novel Significant Feature Selection Method for Classification of Gene Expression Data Using Support Vector Machine and t Statistic, *Frontiers in Genetics*, 11(247), 1–12.

Dekker, G., Pechenizkiy, M., & Vleeshouwers, J. (2009). Predicting Students Dropout: A Case Study, *In 2nd International Educational Data Mining Conference (EDMOG)*, 41–50.

Friedrichs, F., & Igel, C. (2005). Evolutionary Tuning of Multiple Sum Parameters, *Neurocomputing*, 64, 107–117.

Guo, B., Zhang, R., Xu, G., Shi, C., & Yang, L. (2015). Predicting Students Performance in Educational Data Mining, *In 2015 International Symposium on Educational Technology (ISET)*, 125–128. 10.1109/ISET.2015.33

Herzog, S. (2005). Measuring Determinants of Students Return Vs. Dropout/Stopout Vs. Transfer: A First-to-Second Year Analysis of New Freshmen, *Research in Higher Education*, 46, 883–928.

Herzog, S. (2006). Estimating Student Retention and Degree Completion Time: Decision Trees and Neural Network Vis-à-Vis Regression, *New Directions for Institutional Research*, 131, 17 -33.

Huang, M., Hung, Y., Lee, W. M., Li, R. K., & Jiang, B. (2014). SVM-RFE Based Feature Selection and Taguchi Parameters Optimization for Multiclass SVM Classifier, *The Scientific World Journal, Hindawi Publishing Corporation*, 1–10.

Huang, S. (2011). A Predictive Modeling and Analysis of Student Academic Performance in an Engineering Dynamics Course, *PhD Thesis*, Department of Engineering and Technology Education, Utah State University.

Kabakchieva, D. (2012). Student Performance Prediction Using Data Mining Classification Algorithms, *International Journal of Computer Science and Management Research*, 1(4), 686–690.

Kim, K.J. (2003). Financial Time Series Forecasting Using Support Vector Machines, *Neuro-Computing*. 55(1/2), 307–319.

Kotsiantis, S.B., Pierrakeas, C.J., & Pintelas, P.E. (2003). Preventing Student Dropout in Distance Learning Using Machine Learning Technique, Paper Presented at the *AI Techniques in Web-Based Educational System at Seventh International Conference on Knowledge-Based Intelligent Information Engineering Systems*, Oxford, England.

Kotsiantis, S.B., Pierrakeas, C.J., & Pintelas, P.E. (2004). Predicting Students' Performance in Distance Learning Techniques, *Applied Artificial Intelligence*.

Kovacic, Z.J. (2010). Early Prediction of Student Success Mining Student Enrolment Data, *In Proceedings of Informing Science and IT Education Conference (INSITE) 2010*.

Kuyoro, S.O., Nicolae, G., Oludele, A., & Samuel, O. (2013). Optimal Algorithm for Predicting Students Academic Performance. *International Journal of Computer and Technology*, 4(1), 63–75.

Lau, E.T., Sun, L., & Yang, Q. (2019). Modelling, Prediction and Classification of Student Academic Performance Using Artificial Neural Networks. *SN Applied Sciences*, 1(9), 982. 10.1007/s42452-019-0884-7

Luts, J., Ojeda, F., Van de Plos R., De Moor, B., & Van Huffel, S. (2010). A Tutorial on Support Vector Machine-Based Methods for Classification Problems in Chemometrics, *Anal Chim Acta*, 665, 129–145.

Lykourentzou, I., GiannouKos, I., Nikolopoulos, V., Mpardis, G., & Loumos, V. (2009). Dropout Prediction in E-Learning Course through the Combination of Machine Learning Techniques, *Computers and Education*, 53, 950–965.

Minaei-Bidgoli, B. (2003). Predicting Student Performance: An Application of Data Mining Methods with an Educational Web-Based System, *In 33rd ASEE/IEEE Frontiers in Education Conference*, 1–6.

Oeda, S., & Hashimoto, G. (2017). Log-Data Clustering Analysis for Dropout Prediction in Beginner Programming Classes, *Proceedings of International Conference on Knowledge Based and Intelligent Information and Engineering Systems, Procedia Computer Science, Elsevier, Marseille, France*, 112, 614–621.

Oludare, O., Olabiyisi, S., Olaniyan, A., & Fagbola, T. (2014). An Optimized Feature Selection Technique for Email Classification, *International Journal of Scientific and Technology Research*, 3(10), 286–293.

Omidiora, E.O., Fenwa, O.D., Adeyanju, F.A., Babalola, O.V., Opeyemi, E.D. & Jimoh, H.O. (2014). Performance Evaluation of Support Vector Machines and Multilayer Perception for Recognition of Handwritten Digits, *Proceedings of Third International Conference on Engineering and Technology Research, Ladoke Akintola University of Technology, Ogbomoso*, 3, 141–148.

Ovidiu, I. (2007). Application of Support Vector Machines in Chemistry, *In Reviews in Computational Chemistry*, 23, 291–400.

Oyedele, O.J., Oladipupo, O.O., & Obagbuwa, I.C. (2010). Application of K-Means Clustering Algorithm for Prediction of Students' Application Performance, *International Journal of Computer Science and Information Security*, 71(1), 292–295.

Pathom, P., Anongnart, S., & Prasong, P. (2008). Comparisons of Classifiers Algorithms: Bayesian Network, C4.5, Decision Forest and NBTree for Course Registration Planning Model of Undergraduate Students' Scripatum University Chonburi Campus, Chonburi, Thailand, *IEEE*.

Ramaswami M., & Bhaskaran, R. (2010). CHAID-Based Performance Prediction Model in Education Data Mining, *International Journal of Computer Science Issue*, 7(1), 10–18.

Romero, C., Ventura S., Hervas, C., & Gonzales, P. (2008). Data Mining Algorithms to Classify Students, *In Proceeding of International Conference on Education Data Mining Canada*.

Romon, M.M., & Christodoulou, C. (2006). *Support Vector Machines for Antenna Array Processing and Electromagnetics*, San Rafael, CA: Morgan and Claypool.

Sampon, D.L., Parker, T.J., Upton, Z., & Hurst, C.P. (2011). A Comparison of Methods for Classifying Clinical Samples Based on Proteomics Data: A Case Study for Statistical and Machine Learning Approaches, *PLoS One*, 6(9): e24073. 10.1371/journal.Pone.0024973.

Sujitparapitaya, S. (2006). Considering Student Mobility in Retention Outcomes, *New Directions for Institution Research*, 131, 35–51.

Teukolsky, H.W., Vetterling, A.S., & Flannery, T.W. (2007). *Section 16.5 Support Vector Machines: Numerical Recipe: The Art of Scientific Computing*, 3rd ed., New York: Cambridge University.

Vandamme, J.P., Meskens, N., & Superby, J.F. (2007). Predicting Academic Performance by Data Mining Methods, *Education Economics*, 15(4), 405–419.

Vapnik V.N. (1995). *The Nature of Statistical Learning Theory*, New York: Springer.

Vapnik, V.N. (1998). *Statistical Learning Theory*, New York, USA: John Wiley & Sons.

Zaffar, M., Ahmed Hashmani, M., Habib, R., Quraishi, K., Irfan, M., Alqhtani, S., & Hamdi, M. (2022). A Hybrid Feature Selection Framework for Predicting Students Performance. *Computers, Materials & Continua*, 70(1), 1893–1920. 10.32604/cmc.2022.018295

Zhang, Y., Qussena, S., Clark, T., & Kim, H. (2010). Use Data Mining to Improve Student Retention in Higher Education: A Case Study, *In 12th International Conference on Enterprise Information Systems (ICEIS)*.

# 8

## Survey of Sensors and Techniques in Microwave Imaging for Through-Wall Imaging for Detecting Trapped Humans under Rubble

*Jiya A. Enoch[1], Ilesanmi B. Oluwafemi[2], and Paul K. Olulope[1]*

[1]Department of Electrical and Information Engineering, Landmark University, Omu-Aran Kwara, Nigeria
[2]Department of Electrical and Electronic Engineering, Ekiti State University, Ado Ekiti, Nigeria

## 8.1 INTRODUCTION

According to the Anthropocene principle, the world is encountering more environmental hazards and harsh precipitation than it has in the past, caused by human impacts on ecosystems (Jon, 2020; Marjanac & Patton, 2018; Mazzoleni et al., 2021; Thi & Thanh, 2020). Different continents ranging from Asia, Europe, and Africa, have been hit by many structural collapses. Building/structural collapses are not uncommon around the world. Many countries, including the United States of America (USA), have had their fair share of failures that have resulted in the collapse of buildings (Boateng, 2021; Shen & Hwang, 2019). Major catastrophes like the Indian Ocean Tsunami of 2004 have also struck other places, such as Asia. Structural building collapses have been a common occurrence in Nigeria, a West African superpower where corruption is widespread and infrastructures are sometimes inadequate (Anthony

DOI: 10.1201/9781003346326-8

Nkem Ede, 2013; Kaul & Kant; Omran, Bamidele, & Baharuddin, 2016). The earth experiences more natural disasters and extreme weather than before due to the human impact on nature as explained by the Anthropocene theory (Jon, 2020; Marjanac & Patton, 2018; Mazzoleni et al., 2021; Thi & Thanh, 2020).

When a structure fails to fulfill the reasons for which it was created, it collapses (Adetunji, Oyeleye, & Akindele, 2018; Anthony N Ede, 2010; Awoyera, Alfa, Odetoyan, & Akinwumi, 2021). In Savar, Dhaka, Bangladesh, an 80-story commercial skyscraper called Rana Plaza, collapsed in 2013, leaving over 1,200 people dead and injuring over 2,500 more (Akinyemi, Dare, Anthony, & Dabara, 2016). The 2014 Synagogue House of Worship fell in Lagos, Nigeria, killing not less than 116 people; the 2015 Hajj crane disaster in Mecca city, Saudi Arabia, killing 184 lives; as well as the Church at Uyo in Nigeria that collapses, and also claimed 60 lives and affected a significant number of people (Mathebula & Smallwood, 2017). The 2019 Lagos School building disaster in Lagos, Nigeria, commercial city, injured over 60 people and claimed the lives of 20 others. On May 25, 2015, an earthquake caused the 19th-century Tower, Dharahara, skyscraper in Kathmandu, Nepal, to fall, killing 200 victims. A multi-storeyed oceanfront condominium structure in Miami partly toppled on late June 24, 2021, harming 98 people. On November 1, 2021, another of the multiple tall structures in the 360 Degrees Towers Complex located at 44, Gerrard Street, Ikoyi, Lagos, fell to the ground like a pack of card numbers killing 46 lives. Those were just a few examples of worldwide collapses (Anthony Nkem Ede, 2013). Due to urbanization and the necessity to provide actual shelter for the steady migration of people into city centers, these incidents are becoming increasingly frequent in developing cities (Boateng, 2020; Gough, Yankson, & Esson, 2019). As indicated by the Anthropocene theory (Jon, 2020; Marjanac & Patton, 2018; Mazzoleni et al., 2021; Thi & Thanh, 2020), humans' impact on nature has resulted in more extreme weather than before. Many structure collapses have occurred on various continents, including Asia, Europe, and Africa. Buildings and architectural failures are commonplace all around the world. Many countries, as well as the government of the United States (USA), have also experienced structural failures that culminated in major collapses. Other places, including Asia, are also being impacted by severe catastrophes, such as the tsunami in the Indian Ocean in December 2004. Building collapses have become a common occurrence in Nigeria, which is known as a West African superpower where unethical behavior is pervasive and infrastructures are typically inadequate (Anthony Nkem Ede, 2013; Kaul & Kant; Omran et al., 2016). On several occasions, it has led to unnecessary loss and destruction of people's properties (Franke et al., 2019; Martínez-Gomariz, Forero-Ortiz, Guerrero-Hidalga, Castán, & Gómez, 2020; Silva & Horspool, 2019), thus becoming an issue of major concern since it poses a threat to the national development of our great nation because, on every occasion, affected individuals are rendered homeless while businesses are lost and much more leads to fatality (Asante & Sasu, 2018; Ayodeji, 2011).

In either of these disasters, time has been the most formidable foe in a search-and-rescue (SAR) mission. Each moment is the difference between life and death (Kibuuka, 2006). According to Ferrara (2015), victims buried under rubble have a three-day survivability duration; however, this time frame might be reduced depending on environmental factors, structural building elements rapid depressurization, and the nature of the blockage. In the case of extreme weather events, the very same life expectancy drops to very remarkably short amounts. If the trapped individual is retrieved from the snow within 15, 30, or 60 minutes, the chances of survivorship drop from 90 percent to 40 percent and 30 percent, respectively. As a result, among the key emergency priorities in catastrophe scenes, which include collapsed cement or concrete-based materials, landslides, and tremors, locating and rescuing submerged or entrapped individuals must take precedence (Restuccia, Thandu, Chellappan, & Das, 2016).

Numerous methods are already being used both for information collection and on-site rescue operations, such as the traditional method of site assessment by professionals and an instrument called FINDER for victims' localization respectively. This later only provides single-dimensional scope information. This is because it is monostatic, with just a single transmitter-receiver (TX-RX) pair. Conversely, in poor countries such as Nigeria, several inappropriate and unprofessional practices are often used (Khan, Wang, & Bhuiyan, 2019; Okunola, 2021; Vlachakis, Vlachaki, & Lourenço, 2020). For example, according to reports, it took several minutes for emergency crews to arrive on the scene of the Ikoyi, Lagos, major disasters due to ineffective means of accessing disasters through crowdsourcing or social media. Witnesses reported seeing personnel viewing Internet videos to learn how to use the excavators to save lives, with the machines occasionally scooping up victim's body pieces with the blood of the ruins before even being deposited in sachets for further diagnosis and identifications by healthcare practitioners of the Nigerian Red Cross (Omran et al., 2016).

As a result, if the system can be updated to at least three different TX-RX pairs, it could be built and operated in such a multi-static mode. This would enable three-dimensional target identification and localization. Also, making it possible for the public to participate in scientific issues like building collapse assessment and reporting in the early time after a disaster will enable a human subject to be found in far less time. This follows a current development in ultra-wideband technologies, in which many, less complex and costly devices replace a single, more efficient, and expensive system.

However, to obtain a particular successful detection rate and positioning precision, preparatory studies are necessary to predict the system's needs, such as transmitting power, central frequency, bandwidth, number of sensors per pair, and positions. Secondly, the integration of real-time location-based social media messages inside the spatial decision-making techniques such as this seems to have significant possibilities for resource allocation and management, allowing damaged regions to be swiftly established, the number of causalities to be evaluated, and designated routes for assistance or evacuation to be specified. To help emergency management and the many sensors utilized in SAR during emergencies, this work surveys how crowdsourced data and participatory platforms including Twitter may be extensively used for near-real-time mapping. Secondly, the integration of real-time location-based social media messages inside the spatial decision-making techniques such as this seems to have significant possibilities for resource allocation and management, allowing damaged regions to be swiftly established, the amount of damage to be evaluated, and evacuation and/or help routes to be specified. To help emergency management and the many sensors utilized in SAR during emergencies, this work surveys how crowdsourced data and participatory platforms including Twitter may be extensively used for near-real-time mapping.

## 8.2 BUILDING COLLAPSE INFORMATION-GATHERING TECHNIQUES

Structure collapse charts that display a structure's level of destruction are indeed a crucial informational tool for numerous emergency preparedness procedures like evacuation, recovery, and rehabilitation (Atalić, Uroš, Šavor Novak, Demšić, & Nastev, 2021; Giuliani, De Falco, & Cutini, 2021; Marasco et al., 2021; Shishido, Kobayashi, Kameda, & Kitahara, 2021). These must be produced as soon as feasible. Specialists, trained personnel, and surveillance crews frequently carry out these evaluations by directly assessing the infrastructure and collapsed structures in the impacted area. To evaluate the extent of harm off-site or to use it in the authentication and confirmation of its on-site evaluations, inspection crews mostly depend on photos and videos that were taken during the investigation. The efficiency and scope of visual information gathered in the wake of a catastrophe have multiplied due to new developments in remotely sensed data and imaging, particularly when leveraging satellite and unmanned aerial vehicle (UAV) photos for disaster assessments and examination. This breakthrough may speed up the process of performing post-disaster evaluations. But relying on certain specialists and skilled workers to conclude the condition of the structures' damages from the visual information has several drawbacks in regards to cost, human capital, geographical area, ease of access, and timeliness. It can also postpone the resolution of other expert-dependent requests that may come up in emergency preparedness (Khajwal & Noshadravan, 2021). Such difficulties necessitate the use of unconventional tools or more effective but trustworthy methods to undertake an immediate damage evaluation and retrieve the necessary details from the survey data gathered in the disaster-affected neighborhood.

However, reducing disaster risk and damage through practical means has grown to be a crucial challenge for humanity. The effectiveness of making emergency judgments can be increased by conducting a proper disaster impact evaluation, which can assist minimize or mitigating loss of life and property (Tan, Guo, Mohanarajah, & Zhou, 2021; Xing et al., 2021). Unfortunately, issues including a lack of information and inconsistent guidelines make evaluation more challenging. The aforementioned post-disaster measurement for data gathering is typically time-consuming and focuses mostly on static or structured data (Xing et al., 2021; You et al., 2022; Zhang & Pan, 2022).

It is noteworthy that the perceptual and psychological traits of individuals, obtained from crowdsourced records including social media and cell phone signals, can serve as sources of information for catastrophe evaluation and support disaster response planning. Additionally, there have been multiple attempts to gather useful information with the aid of modern technology (crowdsourcing images through social media). As quickly as an earthquake occurs, pictures of the destruction can be captured and published on the Internet, making it simple for individuals in other countries around the world to look through these pictures and videos to get a feel of the disaster's impacts. Pictures or videos such as these, which were captured by people or news organizations, frequently reveal crucial details about the devastation, like demolished structures, bridges, roads, and other facilities (Chachra et al., 2022; Feng, Huang, & Sester, 2022; Khatoon, Asif, Hasan, & Alshamari, 2022; Li, Bensi, Cui, Baecher, & Huang, 2021; Mavrodieva & Shaw, 2021).

Crowdsourcing has been heavily utilized in the past few years to comprehend the damaging issue. Crowdsourcing accomplishes enormous labor by breaking it down into manageable smaller tasks that may be distributed between an arbitrary group of individuals. This is appropriate for acquiring data and evaluating disaster scenarios since it can scale up the size and kinds of personnel while allocating resources following the scale of the tragedy. As a result, crowdsourcing has been employed in crisis response to collect data and evaluate the situation (Ang, Seng, & Ngharamike, 2022; Shishido et al., 2021).

Crowdsourced geographical intelligence, also known as volunteered geographic information (Young et al., 2021), is a major repository of knowledge on tragedies in the meantime (Moghadas, Rajabifard, Fekete, & Kötter, 2022; Xing et al., 2021). Text, photos, and positional information from social networking websites, as well as information from cell phone signals, are examples of this type of information. The ability to effectively mine this information can help with disaster response planning, disaster evaluation, and rapid judgmental call, according to various research (Asif et al., 2021; Li & Wang, 2022; Onifade, 2021). The public can read detailed narratives of the catastrophe with geographical signs or geographical details on social media sites, which also offer genuine disaster information exchange and transmission (Jayathilaka, Siriwardana, Amaratunga, Haigh, & Dias, 2021; Mittal, Jahanian, & Ramakrishnan, 2021; Wang, Xiong, Wang, & Chen, 2022). Such data increase the capacity for emergency preparedness and recovery while providing sources of knowledge about the locations of disasters (Jayawardene, Huggins, Prasanna, & Fakhruddin, 2021). Additionally, this data is excellent for information gathering and catastrophe environmental damage studies in the crisis period of a catastrophe and is frequently revised quicker than the material on traditional channels (Mohanty et al., 2021).

## 8.3 REVIEW OF RELATED WORKS

Thi and Thanh (2020) employ a sensing system for the identification of human vital signs with the help of the Doppler radar system in the microwave frequency range in their study. This technique assessed the models' accuracy concerning the intelligent system. When the frequency at which it operates (various frequencies) and distance change (different places and surroundings), the mathematical model was used to determine the effectiveness of the radar vital sign detection approach. This was utilized to locate survivors who had been trapped behind the debris. The transmitter sends out radio-frequency waves to the human heart and gathers the reflected energy. The position of humans is determined by analyzing transmitted and received signals and extracting valuable parameters such as respiratory rate, heartbeat, and location. In his research, he meticulously considers the combination of AI techniques and radar sensors. This arrangement helps make the system better, allows for more applications, and provides consumers with greater benefits. A buried individual under collapsed structures is more often motionless, either because he is unconscious or because the ruins are blocking him (Ferrara, 2015). As a result, this technology fails to capture the breathing and cardiac signals of victims who have passed out and are unable to respond.

Shah (2017) proposed a microwave reflectometer as a prototype for detecting human bodies beneath the rubble of a structurally collapsed building. They ran software models and ran a link budget investigation. In this study, a fully integrated 2.4 GHz frequency-modulated continuous wave (FMCW) radar transceiver is designed and manufactured. Following the creation of the transmitter/receiver and horn antennas, various studies on human living tissue and many other substances (concrete, wood, glass, and sand) were conducted to ascertain if a living or nonliving organism exists behind the medium. When the body was close to the substances, the body seemed identifiable and the materials were easily identified, according to the results of the trials. The vector network analyzer (VNA) was also used to examine individual components as well as the transmitting and receiving chains. An anechoic chamber was used to assess antenna gain and radiation form. The performance of the transceiver was also evaluated, detection capability, range accuracy, signal-to-noise ratio (SNR), and so on are all factors to consider. Various modulation techniques were used to analyze and simulate FMCW within the system. Finally, a prototype FMCW transmitter is provided that can localize human bodies beneath wreckages or behind a wall, be it alive or lifeless, and is capable of broadcasting and receiving reflections, as well as providing information in an audio format for additional signal processing. Nonetheless, beyond a distance of 7 feet, it was difficult to discern the body as it moved away from the material (2.1 m). Second, by employing the XR 2206 IC as an FMCW engine and employing module-based devices with SMA connectors, the circuit and hardware design complications can be considerably reduced. Furthermore, the energy needs of a transceiver capable of identifying a human body behind the debris are reliant on the working atmosphere. Simulating a time domain based on a microwave inbuilt transmitter/receiver, radiation pattern, wireless transmitter, energy demand, maximal potential input power, voltage regulations, and modulation mode is required.

The work by Xu, Wu, Chen, Chen, and Fang (2012) presents a novel approach for automatically detecting entrapped victims utilizing vital-sign detection created by clustering, continuous erroneous alarm rate (CFAR), and grouping in ultra-wideband radar frequency. The approach is reliable and suitable for identifying respiration in both complicated and low-y improved environments. The non-static clutter in the environment can be removed (SCNR). Clutter, which has the same frequency and energy spectrum as breathing, could be successfully eliminated. It is possible to extract the properties of vital signs automatically and correctly, which is important for natural catastrophe rescue. The suggested algorithm is said to be suitable for narrowband, wideband, and ultra-wideband sensing signals, although the range of living people's number estimated is dependent on the radar's bandwidth. When it comes to narrowband sensing signals, our suggested algorithm can identify numerous live signs with varying breath frequencies as well as a single life sign. The transmitted signal has about a 2 GHz bandwidth. The chest model's simulated range is 2.5 m and the frequency of the model is 0.2 Hz. Three genuine signals and two erroneous signals are recognized when the threshold is set to 0.45. The genuine life sign will go undetected when the threshold rate is bigger than 0.5. If the energy of non-static clutter is greater than the energy of the life sign, this method will fail. Increasingly, work should be done to suppress or isolate any clutter, as well as to develop a real-time and reliable approach for detecting vital signs in more complicated environments. Multiple live signals with the very same breathing frequency can't be detected within the margin of error due to the narrowband signals and low-range resolution.

Another significant attainment on post-emergency rescue was that of Yılankıran and Guney (2021), the work present creation, and development of WITNER. WITNER is a geo-enabled cloud-native application. The benefit of WITNER is that it just serves as an intermediary, preserving the accessibility and integrity of the underlying social network post notifications while converting them into a format that can be viewed in space. This approach identifies better practical and inexpensive needs for assistance, which would need prospective support providers a lesser period to respond. Even though WITNER has begun using the geo-parser.io function, the position data it returns is not precise. A study is needed on the best ways to extract accurate and precise disaster-related geolocation data from tweets. To enable WITNER to track and identify better assistance, data analysis, and natural language decoding, methods need to be developed.

In another advancement, Liang, Zhang, Fang, Ye, and Gulliver (2017) use an impulse radar within ultra-wideband frequency to do image reconstruction with an improved model for through-wall target identification and detection of a human subject in difficult surroundings. Micro-motion data is gathered and used to detect the individual remotely, such as breathing and pulse rate frequencies. Its goal is to make localization more accurate. The distance is calculated using a short-time Fourier transform of the kurtosis and standard deviation of the received frequencies. The frequency of human slight movement is also determined using a multiple frequency aggregation technique and enhanced arctangent demodulation techniques. This method's performance was evaluated using data sets collected under various situations and compared to many well-known approaches. According to the results, the suggested technique effectively reduces dynamic and non-dynamic clutter, linear development, harmonics, and the product of respiratory and cardiac signals. It's also simple to put into practice. The fundamental issue is that it is difficult to recover this information in typical catastrophe scenarios because of the poor signal-to-noise and clutter-to-signal ratio.

Layout reconstruction is performed employing UWB TWI radar under only one observation while taking into consideration real-time human input. This technique is used as the pre-processing throughout the proposed framework, with a cohesive processing duration made up of a large number of received echoes being used to create a Range

Doppler (RD) spectrum in the initial stage. A sequence of digital Doppler frequency signals is then used to produce Doppler Back projection (BP) images in the RD spectrum. To capture the structural architecture from the Doppler BP picture stack, a 3-D consistent erroneous alert rate detector was constructed. Once accomplished, the acquired architecture is combined as auxiliary information with the concurrent human signal. Through-wall studies reveal that the suggested technique can efficiently bring out the protected layout of several walls from a single perspective, providing significant support for hidden human sensing. Finally, the acquired designed organization is combined with the live human indication outcome. One of the biggest flaws is that it can't tell the difference between walls and other immobile objects. This effect has the potential to influence the target's location and precise distance (Song et al., 2018).

More interestingly, the traditional ground penetrating radar (GPR) system, the antenna invariance, the electromagnetic wave's multi-polarization properties, target scattering sections (RCS), and other characteristics have all significantly influenced the detection outcome (Akbari, 2013; Tebchrany, 2015). The Zeng, Li, Huang, and Liu (2012) team worked on improving target imaging quality using several multiple-input multiple-output (MIMO) line-ups of antenna GPR technology, which can successfully counteract the impacts of RCS and electromagnetic divergence while improving target imaging resolution. They proposed MIMO GPR, which would be built on "plane wave-like PWL," and employs a traditional radar system that includes several antennas as well as a "plane wave-like" broadcasting resource. This technology is more stable and has a better SNR. The several-polarization uncovering option allows for a more exact waveform of the incident wave to be obtained. We can obtain better exact targeted area parameters and improve detection accuracy by combining multi-polarization phase information of the target signal. The specific location features of the target raise the detection accuracy of the target. Also, more than one polarization and more than one input signal can reduce the target response polarized wave's breath and boost the target-range resolution of the antenna spacing is significantly shorter than the wavelength of the source signal. Compared to the traditional GPR system, the MIMO GPR's multi-polarization detection mode offers greater target imaging efficiency, according to simulation and testing. Though this system can effectively and quickly detect shallow targets, it generates a good suggestion for improving system performance and lowering system design requirements and manufacturing costs.

Another important achievement in microwave imaging was that of (Qi et al., 2019), who demonstrated that their technology is robust and reliable, with broad application to many classifiers through experiments. They suggest a position-information-indexed classifier as a strategy for enhancing classifiers position-information-indexed classifier (PIIC). Its goal is to improve the recognition and classification contribution of different classifiers. This approach extensively utilizes the location data earned by UWB bio-radar to produce a sub-segmented library of micro-Doppler signatures (MD) characteristics that are position-labeled. It also directs adaptive searching for the best-predicted sub-model at a random position of PIICs for performance characterization. The suggested method addresses two key situations of classification confusion (Case 1 and Case 2) caused by MD characteristics being perplexed across different detection locations by fully leveraging position information. The results of five actions within a 6 m range were reported using the wall detection and categorization method. The outcomes, which are based on four widely used predictors, with classifiers rely on PIIC and may effectively minimize misinterpretation classifications. Furthermore, when compared to overall model-based classifiers, all PIIC-based predictors have a higher level of categorization accuracy, with an average increase of 8.16 percent. However, the work was unable to investigate the proposed method's prospective practical application influence on other classifiers, including advanced versions. Furthermore, to target more practical application scenarios, it is necessary to concentrate on the categorization of a variety of subjects engaged in similar or dissimilar activities to determine their detectability based on radar visual angle limitation, as well as the interaction of the shadow effect of several targets.

Gennarelli's research team at the National Research Council of Italy employed a microwave Doppler radar sensor for real-time TWI scenario awareness (Gennarelli, Ludeno, & Soldovieri, 2016). The technology is focused on the creation of short-range radar that can identify people behind optically obscure barriers like building walls. A continuous wave Doppler radar operating in the S-band of the electromagnetic waves is employed in the system to guarantee optimal signal transmission through the walls. The interplay of electromagnetic waves with moving human targets and small routine chest displacements brought on by breathing effort causes phase modulation of the radar signal. The existence of one or more human beings in the through-wall scenario is detected in real-time, utilizing a straightforward and efficient radar data processing method. The system automatically detects whether the subjects are stationary or moving in their surroundings. The suggested gadget for sensing and accompanying signal processing guarantees rapid and trustworthy detailed information on the situation about the scene in experimental testing carried out in an indoor environment, showing its practical utility. When there are animals involved in the area, the suggested detection technique may create significant false alarms, since animals may be confused with people. Integrating the system with time-frequency analysis to enhance detection performance may also be feasible. Because continuous-wave (CW) radars lack a ranging capacity, detection of scenarios with several targets is tough, especially when involving both animals and humans.

To improve disaster site location, Chachra et al. (2022) propose an autonomous method for locating specific user postings that include photographs of damaged structures following earthquakes on social media sites like Twitter. We built a deep learning algorithm to discern photographs with marred structures in the site via transfer learning and roughly 6,500 hand-tagged imagery. Following the 2020 M7.0 earthquake in Turkey, the trained model performed well when evaluated using recently recorded photos of earthquakes in various areas and subsequently used in nearly real time on a Twitter handle. Additionally, we used the Grad-CAM technique to demonstrate the crucial areas on the photos that aid the judgment to comprehend how the model draws judgments. Nevertheless, the model requires developers to get rid of the false-positive results for collapsed structures, which primarily result from shapes that resemble debris like rock rubble and leaves and branches.

Also, Li et al. (2021) create a text classifier algorithm for quick damage evaluation after defining a text-based impact assessment instrument for earthquake disasters. The suggested damage evaluation method boasts quickness with massive volumes of data at geographical densities that surpass others such as typical sensor networks, even though accuracy still poses a barrier, particularly in comparison to ground-based instrumental measurements and examinations.

To reduce distance uncertainties, Srivastav, Nguyen, McConnell, Loparo, and Mandal (2020) created a non-homogeneous stepped-frequency continuous-wave (SFCW) sweep that has been reported and put to use. The irregular arrangement was used, which provides greater ambiguity mitigation. Analytical evaluation and simulation were used to confirm the ambiguity of plateaus' envelopes. An estimation of the anticipated SCR is provided below. Bistatic testing confirmed the analytical SCR of 15 dB that was anticipated. A multistatic imaging system has satisfactorily used the suggested methodology. The system's evaluations showed that the vagueness intensity was reduced at least from 9 to 11 dB.

The study by Qi et al. (2016) involved wall testing for the SFCW radar's recognition of human activity. To categorize various sharper activities, an ideal self-adaption support vector machine (OS-SVM) grounded on historical human position data is proposed. Data was achieved at a stationary distance (3 m) behind a barrier. For the twin situations, the classification accuracies of six actions carried out by eight people were 98.78 percent and 93.23 percent, accordingly.

Additionally, practical tests using the SFCW radar method to find human victims buried beneath rubble have been done by Labarthe et al. (2009). The usage of an enhanced UWB, continuous wave stepped frequency (CW-SF), and ground penetration radar as rescue apparatus is tested by the writers in this study. Either a regulated environment or actual test sites have been used to test with the radar.

The designed radar device demonstrated the potential to find a victim trapped underneath 1 m of dense rubble using the frequency range of 100 MHz to 1 GHz. As this radar system can monitor a variety of human vital signs and is Doppler sensitive (Liu & Liu, 2014; Su, Tang, El Arif, Horng, & Wang, 2019), it has been explored how to identify human vital signs using SFCW radar technology through practical investigations in a lab setting. An SFCW radar system comprised of two bowtie antennas and a VNA managed by a computer system was used to gather the experiment's information. The time domain data were obtained by processing the frequency domain data using an inverse FFT along the propagation time; the resulting data set resembles that of a commercial impulse GPR but has a wider frequency range. At a predetermined propagation time, the time domain recordings were then taken using FFT once more along the sampling time axis. However, there was a need to increase the signal processing's overall sensing performance.

At a predetermined propagation time, the time domain recordings were then taken using FFT once more across the recording time axis. However, there was a necessity to increase the thorough and systematic system's overall effectiveness. Gaikwad, Singh, and Nigam (2011), with the aid of a UWB TWI system, performed research on clutter minimization strategies presented for the identification of metallic and non-metallic (low dielectric constant) targets behind a brick barrier. A UWB stepped frequency wave radar that operates in the frequency span of 3.95 to 5.85 GHz is built locally using a VNA. To remove clutter, statistically based approaches such as singular value decomposition, principal component analysis, factor analysis, and ICA were taken into consideration. The signal-to-clutter ratio for metal object detection is seen to be significantly improved by all four strategies. Therefore, for low dielectric constant material, the ICA-based method could be used to improve the target signal to clutter intensity. Filtering that employs clutter reduction strengthens the targeted signal, which raises the likelihood that the target will be identified correctly and is therefore helpful for additional identification processing.

The research by Jia et al. (2019) used dual-station SFCW radars to conduct real-time trials for the identification and localization of several stationary human targets behind walls. To efficiently identify different targets and offer a distance-matching technique including dual radars, the cross-correlation technique was proposed in this study.

The research by Li, Cai, Abraham, and Mao (2016) demonstrated the use of GPR for emergency disaster rescue operations that involved the identification and tracking of objects hidden in voids in the wreckage. The proposed technique and the created algorithm produced generally positive outcomes, taking into account both actual and simulated GPR scans with 93 percent precision.

Yuan, Li, Cai, and Kamat (2018) created a novel drop-flow algorithm based on GPR that has a detection accuracy of 84 percent as well as an accuracy of 78 percent for finding subterranean utilities. A brand-new drop-flow technique is presented in the research that optimizes the recognition and breakdown of GPR patterns into feature elements in two-dimensional surveys. The method imitates the action of a raindrop dropping or flowing when it strikes the margin pixels of the scanned picture starting at a strip of pixels from the top of the boundary. The outcomes demonstrate the ability of the drop-flow algorithm to distinguish between linked hyperbolas and to pinpoint the image features and sections of each hyperbola. It explicitly counted the number of hyperbolas and subsequently distinguished each one into an ascending leg, peak, and falling leg—information that is essential for figuring out the placement, arrangement, and geometric measurements of utility pipelines with intricate spatial layouts.

In Diamanti, Annan, and Giannakis (2016), a mathematical method for GPR and estimates of target response severity in complicated lower dimensional, such as those experienced in search and rescue operations, were demonstrated. Additionally, the GPR approach was utilized to find buried human remains. Diamanti et al. (2016) improved the effectiveness and efficiency of aiding victims of natural disasters through modeling and measuring techniques.

A robot system that relies on Internet of Things technology (IoT) for personal identification beneath wreckage was developed. According to the research by De Cubber et al. (2017) and Ko and Lau (2009), the goal of deploying robots is to assist first-aid personnel by giving them a visual representation of a location they are unable to access so they can save any survivors that may be present. The World Trade Center catastrophe rescue operation in New York in 2001 saw the usage of real-time robots for the first time (Casper and Murphy, 2003; De Cubber et al., 2017). Ever since, the use of robots in SAR missions has attracted increasing interest on a global scale. The World Trade Center rescue crew deployed six remote-controlled rescue robots to locate people trapped under the wreckage. Robots are simple to use and control in hazardous scenarios including explosive ordnance disposal, mines, and chemical waste cleanup. The creation of a human detection robot for use in natural disaster rescue operations was revealed in 2019 (Joseph, Parmar, & Bagyaveereswaran, 2019). The robot prototype employed a radar method for object identification that is dependent on electromagnetic wave signal reflection and is guided by a cellular application with a Bluetooth device. Robots today are equipped with a variety of technology for search-and-rescue operations during catastrophic disasters. A prototype TWI system was created using the S-band (2–4 GHz). It entails a real-time collection and analysis framework for a MIMO-phased array radar system that allows for imaging rates of more than 10 Hz, amounting to a video-like radar vision of what's inside a concrete barrier has been created. The comprehensibility of point-to-point and distance from distance range in through-wall and free-space radar imaging is improved with video-rate imaging. Images are created without any prior knowledge. An electrically controlled bi-static setup with high-performance microwave devices, a multi-threaded data pipeline, and quick hardware accelerated processing techniques are employed to accomplish video frame rate imaging. Low radar cross-section (RCS) targets, rapid mobile targets in open space, and a person underneath a 10-cm thick solid concrete wall have all been successfully imaged in experiments. In addition, free-space and through-wall trials should be included to verify the system concept and to build a quick prototype that can be tested in the field (Ralston, Charvat, & Peabody, 2010).

A new time-reversal approach for UWB and TWI is also described. An antenna arrangement collects spatial and UWB frequency data, which is used in the proposed method. Scattering data can be gathered by sending a brief pulse from the central emitter and collecting the reflected signal at every element in the array. The scattering information's fine and coarse frequency samples are cast to create an individual multi-static scattering data matrix for each antenna. The matrix results are calibrated using the transmitter signal and given into the decomposition of the time-reversal operator algorithm. The suggested method's performance is numerically examined using discrete scatterers implanted in a non-heterogeneous and continuous medium at irregular intervals. The numerical outcomes imply that the proposed algorithm for TWI is effective and efficient (Bahrami, 2021).

More intriguing, Bahrami (2021) added a new dimension to UWB TR-based imaging by utilizing a frequency-frequency multi-static data matrix (FF-MDM) that uses UWB frequency data generated by the antenna pattern. The suggested method's effectiveness is numerically examined by implementing it in a sequence of distinct moving targets embedded inhomogeneous and continuous random heterogeneous mediums. As can be shown, the method has statistical stability qualities similar to UWB TR. Its performance in the TWI context is also statistically examined. Results obtained by alternative differential tracking techniques are also offered for comparison purposes. There is a high degree of agreement between the actual and produced traces and the proposed method results in improved resolution. The suggested UWB method is highly suited for on-site applications due to the significant increase in imaging speed. Though the proposed method's acquisition time is quite quick, making it appropriate for real-time tracking, rather than each array of pieces, the tracking method is centered exclusively on the intriguing core element.

Harikesh, Abegaonkar, and Koul (2019) conducted a thorough-the-wall detection of several people utilizing Doppler radar alongside Hilbert vibrational decomposition (HVD). The suggested Doppler radar operates at 2.4 GHz and uses respiration rate estimates to detect numerous human individuals behind a wall. Human subjects' respiration signals are retrieved under various breathing settings that mimic a real-life scenario.

The system recognizes the breathing rate of human beings in a variety of real-life circumstances. It's anticipated that it'll be used in earthquakes, building collapses, and security applications. In addition, the transmission power must be increased, which will enhance the detection range through the wall.

For detecting the object behind the wall, two techniques grounded on space-frequency time reversal (SF-TR) for through-wall imaging are presented. The electromagnetic responses are captured and then used to create a space-frequency multi-static signal information matrix using the antenna pattern's space-frequency measurement (SF-MDM). After implementing the singular value decomposition (SVD) on the SF-MDM, the left single vectors can be used to generate the imaging pseudo-spectrum for the targeted object. For wall clutter reduction, two new SF-MDMs are used instead of the regular SF-MDM. When recognizing stationary targets, the whole SF-MDM is used to improve target response and reduce wall clutter. In the case of moving targets, differential SF-MDM is utilized to eliminate wall distortions and noise (clusters) by leveraging target movement, resulting in high throughput. To assess the performance of the offered methodologies, numerical simulations are performed, and the proposed methods are efficient in detecting targets concealed by the wall as well as tracking targets moving behind the wall in real time. Only a wall with hollows within was used for modeling, and the thickness was only 0.1 m (Mu & Song, 2018).

Li, Zeng, Sun, and Liu (2012) and his colleagues use UWB radar technology to detect and recognize human life features through walls and offer solutions premised on fast Fourier transform and S-transform. From experimental data, we can, for example, identify the center frequencies of actual signals and accurately predict the location of human targets. This article focuses on the analysis and identification of the actual signal under extreme clutter, as opposed to previous through-wall detection research. It offers a high signal-to-noise ratio and is easier to deploy when dealing with complicated environments. During an earthquake, explosion, or fire, we can use the approach to look for and discover the survivor buried beneath the wreckage of the building. The result demonstrates that it has a good range resolution and can help distinguish human targets from other items beneath the wreckage of the building. However, by taking extra observations relating to different locations of the radar antenna, it will be possible to not only detect and detect moving targets but also more accurately determine similar live signals. Improved signal processing and target imaging technologies will also be required. Wang, Zeng, and Sun (2018) employed a time-domain finite element technique to detect a model of moving targets using a technique to replicate single-input multiple-outputs (SIMO) radar information. Changes in body size and physical factors are used to represent human breathing. For radar data, background removal is conducted. Then, using back projection, we re-create the successive target sites that make up the traveling direction or path, resulting in a bend in the radar image that contains vital signs. Because the SIMO radar data is multivariate, we isolate and extract the respiratory characteristic frequencies using multivariate empirical mode decomposition (MEMD) and the fast Fourier transform. The reconstructed frequency is identical to the original model's frequency. The results reveal that combining SIMO radar with MEMD can efficiently identify and collect vital signs from a human being moving behind a wall. On the downside, multiple targets must be studied and the strategy must be tested using experimental data.

UWB combined with TWI radar was employed to tackle the issue of human movement detection, which is a novel approach to range profile serialization TWR. The actual radar-reflected signals are first converted into range measurements. The dimension is subsequently decreased and each range profile's attributes are retrieved using an auto-encoder network (AEN) with three layers. A gated recurrent unit (GRU) network with two opaque tiers deals with the characteristics of each timeslot and delivers the identification outcome in real time at every slice. Ultimately, the self-developed UWB TWR collects experimental data on four distinct beneath-the-wall human movements to evaluate the model's use. According to the findings, the suggested model can accurately identify human movement serialization and achieve ninety-three percent recognition efficiency within the first 20 percent of activity length (average time frames are 4 s, 5.5 s, 3 s, and 4.5 s), which is critical for actual human movement identification. The suggested model differs from existing neural network models in that it does not give the action type until the end of the action (Yang et al., 2020).

Fioranelli, Salous, and Raimundo (2014) introduced frequency-modulated interrupted continuous wave (FMICW) waveforms as a revolutionary barrier removal method for through-wall detection. By selecting appropriate gating sequences to generate the suggested FMICW waveforms, reflections from the barrier can be reduced and target identification improved. Utilizing a radar system specifically constructed for the work and efficient for synthesizing FMICW waveforms using arbitrary waveform generators, numerical models. and practical findings were obtained (AWGs). The results of sensing immobile targets plus persons moving as well as breathing through walls have been reported. To produce faster pictures than the SAR technique, the current bistatic system needs to be improved with a network of antennas and corresponding switching and control units, along with the ability to find and follow moving targets. To improve on this study, the idea of integrating FMICW waveforms combined with wall-removal approaches including subspace projection, spatial filtering, and CD might be examined.

Donelli (2011) describes a lightweight microwave device for searching for and rescuing persons trapped beneath the wreckage of a fallen structure through an earthquake and perhaps other disasters. The proposed approach, which is centered on a continuous wave X-band radar, extracts information from the reflected electromagnetic field using the ICA program, which successfully reduces noise and clutter, and can determine respiratory and cardiac fluctuations. To imitate a realistic situation, a first preliminary test was performed on a human inside a hollow concrete pipe. The suggested rescue radar is tiny enough to fit atop a lightweight unmanned aerial vehicle (UAV) to reach locations that are remote or risky regions. The acquired experimental findings suggest that the suggested intrusion detection approach is capable of effectively and accurately locating imprisoned people. However, more research is now required to link this device with modified scattering technique (MST) probes to provide identify potentialities.

The paper presents an e-nose approach for urban SAR missions. The project's goal is to find stuck individuals in construction debris and to detect airborne threats while entering tight and very interior unsanitary conditions (Anyfantis, Silis, & Blionas, 2021). The e-nose device is part of the instrument payload of a remotely operated robot that penetrates through the collapse of building rubbles during the evaluation, SAR level 4 of a USaR operation. To ensure that the system works, it is put through its paces in real-world scenarios. A user interface is included in the system to present the results clearly and concisely and to assist in the conduction of a search. End-users became involved in the research investigation requirements process as well as the final verification in practical situations. A heuristic algorithm is constructed premised on the sensor's information to produce a simplified outcome. The size, weight, ease of use, and energy consumption of the system are all taken into account when deciding whether or not to use it. Various methods for localizing the human target in constricted areas that should not be occupied are currently under study. Also, to teach an AI system to update the output and account for weather conditions (air currents speed and direction, as well as temperatures), as well as to predict its detection limitations for human presence.

The self-injection-locked (SIL) technique put forth by Wang et al. (2013) involves injecting a signal partly reflected from a targeting reticle into the oscillator that created the transmitted wave. This approach increases demodulation responsiveness, allowing the radar system to achieve greater SNR. Slight body movements of persons who remain motionless may be tracked, and the positions of different people hidden behind the wall can be determined at the same time. Although such a system has only been explored in a simpler setting than that of a rescue operation, it remains an intriguing prospect.

The intriguing usage of a continuous wave stepped frequency radar (CW-SF) to overcome the timing inconsistency of UWB impulse radar caused by instability in the pulse triggering mechanism was proposed by Grazzini et al. (2010). Because of the expanded dynamic range, this type of radar is better at detecting low-frequency vibrations.

Pulse radars send out a series of brief RF pulses, and the time delay of the reflected signals is used to measure the target's range. Short pulses are generated by UWB electromagnetic wave generators, which are used in more contemporary systems and disseminate their energy throughout a wide range of frequencies. These UWB systems exploit the variation in arrival time of the back-reflected wave owing to the person's chest displacement to extract the needed attributes. There is no null-point difficulty with the UWB radar method. With principal component analysis, Zaikov and Sachs built a model UWB radar that can reduce dynamic interference and separate the desired signals from noise (Zaikov, 2010).

The impacts of various kinds of interferences encountered in UWB detection of concealed fatalities are investigated in another paper by the same authors (Sachs et al., 2011). The report mentions a variety of noise sources, including static clutter, dynamic clutter, internal noise, narrowband interference, and random fluctuations. The noise involvement varies according to the type of radar used: pulse, pseudo-noise, stepped frequency, and random noise. In addition, the scientists developed a prototype for a pseudo-random radar that incorporates trilateration and is comparable to GPS.

The idea of employing ultra-wideband radar to locate persons trapped beneath rubble or concealed behind a wall was discussed and demonstrated with some measurements. The premise is that the victim's faint physical movements are detected. M-sequence radar systems look to be viable sensing devices owing to their responsiveness and noise efficiency, as well as their flexibility to integrate with other devices. A significant number of sensors are necessary to explore a sizable search zone in a reasonable length of time in the event of rescue operations. Weak target motions were seen across almost the whole unambiguity scope (17 m) of the radar instrument used in the investigations. As a result, the radar will be sensitive enough to detect massive reflectors from afar. These objects will be convolved into the radar's detectability, obstructing target detection with their movement. Aside from detection capabilities, device costs, as well as equipment size and weight, are major considerations for this search technique's future use. The most disruptive signal is static clutter, which is generally hundreds of times stronger than the optimum motion-modulated individual reflection. Its elimination needs constant antenna placements (Sachs et al., 2014).

The idea behind the survivor localization e-operational nose is to sample and measure the composition of the ambient air to detect concentration levels of specific target gases that seem to be indicators of human presence. The elimination of NH3 during the periods when the subjects slept was an unexpected finding from the NH3 channel, and this will be the subject of additional investigation, as will the full examination of the fatalities detection data collected via the seven devices utilized (Huo et al., 2011).

## 8.4 CONCLUSION

This chapter looked at some of the approaches that researchers came up with to handle the problem of detecting buried persons beneath the rubble of a collapsed structure. The differences between buried people scenarios were detailed, including rubble from a fallen building, the sensor used, and the number of individuals.

Additionally, locating individuals buried under rubble can benefit from efficient data collection. This collection encompasses a wireless sensor network that tracks environmental conditions and provides accurate information about the specific location/scenario. The utilization of crowdsourcing and social media platforms for managing resources following catastrophes, along with the implementation of navigation systems during disasters, can collectively reduce the time spent on real-time operations.

## REFERENCES

Adetunji, Michael, Oyeleye, O, & Akindele, O. (2018). Assessment of building collapse in Lagos Island Nigeria. *American Journal of Sustainable Cities and Society, 7*(1), 18–27.

Akbari, Vahid. (2013). Multitemporal analysis of multipolarization synthetic aperture radar images for robust surface change detection.

Akinyemi, Adebowale, Dare, Gambo, Anthony, Ankeli, & Dabara, Daniel Ibrahim. (2016). *Building collapse in Nigeria: issues and challenges.* Paper presented at the Conference of the International Journal of Arts & Sciences, CD-ROM.

Ang, Kenneth Li Minn, Seng, Jasmine Kah Phooi, & Ngharamike, Ericmoore. (2022). Towards crowdsourcing internet of things (crowd-IoT): Architectures, security and applications. *Future Internet, 14*(2), 49.

Anyfantis, Antonios, Silis, Athanasios, & Blionas, Spyridon. (2021). A low cost, mobile e-nose system with an effective user interface for real time victim localization and hazard detection in USaR operations. *Measurement: Sensors, 16*, 100049.

Asante, Lewis Abedi, & Sasu, Alexander. (2018). The challenge of reducing the incidence of building collapse in Ghana: Analyzing the perspectives of building inspectors in Kumasi. *Sage open, 8*(2), 2158244018778109.

Asif, Amna, Khatoon, Shaheen, Hasan, Md Maruf, Alshamari, Majed A, Abdou, Sherif, Elsayed, Khaled Mostafa, & Rashwan, Mohsen. (2021). Automatic analysis of social media images to identify disaster type and infer appropriate emergency response. *Journal of Big Data, 8*(1), 1–28.

Atalić, Josip, Uroš, Mario, Šavor Novak, Marta, Demšić, Marija, & Nastev, Miroslav. (2021). The Mw5.4 Zagreb (Croatia) earthquake of March 22, 2020: Impacts and response. *Bulletin of Earthquake Engineering, 19*(9), 3461–3489.

Awoyera, PO, Alfa, J, Odetoyan, A, & Akinwumi, II. (2021). *Building collapse in Nigeria during recent years – Causes, effects and way forward.* Paper presented at the IOP Conference Series: Materials Science and Engineering.

Ayodeji, Oke. (2011). An examination of the causes and effects of building collapse in Nigeria. *Journal of Design and Built environment, 9*(1), 37–47.

Bahrami, Sirous. (2021). Through the wall imaging using ultrawideband frequency domain sampling method. *IETE Journal of Research, 67*(2), 281–289.

Boateng, Festival Godwin. (2020). Building safe and resilient cities: Lessons from Ghana. *Moving from the Millennium to the Sustainable Development Goals* (pp. 267–293): Springer.

Boateng, Festival Godwin. (2021). A critique of overpopulation as a cause of pathologies in African cities: Evidence from building collapse in Ghana. *World Development, 137*, 105161.

Casper, Jennifer, & Murphy, Robin R. (2003). Human-robot interactions during the robot-assisted urban search and rescue response at the world trade center. *IEEE Transactions on Systems, Man, and Cybernetics, Part B (Cybernetics), 33*(3), 367–385.

Chachra, Gaurav, Kong, Qingkai, Huang, Jim, Korlakunta, Srujay, Grannen, Jennifer, Robson, Alexander, & Allen, Richard M. (2022). Detecting damaged buildings using real-time crowdsourced images and transfer learning. *Scientific Reports, 12*(1), 1–12.

De Cubber, Geert, Doroftei, Daniela, Roda, Rui, Silva, Eduardo, Ourevitch, Stephane, Matos, Anibal, Bedkowski, Janusz. (2017). Chapter introduction to the use of robotic tools for search and rescue.

Diamanti, Nectaria, Annan, A Peter, & Giannakis, Iraklis. (2016). *Predicting GPR performance for buried victim search & rescue.* Paper presented at the 2016 16th International Conference on Ground Penetrating Radar (GPR).

Donelli, Massimo. (2011). A rescue radar system for the detection of victims trapped under rubble based on the independent component analysis algorithm. *Progress In Electromagnetics Research M, 19*, 173–181.

Ede, Anthony N. (2010). *Structural stability in Nigeria and worsening environmental disorder: the way forward.* Paper presented at the West Africa Built Environment Research Conference Accra Ghana.

Ede, Anthony Nkem. (2013). Building collapse in Nigeria: The trend of casualties the last decade (2000-2010). *International Journal of Civil & Environmental Engineering, 10*(6), 32–42.

Feng, Yu, Huang, Xiao, & Sester, Monika. (2022). Extraction and analysis of natural disaster-related VGI from social media: Review, opportunities and challenges. *International Journal of Geographical Information Science,* 1–42.

Ferrara, V. (2015). Technical survey about available technologies for detecting buried people under rubble or avalanches. *WIT Transactions on The Built Environment, 150*, 91–101.

Fioranelli, Francesco, Salous, Sana, & Raimundo, Xavier. (2014). Frequency-modulated interrupted continuous wave as wall removal technique in through-the-wall imaging. *IEEE Transactions on Geoscience and Remote Sensing, 52*(10), 6272–6283.

Franke, Kevin W., Candia, Gabriel, Mayoral, Juan M., Wood, Clinton M., Montgomery, Jack, Hutchinson, Tara, & Morales-Velez, Alesandra C. (2019). Observed building damage patterns and foundation performance in Mexico City following the 2017 M7.1 Puebla-Mexico City earthquake. *Soil Dynamics and Earthquake Engineering, 125*, 105708.

Gaikwad, Abhay N, Singh, D, & Nigam, MJ. (2011). Application of clutter reduction techniques for detection of metallic and low dielectric target behind the brick wall by stepped frequency continuous wave radar in ultra-wideband range. *IET Radar, Sonar & Navigation, 5*(4), 416–425.

Gennarelli, Gianluca, Ludeno, Giovanni, & Soldovieri, Francesco. (2016). Real-time through-wall situation awareness using a microwave Doppler radar sensor. *Remote Sensing, 8*(8), 621.

Giuliani, Francesca, De Falco, Anna, & Cutini, Valerio. (2021). Unpacking seismic risk in Italian historic centres: A critical overview for disaster risk reduction. *International Journal of Disaster Risk Reduction, 59*, 102260.

Gough, Katherine V, Yankson, Paul WK, & Esson, James. (2019). Migration, housing and attachment in urban gold mining settlements. *Urban Studies, 56*(13), 2670–2687.

Grazzini, Gilberto, Pieraccini, Massimiliano, Parrini, Filippo, Spinetti, Alessandro, Macaluso, Giovanni, Dei, Devis, & Atzeni, Carlo. (2010). *An ultra-wideband high-dynamic range GPR for detecting buried people after collapse of buildings.* Paper presented at the Proceedings of the XIII International Conference on Ground Penetrating Radar.

Harikesh, Ananjan Basu, Abegaonkar, Mahesh Pandurang, & Koul, Shiban Kishen. (2019). Through the wall respiration rate detection of multiple human subjects using Hilbert vibrational decomposition. *Progress In Electromagnetics Research M, 80,* 83–91.

Huo, R, Agapiou, Agapios, Bocos-Bintintan, V, Brown, LJ, Burns, C, Creaser, CS, Hildebrand, L. (2011). The trapped human experiment. *Journal of Breath Research, 5*(4), 046006.

Jayathilaka, Gaindu Saranga, Siriwardana, Chandana, Amaratunga, Dilanthi, Haigh, Richard, & Dias, Nuwan. (2021). A conceptual framework for social media use during disasters. *Multi-Hazard Early Warning and Disaster Risks,* 659–684.

Jayawardene, Vimukthi, Huggins, Thomas J, Prasanna, Raj, & Fakhruddin, Bapon. (2021). The role of data and information quality during disaster response decision-making. *Progress in Disaster Science, 12,* 100202.

Jia, Yong, Guo, Yong, Yan, Chao, Sheng, Haoxuan, Cui, Guolong, & Zhong, Xiaoling. (2019). Detection and localization for multiple stationary human targets based on cross-correlation of dual-station SFCW radars. *Remote Sensing, 11*(12), 1428.

Jon, Ihnji. (2020). A manifesto for planning after the coronavirus: Towards planning of care. *Planning Theory, 19*(3), 329–345.

Joseph, Alvin, Parmar, Vishal, & Bagyaveereswaran, V. (2019). *Design of human detection robot for natural calamity rescue operation.* Paper presented at the 2019 Innovations in Power and Advanced Computing Technologies (i-PACT).

Kaul, Kavya Kriti, & Kant, Surya. (2019). Natural disasters and their mitigation measures.

Khajwal, Asim B, & Noshadravan, Arash. (2021). An uncertainty-aware framework for reliable disaster damage assessment via crowdsourcing. *International Journal of Disaster Risk Reduction, 55,* 102110.

Khan, Muhammad Faizan, Wang, Guojun, & Bhuiyan, Md Zakirul Alam. (2019). Wi-Fi frequency selection concept for effective coverage in collapsed structures. *Future Generation Computer Systems, 97,* 409–424.

Khatoon, Shaheen, Asif, Amna, Hasan, Md Maruf, & Alshamari, Majed. (2022). Social media-based intelligence for disaster response and management in smart cities. *Artificial Intelligence, Machine Learning, and Optimization Tools for Smart Cities* (pp. 211–235): Springer.

Kibuuka, Kharim. (2006). Save lives, property and the environment: a practical application of the concept of risk management to enhance the effectiveness of the SAR [search and rescue] service provision in developing countries.

Ko, Albert WY, & Lau, Henry YK. (2009). Intelligent robot-assisted humanitarian search and rescue system. *International Journal of Advanced Robotic Systems, 6*(2), 12.

Labarthe, Chistophe, Mutzig, Jean-Paul, Jecko, B, Hamieh, H, Martinod, E, Feix, N,... ... Bertrand, V. (2009). *An ultra-wideband radar concept for the detection of buried victims beneath building rubble.* Paper presented at the 2009 International Radar Conference" Surveillance for a Safer World" (RADAR 2009).

Li, Jing, Zeng, Zhaofa, Sun, Jiguang, & Liu, Fengshan. (2012). Through-wall detection of human being's movement by UWB radar. *IEEE Geoscience and Remote Sensing Letters, 9*(6), 1079–1083.

Li, Lingyao, Bensi, Michelle, Cui, Qingbin, Baecher, Gregory B, & Huang, You. (2021). Social media crowdsourcing for rapid damage assessment following a sudden-onset natural hazard event. *International Journal of Information Management, 60,* 102378.

Li, Shuai, Cai, Hubo, Abraham, Dulcy M, & Mao, Peng. (2016). Estimating features of underground utilities: Hybrid GPR/GPS approach. *Journal of Computing in Civil Engineering, 30*(1), 04014108.

Li, Xianghai, & Wang, Yixin. (2022). Construction of urban flood disaster emergency management system using scenario construction technology. *Computational Intelligence and Neuroscience, 2022,* 1–10.

Liang, Xiaolin, Zhang, Hao, Fang, Guangyou, Ye, Shengbo, & Gulliver, T Aaron. (2017). An improved algorithm for through-wall target detection using ultra-wideband impulse radar. *IEEE Access, 5,* 22101–22118.

Liu, Lanbo, & Liu, Sixin. (2014). Remote detection of human vital sign with stepped-frequency continuous wave radar. *IEEE Journal of Selected Topics in Applied Earth Observations and Remote Sensing, 7*(3), 775–782.

Marasco, Sebastiano, Cardoni, Alessandro, Noori, Ali Zamani, Kammouh, Omar, Domaneschi, Marco, & Cimellaro, Gian Paolo. (2021). Integrated platform to assess seismic resilience at the community level. *Sustainable Cities and Society, 64,* 102506.

Marjanac, Sophie, & Patton, Lindene. (2018). Extreme weather event attribution science and climate change litigation: An essential step in the causal chain? *Journal of Energy & Natural Resources Law, 36*(3), 265–298.

Martínez-Gomariz, Eduardo, Forero-Ortiz, Edwar, Guerrero-Hidalga, María, Castán, Salvador, & Gómez, Manuel. (2020). Flood depth–damage curves for Spanish urban areas. *Sustainability, 12*(7), 2666.

Mathebula, A.M., & Smallwood, JJ. (2017). Religious building collapses: The heavy price of short cuts in places of worship and pilgrimage site construction. *Procedia Engineering, 196,* 919–929.

Mavrodieva, Aleksandrina V, & Shaw, Rajib. (2021). Social media in disaster management. *Media and Disaster Risk Reduction* (pp. 55–73): Springer.

Mazzoleni, Maurizio, Mård, Johanna, Rusca, Maria, Odongo, Vincent, Lindersson, Sara, & Di Baldassarre, Giuliano. (2021). Floodplains in the Anthropocene: A global analysis of the interplay between human population, built environment, and flood severity. *Water Resources Research, 57*(2), e2020WR027744.

Mittal, Viyom, Jahanian, Mohammad, & Ramakrishnan, KK. (2021). *Online delivery of social media posts to appropriate first responders for disaster response.* Paper presented at the Adjunct Proceedings of the 2021 International Conference on Distributed Computing and Networking.

Moghadas, Mahsa, Rajabifard, Abbas, Fekete, Alexander, & Kötter, Theo. (2022). A framework for scaling urban transformative resilience through utilizing volunteered geographic information. *ISPRS International Journal of Geo-Information, 11*(2), 114.

Mohanty, Somya D, Biggers, Brown, Sayedahmed, Saed, Pourebrahim, Nastaran, Goldstein, Evan B, Bunch, Rick,... ...Cosby, Arthur. (2021). A multi-modal approach towards mining social media data during natural disasters: A case study of Hurricane Irma. *International Journal of Disaster Risk Reduction, 54,* 102032.

Mu, Tong, & Song, Yaoliang. (2018). *Through wall imaging based on the space-frequency time reversal.* Paper presented at the 2018 14th IEEE International Conference on Signal Processing (ICSP).

Okunola, Olasunkanmi Habeeb. (2021). Survival of the fittest: Assessing incidents of building collapse and reduction practices in Lagos, Nigeria. *Environmental Quality Management.*

Omran, Abdelnaser, Bamidele, Olojotuyi, & Baharuddin, Amir Hussin B. (2016). Causes and effects of incessant building collapse in Nigeria. *Serbian Project Management Journal, 13,* 13–26.

Onifade, Moshood. (2021). Towards an emergency preparedness for self-rescue from underground coal mines. *Process Safety and Environmental Protection, 149,* 946–957.

Qi, Fugui, Liang, Fulai, Liu, Miao, Lv, Hao, Wang, Pengfei, Xue, Huijun, & Wang, Jianqi. (2019). Position-information-indexed classifier for improved through-wall detection and classification of human activities using UWB bio-radar. *IEEE Antennas and Wireless Propagation Letters, 18*(3), 437–441.

Qi, Fugui, Liang, Fulai, Lv, Hao, Li, Chuantao, Chen, Fuming, & Wang, Jianqi. (2016). Detection and classification of finer-grained human activities based on stepped-frequency continuous-wave through-wall radar. *Sensors, 16*(6), 885.

Ralston, Tyler S, Charvat, Gregory L, & Peabody, John E. (2010). *Real-time through-wall imaging using an ultrawideband multiple-input multiple-output (MIMO) phased array radar system.* Paper presented at the 2010 IEEE International Symposium on Phased Array Systems and Technology.

Restuccia, Francesco, Thandu, Srinivas Chakravarthi, Chellappan, Sriram, & Das, Sajal K. (2016). *RescuePal: A smartphone-based system to discover people in emergency scenarios.* Paper presented at the 2016 IEEE 17th International Symposium on A World of Wireless, Mobile and Multimedia Networks (WoWMoM).

Sachs, Jürgen, Helbig, Marko, Herrmann, Ralf, Kmec, Martin, Schilling, Kai, & Zaikov, E. (2014). Remote vital sign detection for rescue, security, and medical care by ultrawideband pseudo-noise radar. *Ad Hoc Networks, 13,* 42–53.

Sachs, Jürgen, Helbig, Marko, Herrmann, Ralf, Kmec, Martin, Schilling, Kai, Zaikov, E, & Rauschenbach, Peter. (2011). *Trapped victim detection by pseudo-noise radar.* Paper presented at the Proceedings of the 1st International Conference on Wireless Technologies for Humanitarian Relief.

Shah, Syed Daniyal Ali. (2017). A microwave reflectometer prototype for detection of body through the rubble of collapsed buildings. *Advances in Science, Technology and Engineering Systems Journal, 2*(3), 1092–1106.

Shen, Guoqiang, & Hwang, Seong Nam. (2019). Spatial-temporal snapshots of global natural disaster impacts revealed from EM-DAT for 1900–2015. *Geomatics, Natural Hazards and Risk, 10,* 912–934.

Shishido, Hidehiko, Kobayashi, Koyo, Kameda, Yoshinari, & Kitahara, Itaru. (2021). Method to generate building damage maps by combining aerial image processing and crowdsourcing. *Journal of Disaster Research, 16*(5), 827–839.

Silva, Vitor, & Horspool, Nick. (2019). Combining USGS ShakeMaps and the OpenQuake-engine for damage and loss assessment. *Earthquake Engineering & Structural Dynamics, 48*(6), 634–652.

Song, Yongping, Hu, Jun, Chu, Ning, Jin, Tian, Zhang, Jianwen, & Zhou, Zhimin. (2018). Building layout reconstruction in concealed human target sensing via UWB MIMO through-wall imaging radar. *IEEE Geoscience and Remote Sensing Letters, 15*(8), 1199–1203.

Srivastav, Arvind, Nguyen, Phong, McConnell, Matthew, Loparo, Kenneth A, & Mandal, Soumyajit. (2020). A highly digital multiantenna ground-penetrating radar (GPR) system. *IEEE Transactions on Instrumentation and Measurement, 69*(10), 7422–7436.

Su, Wei-Chih, Tang, Mu-Cyun, El Arif, Rezki, Horng, Tzyy-Sheng, & Wang, Fu-Kang. (2019). Stepped-frequency continuous-wave radar with self-injection-locking technology for monitoring multiple human vital signs. *IEEE Transactions on Microwave Theory and Techniques, 67*(12), 5396–5405.

Tan, Ling, Guo, Ji, Mohanarajah, Selvarajah, & Zhou, Kun. (2021). Can we detect trends in natural disaster management with artificial intelligence? A review of modeling practices. *Natural Hazards, 107*(3), 2389–2417.

Tebchrany, Elias. (2015). *Contribution of ultra-wide band and polarization diversity for the non-destructive evaluation of civil engineering structures using the ground penetrating radar (GPR).* Université Paris-Est.

Thi, Phuoc Van Nguyen, & Thanh, Tung Tran. (2020). Microwave Doppler radar sensing system for vital sign detection: From evaluated accuracy models to the intelligent system. ICDAR, Dublin, Ireland Proceedings.

Vlachakis, Georgios, Vlachaki, Evangelia, & Lourenço, Paulo B. (2020). Learning from failure: Damage and failure of masonry structures, after the 2017 Lesvos earthquake (Greece). *Engineering Failure Analysis, 117*, 104803.

Wang, Fu-Kang, Horng, Tzyy-Sheng, Peng, Kang-Chun, Jau, Je-Kuan, Li, Jian-Yu, & Chen, Cheng-Chung. (2013). Detection of concealed individuals based on their vital signs by using a see-through-wall imaging system with a self-injection-locked radar. *IEEE Transactions on Microwave Theory and Techniques, 61*(1), 696–704.

Wang, Houcai, Xiong, Li, Wang, Chengwen, & Chen, Nan. (2022). Understanding Chinese mobile social media users' communication behaviors during public health emergencies. *Journal of Risk Research*, 1–18.

Wang, Kun, Zeng, Zhaofa, & Sun, Jiguang. (2018). Through-wall detection of the moving paths and vital signs of human beings. *IEEE Geoscience and Remote Sensing Letters, 16*(5), 717–721.

Xing, Ziyao, Zhang, Xiaodong, Zan, Xuli, Xiao, Cong, Li, Bing, Han, KeKe,... ...Liu, Junming. (2021). Crowdsourced social media and mobile phone signaling data for disaster impact assessment: A case study of the 8.8 Jiuzhaigou earthquake. *International Journal of Disaster Risk Reduction, 58*, 102200.

Xu, Yanyun, Wu, Shiyou, Chen, Chao, Chen, Jie, & Fang, Guangyou. (2012). A novel method for automatic detection of trapped victims by ultrawideband radar. *IEEE Transactions on Geoscience and Remote Sensing, 50*(8), 3132–3142.

Yang, Xiaqing, Chen, Pengyun, Wang, Mingyang, Guo, Shisheng, Jia, Chao, & Cui, Guolong. (2020). Human motion serialization recognition with through-the-wall radar. *IEEE Access, 8*, 186879–186889.

You, Jianyi, Muhammad, Auwal Sagir, He, Xin, Xie, Tianqi, Wang, Zhiyuan, Fan, Xiaoliang,... ...Wang, Cheng. (2022). PANDA: Predicting road risks after natural disasters leveraging heterogeneous urban data. *CCF Transactions on Pervasive Computing and Interaction*, 1–15.

Young, Jason C, Lynch, Renee, Boakye-Achampong, Stanley, Jowaisas, Chris, Sam, Joel, & Norlander, Bree. (2021). Volunteer geographic information in the global south: Barriers to local implementation of mapping projects across Africa. *GeoJournal, 86*(5), 2227–2243.

Yuan, Chenxi, Li, Shuai, Cai, Hubo, & Kamat, Vineet R. (2018). GPR signature detection and decomposition for mapping buried utilities with complex spatial configuration. *Journal of Computing in Civil Engineering, 32*(4), 04018026.

Yılankıran, Feyzi Çelik, & Guney, Caner. (2021). Emergency response with mobile geosocial sensing in the post-app era. *Transactions in GIS, 25*(2), 897–922.

Zaikov, Egor. (2010). *UWB radar for detection and localization of trapped people*. Paper presented at the 11th International Radar Symposium.

Zeng, Zhaofa, Li, Jing, Huang, Ling, & Liu, Fengshan. (2012). *Improvement of target imaging quality by multi-polarization MIMO GPR*. Paper presented at the 2012 14th International Conference on Ground Penetrating Radar (GPR).

Zhang, Limao, & Pan, Yue. (2022). Information fusion for automated post-disaster building damage evaluation using deep neural network. *Sustainable Cities and Society, 77*, 103574.

# 9

# A Comparative Study on Available Fake Detection Apps

Sakshi Gosain, Shrutika Saxena, Tapas Kumar, and Shweta Mongia

Department of Computer Science and Engineering, Manav Rachna International Institute of Research and Studies, Faridabad, Haryana, India

## 9.1 INTRODUCTION

A false, sensationalized report that aims to garner attention, mislead, deceive, or damage someone's reputation is known as fake news. The extensive dissemination of misleading information made possible by its rising popularity has had extremely negative effects on society [1]. Recent events have shown how social media sites like Facebook, Twitter, and YouTube are changing how news is consumed and shared. Typically, their data is unreliable [2]. They frequently make grammatical errors. They frequently use clickbait, attention-grabbing language, and news formats. Their sources are frequently unreliable [3]. Recent political events, particularly the divisive Brexit vote in the United Kingdom and Donald Trump's narrow victory in the 2016 U.S. presidential election have increased interest in the subject of "fake news." It is generally accepted that this significantly influenced how both political campaigns turned out. Less time has been spent researching and defining the phrase fake news, despite the fact that both academics and commentators have written extensively about its disruptive potential and deceptive nature. Numerous countries' social media networks have been swamped with COVID-19 hoaxes and false information for the past two years. We currently live in the information age, where consumers create material, but the majority of that content lacks credibility and verification since

DOI: 10.1201/9781003346326-9

debunking tools are scarce. Academics from around the world are drawn to the hot research topic of identifying fake news on social media platforms. Just two of the Internet's biggest players, Google and Facebook, are looking for ways to refute online bogus news. Facebook launched a third-party fact-checking initiative in 2016 [4] to rate and evaluate the veracity of content on their site. This program works with fact-checkers from all over the world who have earned the IFCN certification. While this was going on, Google unveiled its News Initiative to address false information and contentious breaking news [5]. Social media posts contain information that is multimodal, or a combination of text, images, and videos. This has transformed traditional print media into an online-based multimedia. The numerous informational channels boost the claim's credibility and offer a variety of options for spotting false news red flags. Many research communities have recently become interested in a strong and reliable strategy for spotting misleading information.

Around 3.6 billion people use social media globally, according to Statistica [6]. In terms of instant information availability, unfettered distribution, no time constraints, and variety, social media websites and networks clearly outperform traditional news providers. But most of these platforms lack any kind of oversight. As a result, it is frequently difficult to decide whether a specific news item is true or false.

## 9.2 LITERATURE SURVEY

### 9.2.1 Features of Fake News

Several studies have used feature-based categorization to more effectively spot fake news reports [7]. False information can be quickly identified using textual characteristics [8].

Semantic characteristics: The semantic or meaning content of the text is described by semantic characteristics. These characteristics make it simpler to spot a meaningful pattern in the data.

Characteristics of the lexicon: Lexical features are mostly used in tf-idf vectorization to summarize the total number of unique words and the frequency of the term. Hashtags, pronouns, verb tenses, and punctuation are examples of lexical elements [9].

Attributes of these characteristics include n-gram strategies, bag-of-words tactics, and part-of-speech techniques. The linguistic traits used in text classification most frequently are sentence-level features.

Psychological and linguistic traits: The word count is one of these attributes that is based on text-mining software that consults dictionaries.

## 9.2.2 Identifying Fake News Methods

Because social media platforms are used more often than ever, there is a historic epidemic of fake news online. Traditional automatic rumor detection systems relied on hand-crafted features, but deep-level characteristics have recently taken over with the rise of big data and a massive amount of user-generated data. The methods for identifying bogus news are depicted in Figure 9.1.

**Content-Based:** To spot bogus information, the article's text, image, or both may be examined by the content-based fake news detection method. The researchers typically rely on latent or purposely constructed characteristics in the article to automatically identify fake news [10].

**Knowledge-Based:** Claims are verified as true by comparing them to outside sources when knowledge-based techniques are used. Fact-checking processes are in two varieties: manual and automatic [11]. Expert-based and crowdsourced fact-checking are the two main categories. Expert-based approaches to decision making rely on real individuals who have specialized knowledge and have an expert-oriented mentality. Fact-checking websites like Snopes, PolitiFact, and Gossip Cop all employ this strategy. These techniques work well, but they are time-consuming and inefficient when handling the vast volume of content that is available on social media.

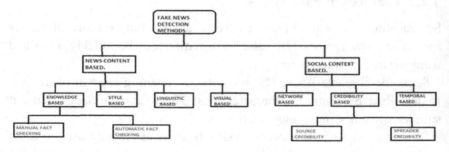

**FIGURE 9.1**
Fake news detection methods.

The "wisdom of crowd" is applied in crowdsourcing methods to crowd-source the verification of news story accuracy. A similar approach is used by Fisk kit, which provides a forum for people to discuss important news stories and evaluate their correctness [12].

Credbank is a widely accessible benchmark data set for false news that includes fact-checker annotations. Contradictory annotations must be addressed in advance, and non-credible users must be excluded from data sets created using this method [13].

The implementation of automatic fact-checking systems has solved the issue that with the enormous volume of data produced, especially with the usage of social media, manual fact-checking procedures do not scale effectively [11]. The two procedures that make up the automatic fact-checking process are fact extraction, which collects information and builds a knowledge base, and fact-checking, which assesses news articles to determine their veracity by contrasting them with facts in the knowledge base.

**Style-Based:** Similar to knowledge-based false news detection, style-based false news identification analyzes news content. However, rather than focusing on the veracity of the news, this method investigates the writer's desire to deceive the reader.

Style-based approaches capture the traits of writing styles to differentiate between real users and anomalous accounts [14].

**Based on images:** People frequently consider images to be evidence that strengthens the reliability of news articles. It is widely used by false news publishers to seduce and dupe viewers. For news authentication, it extracts various features of the statistical and visual picture [15].

In order to uncover false information, a variety of social networks, including friendship, tweet-retweet, and post-repost networks, are examined by network-based fake news identification. It names those who post false material on social media and details who and with whom they collaborate. On the basis of their shared traits and interests, users of online platforms frequently form a variety of networks, which act as channels for the distribution of information. This investigation looks into a number of social media networks and offers helpful details on news spreaders and how they interact with one another. It uses a tree to represent the message propagation pattern, which, when combined with the connections between posts, sheds more light on the posts' temporal behavior and mood [16].

### 9.2.3 Conventional Techniques for Fake News

The conventional techniques for spotting fake news are listed below [17].

Be Skeptical When We See Something That Seems Sensational, it is Even More Important to Be Skeptical. Headlines that overuse capital letters or emotive words should be taken seriously [18].

Going back to the source. If a study is mentioned in an article, go directly to the source to confirm its reliability.

Once more, back to the story: You wrote the story when? What is the circumstance? The breaking news will continue to arrive. Keep a watch on a story as it develops because early reports sometimes rely on sketchy information.

Triangulate: Verify or corroborate the facts with a variety of sources, such as print media and library databases. To start sorting out the hoaxes, look at websites like the nonprofit, neutral FactCheck.org or well-known websites like Snopes or Hoax-Slayer.

What exactly are you reading? Pay attention to the style of writing you're reading, even if you're on a regular news website. Which of the following best describes it: news reporting, a feature piece, an editorial, guest blogging, a review, an op-ed, a veiled ad, or a comment?

Examine your own biases and mindset when searching: Is your search language biased in any way? Are you rejecting evidence in favor of information that confirms your own beliefs?

Prior to sending (or utilizing): If you see a link that has been forwarded or widely shared, be wary of it being a scam or a false report. Can you verify the information found on social media sites outside of those places?

Be cautious while viewing images because not all of them accurately capture reality. Images can be digitally manipulated in addition to being typically edited or processed. Some people grew up with the Internet. You can discover the origin and iterations of an image with a Google reverse image search.

Look at the comments; if many people claim the article is inaccurate or misleading, it probably is.

Visit the "about" and "about me" pages: It should be standard practice in the research process to take the credentials of authors into consideration by clicking on or researching their names.

## 9.2.4 Machine Learning Technique

As depicted in Figure 9.2, an in-depth study has recently focused on the use of various machine learning algorithms to recognize bogus news. The same is summarized in Table 9.1.

**Supervised Learning:** Supervised learning is the process of utilizing machine learning to train a function that translates an input to an output, using input-output pairs as examples. It makes use of tagged training data, a set of training samples, and a function to infer. Using a task-driven approach or when specific goals are set up to be achieved from a predetermined set of inputs, supervised learning is employed. The two most common supervised tasks are classification, which divides the data, and regression, which fits the data. As an illustration, supervised learning can be used to classify text or to determine the tone or genre of a piece of writing, such as a tweet or a product review [19].

**Unsupervised Learning:** Unsupervised learning that is driven by data analyzes of unlabeled data sets without human intervention. This is frequently used for feature extraction, identifying significant patterns and structures, data gathering, and offering explanations for experiments. Clustering, density estimation, feature learning, dimensionality reduction, identifying association rules, anomaly detection, and other unsupervised learning tasks are some of the more prominent ones [20].

**Technique:** Since it uses both labeled and unlabeled data, semi-supervised learning combines the supervised and unsupervised techniques described above. It falls between the two possibilities of "without

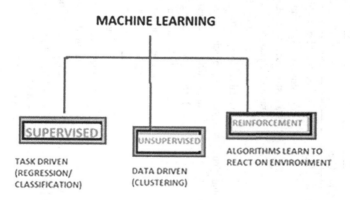

**FIGURE 9.2**
Machine learning techniques for detecting fake news.

**TABLE 9.1**

List of the Algorithms for Machine Learning Used to Detect Bogus News

| ML Algorithm Used | Working/Data Set | Limitations | Result/ Conclusion |
|---|---|---|---|
| Random Forest [23] | Based on the idea of developing different decision tree algorithms, each of which yields a distinct outcome. A training data set is randomly subset by each tree. Any decision tree model uses a random selection of variables to split the data set at each node. | If there are a lot of trees, the algorithm can be too slow and ineffective to make predictions in real time. | Achieved an accuracy of 83% by using Random Forest. |
| Convolutional Neural Network [24] | Accuracy, precision, recall, and f1-score values all fell when k-nearest neighbor was used. However, when using the CNN approach, it was able to achieve a maximum accuracy of 97.15%. The data found at https://www.kaggle.com/c/fake-news/ is a feed-forward neural network, a CNN with one convolutional layer, a CNN with several convolutional layers, and an LSTM can all be used to analyze data to detect fake news. | A significant amount of training data is required because the object's position and orientation are not encoded. | The accuracy of a CNN with more convolutional layers is 97.15%. |
| Support Vector machine [25] | For the SVM algorithm, each data item is depicted as a point in a collection of n dimensions, with the number of given coordinates determining the value of each characteristic. False news was detected using the LIAR Data set. | The support vector machine algorithm fails with huge data sets. When target classes overlap in a data set with more sound, it does not work well. | Achieved an accuracy of 94%. |

| | | |
|---|---|---|
| Simple Bayes [26] | It is assumed that this algorithm, which is based on Bayes theorem, is free of predictors and that it is employed in a variety of machine learning problems. They are interested in forecasting the value of the response variable and the probability distribution of the variables in a data set. | Naive Bayes bases its predictions on the idea that all predictors (or features) are independent because this rarely occurs in reality. The "zero-frequency problem" occurs when an algorithm, a categorical variable whose category was present in the test data set but absent in the training data set is given a probability of zero. | Achieved an accuracy of 90%. |
| Regression Using Logs [27] | It is a classification technique that forecasts the likelihood of a category-dependent variable using machine learning. They used the Liar Data set along with Random Forest, Logistic Regression, and Naive Bayes Classifier to detect fake news. | The linear relationship between the dependent and independent variables | 97% accuracy is displayed via logistic regression. |

supervision" and "with supervision," as a result. Semi-supervised learning is advantageous since labeled data may be hard to find in some circumstances yet unlabeled data is simple to find in the actual world. A semi-supervised learning model's main objective is to provide predictions that outperform those made only using the model's labeled data. Data labeling, machine translation, fraud detection, and text categorization are a few examples of semi-supervised learning applications [21].

**Reinforcement Technique:** The machine learning technique of reinforcement learning, commonly referred to as environment-driven learning, enables software agents and computers to automatically select the behavior that would maximize efficiency in a specific context or environment. Using the knowledge learned from environmental activists to take measures that will increase the incentives or decrease the dangers is the ultimate goal of this type of learning, which is based on rewards or penalties. It is not suggested, nevertheless, to use it to solve straightforward or fundamental issues [22]. The creation of AI models that can improve the operational effectiveness of complex systems like manufacturing, supply chain logistics, autonomous driving, and robots is instead advantageous.

## 9.2.5 Fake News Detection Apps and Websites

Authors have also studied various apps and websites used for detecting fake news. Following is the description of the same. Table 9.2 summarizes the various apps used for fake news detection.

1. **Whatsapp Farzi** [28]: Using a custom logarithm, the app goes through all of the Internet content and gathers news on a specific topic to verify it from an authentic news portal. Through image tampering algorithms, the app can also verify and scan the authenticity of photos [29].
2. **Listle (Android, iOS)** [30]: Listle curates content from reputable outlets such as CNN, Vox, The Guardian, and others. Look through the headlines, as well as the duration of the audio file and the genre or category. You can immediately begin listening to the article or save it to your playlist. Also, check out some of the pre-made playlists. When you are driving or stuck in traffic with your headphones on, the "read-aloud" news is ideal.

**TABLE 9.2**

Summary of Apps Used for Fake News Detection

| App Name | Year | Features | Algorithm | Data set |
|---|---|---|---|---|
| Whatsapp Farzi | 2019 | On a variety of instant messaging services, such as Whatsapp, Telegram, and Hike, among others, Whatsapp Farzi strives to halt the spread of misleading information. | It uses a combination of graphics, NLP, machine learning/artificial intelligence, and graphics processing unit (GPU) knowledge to analyze the authenticity of news material and images. | It can use both (Images and text) the features to predict the authenticity of the claims present in the message |
| Listle (Android,IOS) | 2012 | Listle is here to address the issue of not being able to read the news while driving. Enjoy writing that has been converted into brief audio clips by a human, not an AI. | The app will utilize its AI to make an audio file after you copy and paste the URL to the article. | Only text into audio |
| OwlFactor | 2016 | It assesses articles structurally, looking for quantifiable characteristics like the quantity and variety of sources, among other things. As a result, you can find items with varying ratings throughout the political spectrum on almost all news outlets. | OwlFactor tracks the quantity of unique links, their frequency of repetition, and how frequently they link back to the website. | Both image and text-based apps used in determination of articles. |

*(Continued)*

**TABLE 9.2 (Continued)**

Summary of Apps Used for Fake News Detection

| App Name | Year | Features | Algorithm | Data set |
|---|---|---|---|---|
| Credder | 2020 | It aims to fend off clickbait and guarantee information accuracy. | Algorithm focuses on locating the initial piece to be utilized for placement. This component, sometimes known as a seed piece, determines how well an algorithm works to solve a particular puzzle. | Consider the nature of the images and text for defining the fakeness. |
| News Chase | 2019 | Solutions like Google Analytics attached to an app can give you the necessary knowledge about your content popularity among mobile users. | This app is based on Fictometer. It measures the imagination writing styles in any given text in English, using a machine learning algorithm. | Mobile application that seeks to tackle misinformation i.e., is in either image or text with a difference. |
| Trimmed News (Android, IOS) | 2017 | The goal is to create a news reading app for young people today in a style that will appeal to mobile users who want bite-sized news consumption. | The AI keeps track of news coverage on it from many outlets, including Reuters, The Guardian, CNN, Fox News, etc. The AI then summarizes and analyzes the article to provide you with just the details you require. | Only text-based app used for reading. |

3. **OwlFactor (Web)** [31]: Authentic, fact-checked news, OwlFactor is doing everything it can to combat the Internet's scourge of fake news and bad reporting. It has now launched a mini website for all your news needs, following the release of CivikOwl, one of the smartest apps for simplifying important news [32].

4. **Credder (Web)** [33]: Trustworthiness Ratings of Other Journalists Credibility is essential in a time of fake news and simple propaganda. A group of dissatisfied customers developed Credder to address this problem by asking journalists to score the credibility of each item, author, and news source. The website fulfills the same function as the movie review website Rotten Tomatoes. Journalists and other prominent individuals are among Credder's detractors. The response of detractors to an article (as demonstrated by their accompanying tweets) determines its credibility on a scale of 1 to 100.

5. **Medius News(Web)** [34]: This news aggregator makes use of Ad Fontes Media's Media Bias chart, which rates all major news sources according to the originality and veracity of their reporting. The graph identifies news reporters who give more attention to analysis and opinion than to information alone, as well as those who use data that is obviously false or propaganda. Medius News is for people who seek news as information and like making up their own minds about what they think about it and how they feel by focusing on original fact-based reporting. The website now offers general news, business news, sports news, and health news, with nine items in each category.

6. **NewsChase** [35]: This is an AI-based tool that analyzes a given news story's creative writing using a learning algorithm. The news stories are divided into three categories by the app: The content will be reliable if it is written in a straightforward and instructive manner.

7. **Oigetit false news filter** [36]: Oigetit employs artificial intelligence (AI) to fact-check a million articles every hour and provides readers with trustworthy and dependable content.

8. **Trimmed News (Android, iOS)** [37]: A summary of the day's news is presented in story format. Trimmed News makes use of artificial intelligence to handle a range of current events. A news-reading app for today's youth with a design that appeals to mobile users who like bite-sized content is the objective. The newspiece has brief slides that you swipe through to read, just like a social media story.

Other features like group chat and news submission are available, but you should just use the app to browse the news instead.

### 9.2.6 Websites Used for Detecting Fake News

**1. Botometer** [38]: Finding bots (fully automated accounts) on Twitter and other social media channels is crucial and challenging. In fact, computational social scientists must be able to gauge the veracity of a Twitter exchange by spotting harmful botnets or figuring out how many "genuine" (i.e., human) followers a politician has. This is accurate not only in terms of political communication, but also in terms of identifying deception campaigns and boosting platform security.

**2. FactCheck.org** [39]: Fake news is not a recent phenomenon. However, incorrect information can now go faster and farther than it ever could through traditional viral emails because of social media. Some of the inaccurate information that circulates online is false, though not all of it is.

**3. Hoaxy** [40]: On the Internet, hoaxes, rumors, false reports, and conspiracy theories are all spreading quickly. Like any other type of news content, fact-checking information is consumed and shared by social media users, creating a complicated interplay between news memes fighting for viewers' attention. The dynamics of rivalry between Internet misinformation and its rebuttal have not previously been systematically studied.

**4. Politifact** [41]: By going through dozens of social media postings, PolitiFact verified some of the most often made untrue statements about COVID-19. False information concerning a new coronavirus strain originating in China has been reported in anything from Facebook posts that falsify a patent to Bill Gates conspiracy fantasies. Many of the assertions were reposted on Facebook and Twitter, and they were widely disseminated on unpopular conspiracy websites.

The fact-checking website **5-Snopes** [42] is a "well-regarded resource for dispelling misconceptions and misinformation."

## 9.3 CONCLUSION

Due to the rise in popularity and use of social media in recent years, nowadays, a lot of people prefer using social media to acquire their news instead of going to traditional news sources. In light of this, numerous publishers use the Internet and social media in general as a breeding ground for quickly disseminating propaganda and false information, which has negative impacts on society. In this text, we have included a number of free fake news detection tools that should be used to guarantee that we only forward reliable and authentic content. In this research, we analyzed the strategies for detecting false news currently in use by analyzing the literature in two divisions: social context-based and content-based techniques are used to detect fake news. If an article or post has both textual and visual material, or both, it is taken into account when using the content-based strategy. The social context-based strategy takes into account the publisher's credibility as well as the propagation structure. Due to the lack of propagation details, context-based approaches are unable to detect fake news in its early phases, whereas content-based methods are able to do so. Despite the fact that many scholars are working on this issue, there aren't many publicly available benchmark data sets.

## REFERENCES

1. Wang, C. C. (2020). Fake news and related concepts: Definitions and recent research development. *Contemporary Management Research, 16*(3), 145–174.
2. Olan, F., Jayawickrama, U., Arakpogun, E. O., Suklan, J., & Liu, S. (2022). Fake news on social media: The impact on society. *Information Systems Frontiers*, 1–16.
3. Hagiu, A., & Bortoș, S. (2021). Understanding fake news: An interdisciplinary approach. *Acta Universitatis Danubius. Communicatio, 15*(2), 58–71.
4. https://www.facebook.com/formedia/mjp/programs/third-party-fact-checking
5. https://www.theverge.com/2018/3/20/17142788/google-news-initiative-fake-news-journalist-subscriptions.
6. https://www.statista.com/statistics/278414/number-of-worldwide-social-network-users/
7. Raza, S., & Ding, C. (2022). Fake news detection based on news content and social contexts: A transformer-based approach. *International Journal of Data Science and Analytics, 13*(4), 335–362.
8. Bharadwaj, P., Shao, Z., & Darren, S. (2019). Fake news detection with semantic features and text mining. *Journal of Natural Language Processing. 8*, 17–22.
9. Mertoğlu, U., & Genç, B. (2020). Lexicon generation for detecting fake news. *arXiv preprint arXiv:2010.11089.*
10. Ngada, O., & Haskins, B. (2020, December). Fake news detection using content-based features and machine learning. In *2020 IEEE Asia-Pacific Conference on Computer Science and Data Engineering (CSDE)* (pp. 1–6). IEEE.
11. De Beer, D., & Matthee, M. (2021). Approaches to identify fake news: A systematic literature review. In *International Conference on Integrated Science* (pp. 13–22). Springer, Cham.

12. Tschiatschek, S., Singla, A., Gomez Rodriguez, M., Merchant, A., & Krause, A. (2018, April). Fake news detection in social networks via crowd signals. In *Companion Proceedings of the Web Conference 2018* (pp. 517–524).

13. Mitra, T., & Gilbert, E. (2015). Credbank: A large-scale social media corpus with associated credibility annotations. In *Proceedings of the International AAAI Conference on Web and Social Media* (Vol. 9, No. 1, pp. 258–267).

14. Przybyla, P. (2020, April). Capturing the style of fake news. In *Proceedings of the AAAI Conference on Artificial Intelligence* (Vol. 34, No. 01, pp. 490–497).

15. Cao, J., Qi, P., Sheng, Q., Yang, T., Guo, J., & Li, J. (2020). Exploring the role of visual content in fake news detection. *Disinformation, Misinformation, and Fake News in Social Media*, 141–161.

16. Zhou, X., & Zafarani, R. (2019). Network-based fake news detection: A pattern-driven approach. *ACM SIGKDD Explorations Newsletter*, 21(2), 48–60.

17. https://www.kaspersky.com/resource-center/preemptive-safety/how-to-identify-fake-news.

18. de Oliveira, N. R., Pisa, P. S., Lopez, M. A., de Medeiros, D. S. V., & Mattos, D. M. (2021). Identifying fake news on social networks based on natural language processing: Trends and challenges. *Information*, 12(1), 38.

19. Reis, J. C., Correia, A., Murai, F., Veloso, A., & Benevenuto, F. (2019). Supervised learning for fake news detection. *IEEE Intelligent Systems*, 34(2), 76–81.

20. Khanam, Z., Alwasel, B. N., Sirafi, H., & Rashid, M. (2021, March). Fake news detection using machine learning approaches. In *IOP Conference Series: Materials Science and Engineering* (Vol. 1099, No. 1, p. 012040). IOP Publishing.

21. Mansouri, R., Naderan-Tahan, M., & Rashti, M. J. (2020, August). A semi-supervised learning method for fake news detection in social media. In *2020 28th Iranian Conference on Electrical Engineering (ICEE)* (pp. 1–5). IEEE.

22. Petkar, P. B. (2020). Fake news detection: A survey of techniques. *International Journal of Innovative Technology and Exploring Engineering*, 9(9), 383–386.

23. Jehad, R., & Yousif, S. A. (2020). Fake news classification using random forest and decision tree (J48). *Al-Nahrain Journal of Science*, 23(4), 49–55.

24. Yang, Y., Zheng, L., Zhang, J., Cui, Q., Li, Z., & Yu, P. S. (2018). TI-CNN: Convolutional neural networks for fake news detection. *arXiv preprint arXiv:1806.00749*.

25. Tijare, P. (2019). A study on fake news detection using Naíve Bayes. SVM. *Neural Networks and LSTM*.

26. Poovaraghan, R. J., Priya, M. K., Vamsi, P. S. S., Mewara, M., & Loganathan, S. (2019). Fake news accuracy using Naive Bayes classifier. *International Journal of Recent Technology and Engineering (IJRTE)*, 8(1C2), 2277–3878.

27. Nada, F., Khan, B. F., Maryam, A., Zuha, N., & Ahmed, Z. (2019). Fake news detection using logistic regression. *International Research Journal of Engineering and Technology (IRJET)*, 6, 5577–5579. https://www.irjet.net/archives.

28. https://play.google.com/store/apps/details?id=precog.whatsfarzi&hl=en_IN&gl=US&pli=1

29. https://precog.iiit.ac.in/blog/2019/02/11/whatsfarzi-analyzing-fake-manipulated-content-misinformation-on-whatsapp/

30. https://apps.apple.com/us/developer/listle-inc/id1471407807.

31. https://download.cnet.com/OwlFactor-News-Evaluator/3000-2164_4-78319130.html.

32. https://app.dealroom.co/companies/owlfactor

33. https://credder.com
34. https://www.getapp.com/finance-accounting-software/a/mediusflow/
35. https://play.google.com/store/apps/details?id=com.iiserb.fictonews&hl=en_IN&gl=US
36. https://play.google.com/store/apps/details?id=io.scal.oigetit&hl=en_IN&gl=US
37. https://play.google.com/store/apps/details?id=com.trimmednews.lankinen&hl=en_US&gl=US.
38. https://botometer.osome.iu.edu
39. https://www.factcheck.org
40. https://cnets.indiana.edu/blog/2016/12/21/hoaxy/
41. https://www.politifact.com/fake-news/
42. https://www.snopes.com

# 10

## Crowdsourcing Mechanisms for Reviving Cultural Heritage

*Bikram Pratim Bhuyan[1,2] and Ravi Tomar[3]*
[1]School of Computer Science, University of Petroleum and Energy Studies (UPES), Dehradun, India
[2]LISV Laboratory, University of Paris Saclay, Velizy, France
[3]Persistent Systems, India

### 10.1 INTRODUCTION

The term "cultural legacy" is used to describe both the material and immaterial aspects of a culture that have been preserved for future generations [1]. All the things that make up a society and help us learn about its past, present, and varied past are included in this category. However, urbanization, industrialization, climate change, and neglect pose continual threats to cultural heritage. Consequently, revitalizing cultural heritage is crucial for protecting and fostering a society's cultural identity and variety.

The term "crowdsourcing" refers to the practice of contracting work to a large number of individuals, generally through the Internet. It's being utilized more and more in the area of cultural heritage to get people interested in and involved with preserving and promoting their own history. By allowing individuals to actively take part in the preservation and promotion of their cultural heritage, crowdsourcing processes have the potential to be a potent instrument for revitalizing cultural traditions [2].

Crowdfunding has emerged as one of the most prominent crowdsourcing tools for revitalizing historical sites. Crowdfunding is a method by which many people may pool their resources to protect and restore a piece of cultural history. As an example, the Isabella Stewart Gardner Museum in Boston and the Grand Palace in Bangkok have both received

DOI: 10.1201/9781003346326-10

funding via the crowdfunding platform Kickstarter [3]. New cultural heritage initiatives, such as a virtual reality experience of Petra, Jordan's historic city, may be funded via crowdfunding as well.

Crowdsourced mapping [4] is another crowdsourcing tool that has been put to use in the preservation of historical sites. Through crowdsourced mapping, users may contribute data and media to comprehensive maps and databases of cultural heritage places. For instance, the ancient city of Persepolis in Iran and the medieval city of Rome in Italy have both been mapped in great detail, according to the website OpenStreetMap [5]. This paves the way for the safeguarding of historically significant locations that could otherwise be disregarded.

Reviving cultural heritage via crowdsourcing has also been accomplished through citizen science. Citizens may take part in cultural heritage study and data collecting via citizen science. Examples include using Zooniverse [6] to catalog dying tongues like India's Aka or to catalog and keep an eye on endangered heritage places like Australia's Great Barrier Reef.

Another crowdsourcing tool that has been utilized to revitalize cultural artifacts is crowdsourced translation. With the help of crowdsourced translation, more people will be able to read and understand cultural heritage texts, inscriptions, and other written items. For instance, the UNESCO World Heritage Convention and the Convention for the Safeguarding of the Intangible Cultural Heritage have both been translated using the website Translatewiki [7].

Last but not least, crowdsourced archiving is another approach employed for revitalizing cultural assets via crowdsourcing. When it comes to cultural heritage, crowdsourced archiving is a great way to get people involved by having them submit their own images, papers, and other primary materials for digital archives and virtual exhibits. A digital collection of European cultural items, books, paintings, and manuscripts is available online, thanks to a platform like Europeana [8]. We now explore the advantages of using such mechanisms.

## 10.2 ADVANTAGES OF USING CROWDSOURCING-BASED TECHNIQUES

In its simplest form, crowdsourcing is the practice of obtaining resources, such as information or labor, from a large group of individuals. It's a method of soliciting input from a larger pool of minds rather than relying on an organization's or company's internal creative resources. Although the terms are similar, crowdsourcing and crowdfunding are extremely different in practice. Although crowdfunding platforms like Kickstarter [9], GoFundMe [10], and RocketHub [11] help people raise money for creative endeavors, crowdsourcing is different since it focuses on soliciting information and expertise rather than financial assistance. Crowdsourcing is being used by a growing number of corporations and organizations to identify innovative solutions to problems in many fields, including space exploration, healthcare, and historical preservation.

The benefits of crowdsourcing include time and money saved, as well as access to expertise that might be lacking in an in-house team. If one person needs a week to complete a task, the same work may be completed by a large group of people in a couple of hours if the activity is divided into numerous smaller portions.

Crowdsourcing is useful for a wide variety of tasks, including developing websites and transcribing audio and video. When developing new goods, many firms seek public feedback. Instead of polling a select group of customers, businesses may poll millions of people from all over the world using social media. This guarantees a more representative sample of customers from all walks of life. Consumer-facing businesses might also gain from increased audience feedback and engagement or loyalty.

However, businesses who seek to reduce their effort while searching for the next big thing may be disappointed to learn that crowdsourcing isn't the answer. It's not uncommon for someone to have to filter through all the ideas being presented, for fundraising targets to fall short on all-or-nothing financing platforms and for it to be challenging to locate and enlist the assistance of the appropriate audience.

It is easy for a company or organization to become stuck in its ways of thinking when it examines its own internal issues. It's understandable that a firm would find it challenging to alter its long-standing practices. This kind of complacency in the face of the status quo is a serious issue for companies of all stripes. This is why innovation masterminds like Steve Jobs put a premium on bringing in outsiders who can question established ways of doing things. Due to this, crowdsourcing offers tremendous benefits. The more individuals an organization gets involved in finding a solution, the more likely they will get hundreds, if not thousands, of unique viewpoints. Crowdsourcing has many advantages, and

Unilever's Open Innovation [12] site is a fantastic illustration of those advantages. Here, the firm solicits input from specialists all across the globe to develop novel approaches to old challenges, such as sustainable packaging and product cooling technologies, with surprising outcomes.

Many companies, particularly those on a smaller scale, may lack the variety of ideas necessary to tackle genuinely intractable challenges due to a lack of personnel. The power of the crowd may alter all of that. A business may benefit from a greater diversity of perspectives, ideas, and solutions to an issue if it solicits input from a wider range of employees in the process of problem-solving.

Indeed, the managerial benefit of crowdsourcing isn't as well-known as the others, but it's no less important for that. When companies develop new products in-house, the people in charge of the project usually have a lot on their plate. To keep creative minds and designers engaged, it's helpful to remind them of the importance of their input and, at times, to provide a little extra encouragement. Through crowdsourcing, a company or organization lays out the ground rules and then sits back and takes suggestions. This less-intrusive alternative to conventional brainstorming methods saves time and allows individuals to pursue other, more exciting pursuits. More on this later, but for now, know that this implies you have less say over your own creative process.

Crowdsourcing is a collaborative and competitive alternative to conventional methods of commercial issue resolution. This does double duty by providing individuals with conversation fodder and a means to expand their support system. Companies like Frito-Lay need publicity like this, so they hold contests like "Do Us a Flavor," in which chip lovers submit their greatest (and craziest) suggestions for new flavors of potato chips [13].

When companies look inward for answers, they are limited by the speed with which their people can get things done. After all, there is a limit to how quickly even the company's most brilliant minds can work. Companies may save a lot of time and money by opening up the process to more individuals at once. This is especially important for time-sensitive undertakings like medical research or urgent software fixes. A good case in point is the multinational Human Genome Project [14], which set out to decipher the human genetic code in its entirety. After 13 years of labor, this project was finished in 2003, thanks to the efforts of scientists from 20 institutions in six nations. Crowdsourcing this effort among several universities would have prevented this initiative from becoming stuck in its early phases. That's the effectiveness of group effort.

Crowdsourcing is much more than simply a technique to generate excellent new ideas for firms like Starbucks with its My Starbucks Idea platform [15]. Participant data analysis may provide Starbucks with invaluable insights into its customer base. What are the main characteristics of the people who have submitted? How do you recommend reaching out to them? And what can we learn about the interests and preferences of the company's most devoted supporters from the comments themselves? Proof that crowdsourcing has more to offer than simple solutions. Crowdsourcing, when executed properly, may also provide valuable information about the needs of the client. In the next section, we explore the various types of crowdsourcing mechanisms for reviving cultural heritage.

## 10.3 TYPES OF CROWDSOURCING MECHANISMS FOR REVIVING CULTURAL HERITAGE

Several forms of crowdsourcing have been used for the purpose of revitalizing cultural artifacts.

1. **Crowdfunding:** Funding from a large number of people is pooled to cover the costs of restoring or maintaining a piece of cultural property. This may be used to buy property to prevent a historic site from being developed or restore an aging monument.

2. **Crowdsourced mapping:** Crowdsourced mapping is a method wherein a large number of people work together to compile and organize data on cultural heritage places to make comprehensive maps and databases. The information may be used to produce more accurate maps of historic areas or to record the whereabouts of sites that are in jeopardy.

3. **Citizen science:** Citizen science is a technique that empowers everyday people to take part in cultural heritage-related scientific studies and data collecting, such as the recording of dying languages or the tracking of potentially dangerous historical locations. This may be used in the documentation of disappearing languages and customs and the collection of data on historic locations.

4. **Crowdsourced translation:** Individuals may participate in the translation of cultural heritage texts, inscriptions, and other written

materials via this process, increasing the audience for these works. This may be put to use by translating important historical materials or promoting the accessibility of cultural heritage locations.

5. **Crowdsourced archiving:** Individuals may participate in the creation of digital archives and online exhibits by submitting images, papers, and other original materials relating to cultural heritage. This may be used to preserve local history and create digital archives of historic locations.

Mechanisms of crowdsourcing have proved effective in revitalizing cultural artifacts. They have been used in the following ways: to protect and promote historic sites; to collect data on endangered heritage; to chronicle endangered languages and traditional practices; to make heritage sites available to a larger audience; to record the history of a community or area. However, while employing crowdsourcing techniques for revitalizing cultural assets, it is also crucial to address critical ethical and practical considerations. Protecting the rights of communities and persons participating in the process and ensuring the accuracy of the information acquired is of paramount importance. In addition, we must guarantee that everyone in the community has an equal opportunity to participate and reap the advantages of crowdsourcing.

## 10.3.1 Crowdfunding

The preservation of cultural artifacts is crucial for making sense of the past and planning for the future. Traditional techniques of conservation, however, are becoming more insufficient as both resources and the number of cultural assets continue to expand. Crowdfunding as a means of revitalizing cultural traditions is one approach to addressing this issue.

The term "crowd financing" refers to the practice of collecting monetary contributions from a large number of people for a particular purpose or endeavor with the use of a digital platform. In recent years, this mechanism's usage has skyrocketed, and it now finances a broad range of initiatives, including the upkeep of historic landmarks.

Using crowdfunding to revitalize historical sites has several advantages. First, it facilitates the rapid amassing of a sizable sum of money, making it a time and money-saving strategy for the protection of historic places. Plus, it encourages locals to pitch in throughout the preservation effort, which strengthens their emotional connection to the landmark. As a result, there may be more people who care about keeping historical sites and artifacts around for future generations.

Restoration of historic landmarks, buildings, and artworks may also be aided via crowd financing. Crowd fundraising may assist in guaranteeing that these places are accessible to future generations by giving cash for their repair. Additionally, property or buildings that are in danger of being demolished due to development might be purchased with the help of crowd fundraising.

Crowd financing for cultural assets also can strengthen public support for the preservation of historic places at risk of being lost. Crowd fundraising initiatives may assist in increasing awareness and building support for the protection of endangered historic sites by offering information about the sites and the need to preserve them.

As governmental and private investments in cultural assets throughout the world have declined, crowdsourcing has emerged as a viable alternative financing mechanism for the cultural sector [16]. The GDP utilization of European countries in Cultural Heritage in the year 2021 is shown in Figure 10.1.

More and more arts groups and artists have been soliciting money from the wide-ranging and scattered population of Internet users in recent years. In the report [17], we find that, since 2013, over 75,000 cultural assets have undertaken crowdfunding projects, raising over 247 million euros. Between 2013 and 2016, the United Kingdom dominated the cultural heritage crowdfunding industry, accounting for 36 percent of all campaigns and 41 percent of all transaction volume. This was followed by France, which accounted for 30 percent of all campaigns and 22 percent of all transaction volume.

Crowdfunding has gained a lot of interest from practitioners, policymakers, and scholars in the crowdfunding cultural heritage because of its recent meteoric ascent [18]. Crowdfunding in crowdfunding in cultural heritage literature has mostly concentrated on exploring what factors influence the success of various crowdfunding initiatives [19]. One of the first empirical investigations of the Kickstarter platform, [20] data on projects in crowdfunding in cultural heritages, is both intriguing and informative. The author finds, in particular, that the majority of supported campaigns only meet their minimum target amounts and that the majority of successfully funded campaigns fail to meet their entire seven target amounts. Indicators of campaign quality include the existence of a pitch video, the founder's activity on social media, the frequency of

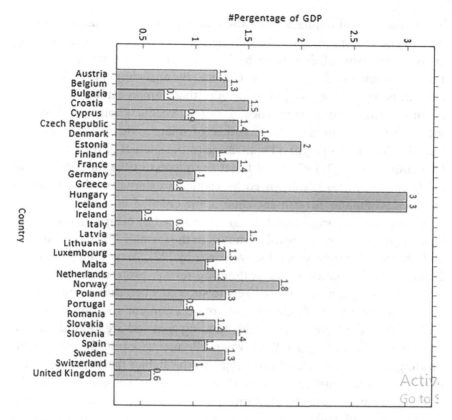

**FIGURE 10.1**
GDP utilization of European countries in cultural heritage in the year 2021.

updates, and the total amount of money raised. [21] conducted a similar study of Kickstarter campaign financing patterns and found that backers are more inclined to give early or late in the campaign. The writers also recognize the so-called Kickstarter effect, in which the likelihood of success grows as the financial target is neared. These findings hold true for every kind of campaign, including KICs. The offer of symbolic rewards, such as public acknowledgment of the donor, is positively associated with the amount of capital raised for a project and its subsequent success, but only when no material rewards are offered, as shown by [22] in a sample of 875 successful theater projects financed through Kickstarter in 2011. [23] analyzed 100 creative Kickstarter projects in the film and video category and concluded that pitch quality, updates, and network management are critical to the success of crowdfunding campaigns. Despite the widespread belief that crowdfunding lessens the chilling effect of distance between donors and entrepreneurs, [24] find the opposite to be true when looking at the propensity of donors to back music production projects on the Brazilian crowdfunding platform Catarse. By analyzing 447 video game crowdfunding campaigns, [25] concludes that human capital in the form of prior professional experience, location, media choice, and media intensity (as measured by the number of images, videos, and graphics included in the campaign) all contribute to the success of the campaigns. In a similar vein, [26] discovered that the success of the film, video, and publishing ventures is influenced by elements external to the initiatives themselves. Funder investment choices for creative initiatives are positively impacted by project quality signals recorded by campaign text length and the propagation of e-word of mouth in the form of "likes," comments, and shares, according to another research by [27]. According to Lin and Phillips's [28] research on crowdfunding for art projects in the United Kingdom, campaigns are more likely to succeed when they feature a clear and transparent video disclosing the project's content and uniqueness, as well as when they have a reasonable funding goal and are located close to the artists. According to [29], when discussing equity-based crowdfunding, the success rate of campaigns in the Italian market is favorably correlated with intellectual capital and strongly correlated with the number of connections the platforms have. According to research by [30], a company's adaptability is a key factor in the success of its equity crowdfunding campaign. As shown by [31], knowledge management encourages equity investment in knowledge-driven business model innovation. According to [32], a large number of supporters who contribute many times to a project is one of the most crucial criteria for the success of campaigns on the Polish music equity crowdfunding site MegaTotal. A project's success may depend on the creator's willingness to keep in touch with possible funders and provide incentives to collaborators (Figure 10.1).

The global community is now facing unseen threats due to the COVID epidemic. Within a couple of weeks, the activities and earnings of creative individuals and entrepreneurs, cultural businesses, and organizations plummeted. The ambiguity and persistence of the epidemic made a bad situation much worse.

A poll found that 52 percent of creative industries saw an 80 percent or more drop in revenue during the first few months of the epidemic [33]. This has significantly impacted their workforce, particularly the most vulnerable segments of the workforce, such as freelancers and the informal economy. Roughly 80 percent of independent contractors saw their pay drop. That's money they won't have for necessities like food, rent, healthcare, or an emergency. The worst hit were those who worked in industries dependent on the public's attention, such as the arts and crafts industry. Meanwhile, the effect was less severe on those who work in fields that are already heavily reliant on digital tools, such as architecture and design.

## 10.3.2 Crowdsourced Mapping

Travelers who seek out cultural experiences have gotten increasingly discerning in recent decades. They need to engage more deeply with the local culture via artistic endeavors. As a result, established tourist hotspots, mostly smaller urban centers and rural locations, need to improve their marketing, boost the value of their tourism resources, and develop new offerings to attract more tourists. Innovation in the travel industry has a lot to thank tourists for. The goal of this emerging field of travel is to make locations more appealing by facilitating tourist participation in original, one-of-a-kind experiences. As a result of this tourism strategy, cultural and creative institutions will be responsible for developing, enhancing, and promoting existing tourist resources and destinations.

Experts often use specialized equipment to record historic builds in emerging national gathering, and excellent data quality in terms of geometric precision and completeness has made laser scanners standard equipment for such jobs [4]. However, it works well for localized documentation but not at a national or even city level. In addition, high-end laser scanners are often pricey and may not be hired for large-scale projects. Advantages of image-based historical recording over laser scanning include its mobility, cheap cost, photorealism, and ubiquity [34]. The quality of photogrammetric models is sufficient for documentation purposes, including geometric extraction, thanks to recent advancements in photogrammetric 3D reconstruction, such as structure from motion and dense image matching. As a result, it is crucial that emerging nations have access to low-cost photogrammetry for historical recording.

The process of cultural mapping may be used to plan out creative tourism projects. Cultural mapping can be broken down into two distinct categories: (a) asset mapping, which uses GIS to document the locations and identities of physical and cultural artifacts; and (b) community identity mapping, which uses the knowledge and experiences of residents to uncover hidden treasures of intangible cultural artifacts. Planning, community awareness, and the growth of the cultural sector may all benefit from this method, as can the communication skills of people [34]. Future decision-making, scenario building, and planning are all aspects of informing innovation planning. Raising public awareness helps in advertising and promoting these features to locals and tourists alike. Lastly, expanding the cultural sector improves communication and cooperation between diverse cultural entities.

There are primarily two methods used in the cultural mapping. In contrast to the top-down paradigm (in which specialists lead the way), the bottom-up paradigm is driven by the input of the general public (bottom-up). A collection of distinguishing features distinguishes the scientific reduction method based on quantitative indicators from the qualitative criteria associated with the social sciences, which is the paradigm at issue here. Experts in the top-down method utilize indicators to quantify the many facets of reality being studied, but stakeholder concerns are often ignored. Efficiency, effectiveness, and instrumentality are its motivating factors. Various research in this domain is shown in Figure 10.2.

The bottom-up strategy is grounded in a participatory philosophy that emphasizes many of the same features that define the bottom-up method, including the significance of knowing the local context when determining objectives and priorities. Bottom-up techniques are more decentralized and concentrate on addressing the unique needs of local populations and examining the consequences of policy initiatives on these concerns, whereas management-led, top-down approaches are more concerned with enhancing production efficiency. Bottom-up methods

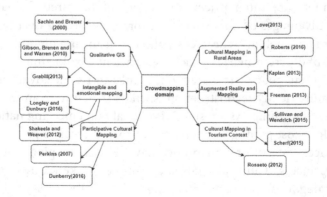

**FIGURE 10.2**
Research in the crowd mapping domain [35].

focus on processes, outcomes, and implications across several industries. The goals of self-determination and public engagement are central to its guiding principles. The increasing popularity of social computing is having an impact on both the supply and demand of vacation destinations.

In this context, mapping serves as an effective method for the neighborhood to guarantee its long-term viability. However, politicians tend to disregard bottom-up methods since their findings are typically at odds with the prevailing macro-level paradigms and development paradigms. However, top-down techniques may generalize from a collection of indicators and capture wider aspects of the territory's reality, whereas bottom-up approaches have more trouble mapping settings overall and tend to concentrate on the local level.

Researchers have made use of maps to investigate such questions as where a story takes place geographically, how an author was inspired by their surroundings, and whether or not the story itself "blocked" certain landscapes. You can use the maps for more than just figuring out where things are on the ground; you can also use them to make tales. Many authors and filmmakers have examined the potential of story maps [36]. Movies and books often include "interior maps" [37] to assist their audiences in visualizing key locations and better following the action. Journalists, academics, and activists have all taken use of the argumentative potential of maps by using them as a narrative tool in their reporting and activism. That is to say, there is a practically infinite amount of information and tales hidden inside maps [37].

Two vantage points are used to create the cartographic image. In the first, tales' spatial patterns are represented by maps, and the accompanying cartographic projects are then utilized to pinpoint the whereabouts of story components across genres and settings (fictional or factual). We also map a sad occurrence with profound emotional elements and discuss the mapping of indigenous oral legends and fictional locations from literature. The second view emphasizes the role the map plays in the story. Photos taken at specific locations throughout the world accompany this story. The community has to be mapped so that the usefulness of the storytelling applications can be recognized and the mapping process as a whole can be enhanced. Recent developments in geo-crowdsourcing have elevated the study of collaborative GIS to the forefront of academic interest. We were able to create a more nuanced profile of the creative tourist thanks to the fact that we knew events catering to this genre of tourism (unlike mass tourism) often attract smaller groups

**FIGURE 10.3**
Crowdsourced mapping tool [35].

of people. Twelve photos were posted to the Encontrarte Amares website as part of our crowdsourced investigation, as shown in Figure 10.3.

### 10.3.3 Citizen Science

The concept of "citizen science" is gaining ground as a way for individuals to participate in scientific endeavors without having received formal training in the field. The proliferation of mobile devices and the rise of social media have created ideal conditions for creative new approaches to enlist the help of huge numbers of amateur researchers. Nevertheless, it's worth noting that citizen science is not a recent phenomenon; rather, it flourished throughout the 19th century.

To fill in the gaps in our understanding of ancient earth-building methods and to get insight into the local architectural history for future sustainable usage, citizen science may prove to be an effective method. Rapid technological advancements in recent years have paved the way for a new profession called "Citizen Science," which encourages and equips ordinary people to take part in scientific operations. Web services, applications, and mobile devices are not essential to the practice of citizen science; rather, they are tools that help facilitate teamwork and data collection. The latest smartphones and tablets have GPS, compass, gyroscope, and camera, allowing for capturing precise location-based environmental data. The data is entered by the participants using simple survey forms, and the participants' access to the internet enables prompt transmission to the project database and the seamless integration of data from other contributors. The design and usability of a successful app must be tailored to its intended audience, and a transparent framework must be established for the ethical and legal considerations of data collecting.

What sets citizen science apart from other types of research is the need for initiatives to be attractive to the community on both an intellectual and a practical level. In the process of developing a crowdsourcing project, community scoping is crucial. Researchers need to begin by deciding who to consult in order to collect the necessary data.

Analyzing relatively simple image data, such as pictures, allows for efficient long-term monitoring of physical change. In popular cultural heritage sites, tourist pictures are a significant data source. The second question that needs to be answered is what are the key considerations in planning crowdsourcing data collection once it has been established that there is potential for a citizen science project given (1) the adequacy of the task and (2) the existence/availability of a relevant and interested community.

The chapter presents a comprehensive list of considerations, such as how to mobilize participation, collect photograph settings and metadata, ensure the entire site is covered, and not just the popular areas, and create privacy policies and image processing approaches of people featured in photographs. The conversation underscored the intricacy of the undertaking.

From a technical standpoint, a crucial stage that has to be adequately planned and scoped before the project starts is arranging end-user access to the provided data. Budgeting and planning for data storage should begin at the outset of a project, taking into account the likely length of the project and the data's potential usefulness. Careful attention should also be given to how data is transferred from collectors to users; although social media may seem easy to channel user interest, most of these platforms compress photos and remove their information, making them potentially worthless for the study in question. Finally, the point of view of the contributors should be taken into account. How detailed the data need to be and how it will be presented to participants are two concerns that must be answered when defining the needs of the photos that are gathered for a project.

Crowdsourcing may also be useful in research that involves the processing of vast volumes of data, where that processing needs a degree of human validation, such as in the digitalization of hand-written manuscripts. Workshop participants contributed to defining the major concerns to address in a data tagging project tied to the processing of personal diaries and letters. Again, a wide variety of obstacles was considered, from the readability of the texts to ethical considerations deriving from the contents or authenticity concerns.

Once again, the eventual purpose of the digital documents has to be fully understood while organizing the crowdsourcing data tagging process. Enhancing data and making it searchable are two crucial features. To this goal, keywords might be considered as part of the participatory process. Researchers may aid themselves by employing platforms created for citizen research, like Zooniverse, that provide options for boosting searchability. However, technological competence is needed to make sense of the data generated by these systems.

The requirements for participant abilities and degree of participation are different for the two case studies presented in this chapter. While it is possible to arrive at a straightforward method of involvement in a data-gathering project, participants in a data tagging activity may need to make more substantial contributions, which may include training and input validation. Due to these distinctions, community involvement must be approached differently, and additional non-technical problems must be met.

Involving members of the community in heritage science projects is a fun and efficient approach to teaching people about the importance of preserving and managing historic assets. The chance to take part in scientific study and have a direct impact on the preservation of a cultural resource is generally the driving force behind people signing up to help.

Researchers should see community engagement as a two-way street, with both parties obligated to provide and receive frequent input and account for how their involvement has benefited the study. This not only complies with ethical ideals, but it also has the potential to keep people interested in the project all the way through.

## 10.3.4 Crowdsourced Translation

A crowd-generated translation is the result of a group of people pooling their resources to convert a text, such as a historical record or a folk narrative, into a number of other languages. For the most part, this is done using an online platform that lets contributors submit translations, work together on edits, and then vote on the final version.

The crowdsourced translation is useful because it produces more reliable and genuine accounts of cultural traditions. The translator's cultural assumptions and ignorance of the context may easily creep into a literal translation. On the other hand, crowd-generated translation encourages a wide range of people to work together to produce a translation that is accurate to the source text.

Increased access to cultural material is another advantage of community-based translation. With the aid of volunteers, texts may be translated into several languages, making them accessible to a larger audience. As a result, this may be especially useful for spreading awareness about and knowledge of marginalized communities, which can help to protect their languages and traditions.

Finally, crowd-based translation is an opportunity to get people involved and excited about preserving cultural traditions. The crowd-based translation may instill a feeling of pride and responsibility in the preservation of cultural heritage by enabling everyone to contribute their own knowledge and talents.

The digital cultural legacy of Europe is made available via the Europeana platform [38]. Currently, it is home to over 58 million digitized artifacts from over 3,500 museums, libraries, archives, and galleries throughout all EU member states. Metadata fields provide crucial information about an item, including its title, free-text description, inventor, etc., and enable users to find and learn more about the things of their interest. Most records only include words in one language for now, and that's the language of the data suppliers. Europeana's ambition to provide cross-lingual access to its collection is hampered by the absence of multilingual metadata. Metadata records from the Europeana platform that have been translated into parallel languages serve as the primary source of training data. When there is not enough bilingual data, we will utilize monolingual data to specialize the models by creating synthetic data. Europeana's multilingual vocabularies utilized for semantic enrichment in the domain are leveraged alongside the training data corresponding to metadata records to facilitate domain adaption of the translation engines. If used properly, Europeana Translate might greatly enhance goods' existing multilingualism. The project is based on a well-defined architecture, and it has looked at the raw data that may be used for in-domain training. Experiments conducted thus far show an increase in accuracy when translating French metadata into English, as compared to results obtained using generic models. There are still a number of obstacles to overcome, including the need to collect more training data for underrepresented languages and implement suitable assessment methodologies.

## 10.3.5 Crowdsourced Archiving

Information, artifacts, and other resources relevant to a culture or community may be collected, preserved, and made available via a method called "crowd-generated archiving." An online platform is generally used to ease this process since it enables people to upload data, cooperate on categorization and annotation, and ultimately vote on the archive's final edition.

Among the many advantages of crowdsourced archiving is the improved accuracy and completeness of cultural heritage representations. Sometimes the archivist's own cultural prejudices or inability to grasp the context might creep into the preservation process while using traditional archival methods. Alternatively, crowd-based archiving encourages a wide range of people to work together to preserve an archive that is accurate to its original setting.

The increased availability of historical records is another perk of crowdsourced archiving. Archives may be made available online to a broader audience with the support of a community of persons. As a result, this may be especially useful for spreading awareness about and knowledge of marginalized communities, which can help to protect their languages and traditions.

In addition, crowd-generated archiving may motivate people to become involved in the process of preserving cultural artifacts. Crowd-generated archiving may inspire people to care about the preservation of cultural history by enabling them to contribute their own knowledge, memories, and artifacts. As a result, a community may have a hand in shaping the story spoken about and the images depicting their own cultural history, which is significant for purposes of both identity and self-determination.

A significant portion of urbanites' intangible cultural legacy consists of the sounds they hear on a daily basis. Cultural memory, which stores feelings and ideas about one's own people, relies heavily on auditory cues as well. We need to record the sounds of cities and cultures on a regular basis if we are to preserve their significance. Urban life is changing so quickly that if sounds aren't maintained or adapted, they will be lost. To that end, we've opted for the tried-and-true strategy of archiving our audio records for future generations to enjoy. The preservation of our musical history depends on the recording and archiving efforts. However, the sounds of cities and cultures are recognized as intangible cultural heritage. As society evolves at a quick pace, so do the customs that people practice on a regular basis. Therefore, it's essential to preserve urban acoustic legacy by making sure it continues to be used in modern society [39]. The reason is that once a culture stops upholding a particular custom, it fades away from everyday life. To reintroduce it would be difficult, and protecting a long-lost custom would be pointless [39]. To prevent the irretrievable loss of these one-of-a-kind sounds, an online archive was set up. An online crowdsourced sound archive was developed in the same vein as several previous sound archive examples [40]. While the project's primary outcome is an auditory database of the city's soundscape for the preservation of symbolic and cultural sounds, it also raises people's consciousness of urban sounds, provides a scalable process of collecting urban sounds for the preservation of sonic heritage in a crowdsourced manner, and crafts an interface design to present the archive.

## 10.4 CHALLENGES

While crowdsourcing has the potential to be a game changer for revitalizing cultural traditions, it also presents certain limitations that must be overcome.

Verifying the reliability of the data gathered via crowdsourcing is a significant obstacle to this method's use. However, not everyone who contributes to a crowdsourced project will necessarily have the requisite skills or experience to provide reliable data. Inaccuracies and mistakes, in the end, the output might cast doubt on the authenticity of the cultural artifacts being maintained in this way. There has to be a well-defined procedure in place for examining and verifying participant submissions in order to overcome this obstacle.

Maintaining diversity and broad representation is another difficulty of crowdsourcing. A common criticism of crowdsourcing is that it often depends on an unrepresentative subset of the population. This has the potential to marginalize or silence specific groups or individuals. In order to find a solution to this problem, it is crucial to reach out to and include members of marginalized communities.

Additionally, there are ethical and legal considerations that must be made when crowdsourcing cultural assets. Some artifacts may be regarded sacrosanct and hence should not be preserved or shared with the general public, and copyright difficulties may also emerge. There must be an open and honest procedure for getting permission and resolving any potential legal or ethical issues.

By exposing a vast and diversified sample of spare parts (mechanical or conceptual) and encouraging inventive methods of recombining those components, a creative ecosystem may play a key role in realizing an open, linked, and intelligent cultural heritage in which consumers and suppliers are directly integrated. Here, we zero in on a few of the technical hurdles that must be overcome by cross-functional teams across the whole Digital Content Life Cycle if we're ever going to see a successful and effective implementation of crowdsourcing anywhere in that process.

There seems to be a lot of enthusiasm behind the use of Semantic Web approaches [41] and methodologies in Social Web apps [42] and other popular resources right now [43]. Facebook's usage of Open Graph to facilitate cross-application connections between users and content items; Google's semantic search and auto-completion, to name just two. In this piece, we go further into the difficulties of using such methods for crowdsourcing in the realm of cultural heritage.

Despite the proliferation of user-generated material on the Internet, much of it is still produced by a very small group of individuals. The vast bulk of user-generated material comes from only 1 percent of the remaining 10 percent of Internet users who do nothing except consume it. The poor quality of this material is another problem. The vast majority of these postings are spam or malicious software. Consequently, it looks to be a significant problem to motivate not just to participate but also to promote excellent contributions. In today's information-sharing world, when masses of people generate material through social media, collaborative platforms, and other types of crowdsourcing, the emergence of "information disorder" has become a serious problem [44]. Everyone with access to the Internet may create knowledge, and anybody can seem to be an expert on any given topic just by virtue of having a high profile online. In this research, we examine the chaos that might arise in knowledge and cultural heritage organizations like museums, libraries, and archives when visitors contribute material online (GLAM) [45].

Any misinformation, deception, or mal-information contributed by the crowd in the GLAM sector has the potential to inflame racial, ethnic, and political tensions. A person's sense of ethnicity, culture, and nationhood are often deeply intertwined with their interest in the GLAM arts and sciences. As a result, the goal of this study is to discover quality assurance procedures that may be used to avoid future issues. Our goal is to undertake case study research to determine the many forms of information disorder, the various stakeholders' roles, and the best ways to avoid or mitigate the disorder via the use of quality control systems. In the near future, we want to delve more into the prospects and obstacles that the GLAM sector faces in addressing the information chaos. Our in-depth case studies should help us learn more and improve the quality control system we've presented. We anticipate that the results of this study will help both scholars and practitioners better manage their crowdsourcing processes, leading to a deeper knowledge of the phenomena of crowdsourcing.

## 10.5 CONCLUSION

Preserving one's cultural legacy is crucial to every civilization since it is the only way to ensure the continuation of one's own distinct set of norms and practices. Cultural revival and preservation are becoming more challenging tasks as the globe becomes more globalized and linked. Crowdsourcing is one approach that might be used to solve this issue since it makes use of a community's collective intelligence to document and spread historical information. The various benefits of this approach make it a powerful strategy for revitalizing historical artifacts. While crowdsourcing is an effective method for revitalizing cultural traditions, it does present certain obstacles that must be overcome. There are a number of essential things to keep in mind, such as following the law and acting ethically. By overcoming these obstacles, crowdsourcing may be utilized to conserve and transmit cultural material in a form that is accessible to everyone, faithful to historical records, and respectful of local customs.

## REFERENCES

[1] M. Ridge, S. Blickhan, M. Ferriter, A. Mast, B. Brumfield, B. Wilkins, D. Cybulska, D. Burgher, J. Casey, K. Luther, et al., "The collective wisdom handbook: Perspectives on crowdsourcing in cultural heritage community review version," *The Collective Wisdom Handbook: Perspectives on Crowdsourcing in Cultural Heritage-Community Review Version*, 2021.

[2] S. Reinsone, "Searching for deeper meanings in cultural heritage crowdsourcing," *A History of Participation in Museums and Archives. Traversing Citizen Science and Citizen Humanities*, pp. 186–207, 2020.

[3] H. Barnes, "Kickstarting archives: Crowdfunding and outreach in the digital age," *Participatory Archives: Theory and Practice*, pp. 117–130, 2019.

[4] B. Hannewijk, F. L. Vinella, V.-J. Khan, I. Lykourentzou, K. Papangelis, and J. Masthoff, "Capturing the city's heritage on-the-go: Design requirements for mobile crowdsourced cultural heritage," *Sustainability*, vol. 12, no. 6, p. 2429, 2020.

[5] G. Mauroa and M. Ronza, "Cultural heritage and awareness: Differences between volunteered geographic information of openstreetmap and an official cartography. The case of caserta in South-Italy," *Abstracts of the ICA*, vol. 3, p. 199, 2021.

[6] V. Van Hyning, "Curating crowds: A review of crowdsourcing our cultural heritage (ashgate, 2014)," *DHQ: Digital Humanities Quarterly*, vol. 13, no. 1, 2019.

[7] Y. Gil and V. Ratnakar, "Knowledge capture in the wild: A perspective from semantic wiki communities," in *Proceedings of the Seventh International Conference on Knowledge Capture*, pp. 49–56, 2013.

[8] V. Petras, T. Hill, J. Stiller, and M. G"ade, "Europeana – A search engine for digitised cultural heritage material," *Datenbank-Spektrum*, vol. 17, no. 1, pp. 41–46, 2017.

[9] D. Steinberg, "The kickstarter handbook," *Real-Life Crowdfunding Success Stories*, 2012.

[10] N. J. Klein, M. Tran, and S. Riley, ""Desperately need a car": Analyzing crowdfunding campaigns for car purchases and repairs on gofundme.com," *Travel Behaviour and Society*, vol. 21, pp. 247–256, 2020.

[11] M. Castelluccio, "Opening the crowdfunding release valves," *Strategic Finance*, vol. 93, no. 2, pp. 59–61, 2012.

[12] D. Oughton, L. Mortara, and T. Minshall, "Managing asymmetric relationships in open innovation: Lessons from multinational companies and SMEs," in *Open Innovation in the Food and Beverage Industry*, pp. 276–293, Elsevier, 2013.

[13] A. S. Bal, K. Weidner, R. Hanna, and A. J. Mills, "Crowdsourcing and brand control," *Business Horizons*, vol. 60, no. 2, pp. 219–228, 2017.

[14] R. A. Gibbs, "The human genome project changed everything," *Nature Reviews Genetics*, vol. 21, no. 10, pp. 575–576, 2020.

[15] M. Hossain and K. Z. Islam, "Generating ideas on online platforms: A case study of 'my starbucks idea,'" *Arab Economic and Business Journal*, vol. 10, no. 2, pp. 102–111, 2015.

[16] E. Lazzaro and D. Noonan, "A comparative analysis of US and EU regulatory frameworks of crowdfunding for the cultural and creative industries," *International Journal of Cultural Policy*, vol. 27, no. 5, pp. 590–606, 2021.

[17] A. Rykkja, Z. H. Munim, and L. Bonet, "Varieties of cultural crowdfunding: The relationship between cultural production types and platform choice," *Baltic Journal of Management*, vol. 15, no. 2, pp. 261–280, 2020.

[18] J. Tosatto, J. Cox, and T. Nguyen, "An overview of crowdfunding in the creative and cultural industries," *Handbook of Research on Crowdfunding*, pp. 269–302, 2019.

[19] J. Tosatto, J. Cox, and T. Nguyen, "With a little help from my friends: The role of online creator-fan communication channels in the success of creative crowdfunding campaigns," *Computers in Human Behavior*, vol. 127, p. 107005, 2022.

[20] E. Mollick, "The dynamics of crowdfunding: An exploratory study," *Journal of Business Venturing*, vol. 29, no. 1, pp. 1–16, 2014.

[21] V. Kuppuswamy and B. L. Bayus, "Crowdfunding creative ideas: The dynamics of project backers," in *The Economics of Crowdfunding*, pp. 151– 182, Springer, 2018.

[22] A. Hoegen, D. M. Steininger, and D. Veit, "How do investors decide? An interdisciplinary review of decision-making in crowdfunding," *Electronic Markets*, vol. 28, no. 3, pp. 339–365, 2018.

[23] J. Hobbs, G. Grigore, and M. Molesworth, "Success in the management of crowdfunding projects in the creative industries," *Internet Research*, 2016.

[24] W. Mendes-Da-Silva, L. Rossoni, B. S. Conte, C. C. Gattaz, and E. R. Francisco, "The impacts of fundraising periods and geographic distance on financing music production via crowdfunding in Brazil," *Journal of Cultural Economics*, vol. 40, no. 1, pp. 75–99, 2016.

[25] J. Cha, "Crowdfunding for video games: Factors that influence the success of and capital pledged for campaigns," *International Journal on Media Management*, vol. 19, no. 3, pp. 240–259, 2017.

[26] Z. Bao and T. Huang, "External supports in reward-based crowdfunding campaigns: A comparative study focused on cultural and creative projects," *Online Information Review*, 2017.

[27] S. Bi, Z. Liu, and K. Usman, "The influence of online information on investing decisions of reward-based crowdfunding," *Journal of Business Research*, vol. 71, pp. 10–18, 2017.

[28] K. Alexiou, J. Wiggins, and S. B. Preece, "Crowdfunding acts as a funding substitute and a legitimate signal for nonprofit performing arts organizations," *Nonprofit and Voluntary Sector Quarterly*, vol. 49, no. 4, pp. 827– 848, 2020.

[29] D. Vrontis, M. Christofi, E. Battisti, and E. A. Graziano, "Intellectual capital, knowledge sharing and equity crowdfunding," *Journal of Intellectual Capital*, vol. 22, no. 1, pp. 95–121, 2020.

[30] N. Del Sarto and D. Magni, "How dynamic capabilities matter for the implementation of a successful equity crowdfunding campaign," in *Cybernetics and Systems*, pp. 96–100, Routledge, 2018.

[31] J. Zheng, H. Qiao, X. Zhu, and S. Wang, "Knowledge-driven business model innovation through the introduction of equity investment: Evidence from China's primary market," *Journal of Knowledge Management*, 2020.

[32] Y. Song, R. Berger, A. Yosipof, and B. R. Barnes, "Mining and investigating the factors influencing crowdfunding success," *Technological Forecasting and Social Change*, vol. 148, p. 119723, 2019.

[33] V. Burke, D. Jørgensen, and F. A. Jørgensen, "Museums at home: Digital initiatives in response to Covid-19," *Norsk Museumstidsskrift*, vol. 6, no. 2, pp. 117–123, 2020.

[34] H. K. Dhonju, W. Xiao, J. P. Mills, and V. Sarhosis, "Share our cultural heritage (SOCH): Worldwide 3D heritage reconstruction and visualization via web and mobile GIS," *ISPRS International Journal of Geo-Information*, vol. 7, no. 9, p. 360, 2018.

[35] R. Magnussen and A. G. Stensgaard, "Knowledge collaboration between professionals and non-professionals: A systematic mapping review of citizen science, crowd sourcing and community-driven research," in *13th International Conference on Game Based Learning, ECGBL 2019. Academic Conferences and Publishing International*, pp. 470–477, 2019.

[36] M. A. Brovelli, P. Hogan, M. Minghini, G. Zamboni, et al., "The power of virtual globes for valorising cultural heritage and enabling sustainable tourism: NASA world wind applications," *International Archives of the Photogrammetry, Remote Sensing and Spatial Information Sciences*, vol. 4, p. W2, 2013.

[37] I. Havinga, P. W. Bogaart, L. Hein, and D. Tuia, "Defining and spatially modelling cultural ecosystem services using crowdsourced data," *Ecosystem Services*, vol. 43, p. 101091, 2020.

[38] D. Nicholas and D. Clark, "Information seeking behaviour and usage on a multimedia platform: Case study Europeana," in *Library and Information Sciences*, pp. 57–78, Springer, Berlin, Heidelberg, 2014.

[39] E. Johnson and C. L. Liew, "Engagement-oriented design: A study of New Zealand public cultural heritage institutions crowdsourcing platforms," *Online Information Review*, vol. 44, no. 4, pp. 887–912, 2020.

[40] K. Hansson and A. N. Dahlgren, "Crowdsourcing historical photographs: Autonomy and control at the Copenhagen city archives," *Computer Supported Cooperative Work (CSCW)*, vol. 31, no. 1, pp. 1–32, 2022.

[41] B. P. Bhuyan, R. Tomar, and A. R. Cherif, "A systematic review of knowledge representation techniques in smart agriculture (urban)," *Sustainability*, vol. 14, no. 22, p. 15249, 2022.

[42] B. P. Bhuyan, R. Tomar, and A. Ramdane-Cherif, "Formal concept analysis and its validity in power reliability engineering,"

[43] I. Nishanbaev, E. Champion, and D. A. McMeekin, "A survey of geospatial semantic web for cultural heritage," *Heritage*, vol. 2, no. 2, pp. 1471–1498, 2019.

[44] S. Qutab, M. D. Myers, and L. Gardner, "Information disorder in the glam sector: The challenges of crowd sourced contributions," in *27th European Conference on Information Systems (ECIS)*, Stockholm & Uppsala, Sweden, June, pp. 8–14, 2019.

[45] T. G. Kumar, "Preserving the distributed fragments of cultural heritage: Need for building a sustainable information system in India," *Preservation, Digital Technology & Culture*, vol. 51, no. 2, pp. 51–61, 2022.

# 11

# *Ethical Issues in Crowdsourcing*

*Bikram Pratim Bhuyan[1,2] and Thipendra P. Singh[3]*
[1]School of Computer Science, University of Petroleum and Energy Studies (UPES), Dehradun, India
[2]LISV Laboratory, University of Paris Saclay, Velizy, France
[3]School of Computer Science Engineering & Technology, Bennet University, Greater Noida, NCR, India

## 11.1 INTRODUCTION

One of the most astounding things to emerge from the so-called Web 2.0 [1] period is not the tools themselves, but rather the manner in which new media technologies have reconfigured the interactions that we have with one another and with institutions. This is one of the most amazing things that has come out of this period. Even though the Internet has always been a hub for participatory culture, it wasn't until the early 2000s that businesses became more interested in harnessing the knowledge of online communities to advance not only their own interests but also the interests of their customers and the public at large [2]. This trend continued throughout the rest of the decade. The transformative potential of online communities is frequently interwoven into the day-to-day operations of corporations, nonprofit organizations, and government agencies. In fact, a number of firms have been founded entirely on the basis of these kinds of arrangements. The practice of combining a top-down organizational goal with a bottom-up, open creative process is referred to as "crowdsourcing" [3].

The term "crowdsourcing" was first used by contributing editor Jeff Howe, as stated in the article "The Rise of Crowdsourcing," [4] which was included in the issue of *Wired* magazine released in June of 2006. Around the same time, he started publishing "Crowdsourcing: Tracking the Rise of the Amateur" on a blog that was separate from the first. This

DOI: 10.1201/9781003346326-11

article and following blog postings by Howe set the foundations for a new organizational structure, which expanded on James Surowiecki's book *The Wisdom of Crowds* [5] and other publications. The new organizational structure was built on the foundation laid by this essay. Several businesses have been successful in outsourcing jobs that were once completed by in-house employees after making a public call for help in Internet discussion groups. The concepts of "outsourcing" and "a large number of individuals working on a project online" were combined to form the concept that led to the creation of the phrase "crowdsourcing." Both in the article and on his blog, Howe presented a number of concrete illustrations of the phenomenon of crowdsourcing. Four of the earliest instances of the crowdsourcing paradigm being utilized in academic research can be found on the websites Threadless.com, InnoCentive.com, Amazon's Mechanical Turk, and iStockphoto.com [6].

The purpose of this research is to first provide an explanation and analysis of the ethical problems that are brought up by crowdsourcing methodologies, and then present normative-ethical solutions for addressing existing concerns as well as ones that may arise in the future (normative considerations). The following is a selection of the more specific inquiries that we would want to look into: Concerns of a moral nature have been voiced in relation to crowdsourcing. What exactly are these concerns? Are new ethical standards being developed, or do new issues keep cropping up that need the establishment of new ethical norms? In addition, in what ways might guidelines for the ethical operation of projects including crowdsourcing be established?

The chapter is organized in such a way that we discuss the background behind crowdsourcing in the next section. The coming of age of the domain is looked upon, followed by the issues in crowdsourcing. Then the article takes a deep dive into the ethical issues, with a focus on the philosophical and domains where crowdsourcing is used. Proper discussions are made and finally we conclude the article with some future comments.

## 11.2 BACKGROUND BEHIND CROWDSOURCING

The history of crowdsourcing is one of combined efforts, the collection of information, the making of communal decisions, and new thinking.

It's a new way of conducting business, but it's also a phenomenon in which, given the right conditions, teams can outperform individuals, outsiders can shed new light on internal issues, and people from different parts of the world can collaborate to create policies and designs that are acceptable to most people.

The first attempts by scholars to offer a formal definition of crowdsourcing in the literature that has been evaluated by peers were made in the year 2008 [7]. The academic explanations of crowdsourcing vary greatly depending on whether the focus is on the participants and their motivations, the technologies that are utilized, the common organizational aspects that are shared by several examples, the degree of difficulty of the task at hand, or the amount of user input that is required. The many attempts that have been made to define crowdsourcing have led to a diversity of definitions for the phenomenon as well as different points of view on what constitutes crowdsourcing and what does not qualify as crowdsourcing.

In 2012, Enrique Estell´es-Arolas and Fernando Gonz´alez-Ladr´onde-Guevara worked together for the *Journal of Information Science* to undertake a study of the scientific literature on crowdsourcing [8]. They discovered that crowdsourcing could be interpreted in roughly 40 distinct ways, with some academics employing meanings of the word that were different from one another and even contradictory within their own studies. After conducting an in-depth study of these several definitions and ensuring that they were accurate, the researchers came up with the following all-encompassing definition for crowdsourcing: "To participate in crowdsourcing, a person, organization, or company must first put out a public appeal to a wide number of individuals who come from a variety of skill sets and backgrounds and are prepared to work on a project without being paid for their time. When members of the audience contribute their time, energy, resources, and experience toward completing a work, everyone comes out ahead, regardless of how complicated or modular the task may be. The user will receive the satisfaction of a certain type of need, whether it be financial, social recognition, self-esteem, or the development of individual skills, while the crowdsourcer will gain and benefit from the contribution that the user makes to the venture, the form of which will depend on the type of activity that is undertaken." Let us observe some cases often misinterpreted as crowdsourcing.

To begin, open-source manufacturing and crowdsourcing are not interchangeable terms in any way. Open-source production is a concept in which members of a self-governing community collaborate to generate a shared resource on their own terms and in their own format. This approach is referred to by the phrase" open-source production." When someone discovers a means by which the common resource might be improved, they contribute their contribution back to the commons without anticipating receiving anything in exchange for it. Examples of software projects that follow this strategy include Mozilla's Firefox web browser and other programs that make their source code readily available to the public. Fixes for bugs and security holes in the Firefox browser are freely provided by users of the Firefox browser. Users also supply add-ons, plug-ins, and new versions of Firefox whenever these things are required. When they are finished, the new code for Firefox is uploaded to a common repository, and the product that is created, therefore, is available for use by anybody. The Firefox community, like the communities around other open-source projects, is self-governing and follows its own set of rules and principles for the management of product versions [9].

Where exactly does crowdsourcing come into play here? The creation of open-source software is not the same as crowdsourcing since there is no established hierarchy to guide the process. It is generally understood that open-source projects take the form of decentralized, self-managed groups of software engineers working collaboratively toward a common goal. Even though large open-source projects have started using a more hierarchical, top-down management approach, the day-to-day operations of open-source production are regulated by the community rather than necessarily by the project or the project sponsor. This is because the community is comprised of people who are actively involved in the production of open-source software. Open-source production is conceptually distinct from "closed" production, the latter of which occurs when an organization maintains control over the design of the product and directs the activities of its employees and independent contractors toward its realization. The authority to control the production process as well as the product's design is given to the workforce when open-source manufacturing is used. In a conventional, hierarchical, and regulated process, the locus of control in the creative creation of commodities and ideas is located in the organization; however, in open-source production, the locus of control in the creative creation of commodities and ideas is located in the dispersed workforce.

Second, the idea of "commons-based peer production," which was suggested by legal scholar Yochai Benkler [10], is not applicable to crowdsourcing in any way. Wikipedia, an online encyclopedia, is a well-known example of peer production under a paradigm that is founded on the concept of commons. Wikipedia is not regarded to be crowdsourcing in the same way as open-source production is not considered to be crowdsourcing. This is due to the fact that there is no central authority that dictates which articles should be published or which subjects should be covered on Wikipedia. To this day, the growth of Wikipedia is solely the result of the contributions made by its community of users. On Wikipedia, users are encouraged to take risks and share what they've discovered with the community. Anyone who is interested in contributing to the construction of the encyclopedia has access to the available tools, which include a wiki that uses a simple markup language. In fact, Wikipedia does not aggressively encourage users to contribute new material to the website. This kind of activity is conceived by and coordinated by the community from the bottom up. The individuals who contribute to Wikipedia are the ones who ultimately have authority over the development of new concepts and products; not the Wikipedia organization as a whole.

For the next case, conventional voting and focus groups are significantly different from crowdsourcing in three crucial aspects [11]. To clarify, crowdsourcing does not cover straightforward activities like voting or expressing opinions. Pepsi decided to have an online vote to choose the next flavor of Mountain Dew, so they came up with the idea for a contest that they termed DEWmocracy. Pepsi offered customers a selection of flavors, and the one that garnered the most votes was chosen to be the company's flagship flavor. Campaigns such as this one are analogous to more traditional methods of market research such as focus groups and taste testing in the sense that they poll consumers and ask them to choose the option that best meets their requirements. Only today, as a result of the broad availability of the Internet, are activities of a similar kind being carried out on a scale that is far bigger. These promotional activities do not qualify as crowdsourcing since there is too much control from the top down and not enough creativity from the bottom up. This stands in contrast to open-source software and peer production that is based on commons. When organizations finally get around to asking for input, the range of possible outcomes has already been drastically narrowed down, and the only kind of feedback that can be considered valid is a straightforward rating or vote. If individuals were asked to suggest new flavors and vote on the one they liked best, this would be an example of crowdsourcing being put into practice. When companies participate in fundamental activities like voting or rating, however, there is no crowdsourcing taking place since these activities provide the public very little creative or decision-making capacity. In this scenario, the organization itself serves as the control hub for the inventive production of goods and ideas, rather than the consumers.

As a fourth and last point, crowdsourcing is not only an updated version of an earlier idea; rather, it is something more than that. Some print media outlets have criticized crowdsourcing on the grounds that it is not much different from traditional offline forms of collaboration, which have been around for decades, if not millennia. Some people believe that the construction of the Oxford English Dictionary in the 1800s was an early example of crowdsourcing [12]. The organizers of the dictionary put out a call for volunteers to provide lists of English phrases and examples of how those terms are used in order to compile the dictionary's index. The actual origin of what is now known as the Alkali Prize may be traced back to the 1700s. Nicolas Leblanc came forward to claim the award that King Louis XVI of France had promised for a better method of making alkali. Even if they don't quite match the standard definition of crowdsourcing, many of the greatest achievements in human history started with an open call for solutions to an urgent issue. Crowdsourcing is a relatively new phenomenon that is wholly reliant on the infrastructure of the internet. Although it may be founded on tried and proven principles about how to solve issues and collaborate, crowdsourcing is nevertheless a very new phenomenon.

Because of the Internet and other new media technologies that increase speed, reach, rich capabilities, and reduce barriers to entry, crowdsourcing is very different from more traditional forms of open problem-solving and collaborative creation. This is because crowd-sourcing capitalizes on the strengths of these technologies. In the same way that the characteristics of the Internet radically altered the business model, legal landscape, and cultural practices of the music industry from its roots in vinyl and cassette tapes, the Internet has accelerated the collaborative production processes and problem-solving into a completely new phenomenon called crowdsourcing. In spite of the widespread belief that all crowdsourcing entails working together with a huge number of people through the Internet, this is not the case. Not only did it not exist in any significant form before the development of the Internet, but it also does not take place in any meaningful fashion outside of the confines of the Internet.

This is neither a synonym for open innovation nor is it a new phrase for traditional marketing strategies or market research that have been adapted for use in the digital era. The term crowdsourcing, as it was originally used by Jeff Howe, has subsequently evolved, such as crowdsourcing, crowd-sourcing, and CrowdSourcing. Jeff Howe was the first person to use the term "crowdsourcing" [4].

## 11.3 CROWDSOURCING'S COMING OF AGE

The concept of crowdsourcing can only become a reality if certain technical and philosophical conditions are met. Applications that use crowdsourcing depend on the infrastructure that is supplied by the Internet and other new media technologies. These technologies, in turn, create particular attitudes and practices that contribute to the establishment of a culture that is more participative. Crowdsourcing may be interpreted in terms of group phenomena such as collective intelligence and the wisdom of crowds, in addition to the processes of problem solving and creation.

Of the numerous reasons, crowdsourcing can only exist in the digital sphere because the Internet makes it possible for a kind of creative thinking that is networked. According to Tiziana Terranova, the Internet is an appropriate technology for distributed thinking because it is "not only a specialized medium but a type of active execution of a design method suited to cope with the openness of systems" [13]. In other words, the Internet is "not only a specialized medium but a type of active execution of a design method suited to cope with the openness of systems." The ability of the Internet to transmit any and all types of mediated information, in addition to its speed, reach, temporal flexibility, anonymity, interactivity, low entry barriers, and ubiquitous accessibility, makes it an excellent medium for stimulating creative participation.

The Internet is an immediate communications platform where messages and, by extension, ideas may flow so rapidly via its channels that the medium almost eliminates the question of time and, as a result, speeds up the generation of new ideas. The Internet is a global network of interconnected computer systems that allows users to send and receive electronic messages over the world wide web. In addition to this, the Internet may really have a worldwide reach if people in all parts of the globe have access to the same technology. This enables people in different areas to communicate with one another in a rapid and simple manner. The global nature of the Internet has the effect of erasing not just the passage of time but also the distance that separates people physically. James W. Carey [14], a communication theorist, pondered the cultural alterations and social potential of time- and space-decoupled communications technologies. He observed that innovations such as the telegraph achieved this erasing and unified countries into one cultural vision. Carey's thoughts can be found in the following passage. When you combine the rapidity of the Internet with its asynchronicity, you are able to achieve a degree of temporal flexibility that would not be achievable in any other setting. The medium adjusts to the demands and uses of the unique user in an online collaborative project that is either synchronous (in "real time") or asynchronous (not in "real time"), bringing together a variety of speeds and usage patterns.

The asynchronous nature of the Internet provides a striking contrast to the instantaneous nature and widespread scope of the Internet. To put it another way, individuals are able to congregate their ideas and viewpoints in a single "location" in cyberspace via the use of online bulletin board systems and other tools of a similar kind. In spite of the fact that the speed of the Internet encourages users to be hasty in their online posts, asynchrony makes it possible for other users to engage those thoughts at a later time and give them meaningful attention. The leaving and taking of notes on a bulletin board in a town square is analogous to the feeling that can be provided by continuing discourse between members of a community via the Internet. However, unlike the former, the latter does not require all of the individuals to be present at the same time.

In addition, individuals have the ability to conceal their identity when they use the Internet. Users have a lot of discretion to shape their online profiles however they choose, including the option to remain completely anonymous if that is what they prefer. Avatars are graphical representations of people and their interests that may be created by participants in online chat rooms and message boards. Avatars can be found in online communities. It is essential for effective collaboration that individuals have the option of contributing their thoughts and ideas to an online commons while maintaining their anonymity. Studies of nonverbal communication have revealed that the allocation of power in a meeting or interaction may be "scripted" by characteristics such as participants' body language, physical placement, and casual chat. This is something that may happen in both formal and informal settings. Those who participate in online arguments or evaluate ideas do not have to worry about nonverbal politics or the power imbalances that come into play with physical manifestations of difference like race, gender, or (dis) ability. These factors are not taken into consideration. The anonymity that is provided by interactive aspects of the internet has the ability to liberate people from the constraints of identity politics and theatrical posturing. This liberation might occur as a result of the Internet. According to John Suler, the Internet gives users the ability to be "uninhibited" and forthright in their communication [15]. The Internet serves as a central location for the convergence of a wide variety of forms of media and interactive technology. In contrast to the straightforward information transmission method that is typical of conventional media (such as newspapers, radio, and television), the Internet encourages ongoing co-creation of new ideas. This is in contrast to the way that most policies are formulated. There is not just one way that information is created on the Internet; rather, it is a combination of top-down (content provided by politicians, businesses, and media organizations) and bottom-up (content provided by individual users) (content from the people). Some individuals are concerned that the Internet would socially isolate them from their neighbors and open the door for companies to exploit them financially. In addition, they fear that the Internet will make it easier for firms to target them. Individuals are learning how to broadcast their own ideas in this era of more content creation, as well as how to find hidden information and remix current ideas and material in unique ways. Internet users are likely to be resourceful thinkers who may develop original approaches to resolving issues that they encounter. Last but not least, the capacity of the Internet to encourage the expansion of crowdsourcing is perhaps the feature that is the most important. A greater number of individuals are now able to participate in activities that were previously beyond their reach because of the Internet. One of the ways in which the Internet has made communication easier is by eliminating the physical and temporal barriers that previously stood in the way of experiencing new things and meeting new people. However, on a deeper level, the Internet has reduced barriers to obtaining information, which has resulted in the exposure of previously hidden troves of expert knowledge and the expansion of the availability of resources that were previously inaccessible. The process of releasing a problem to be solved to an online community over the Internet is known as crowdsourcing. This kind of problem-solving approach enables a business to vastly improve the working environment and broaden the pool of people who can provide a solution. Organizations turn to crowdsourcing when they require assistance with a diverse array of issues, including the development of new products, the resolution of difficult scientific problems, the formation of consensus on contentious public policy issues, and the processing of enormous amounts of data utilizing human intelligence. Crowdsourcing is becoming more popular as a means for businesses to solve problems by drawing on the expertise of many diverse people. These individuals bring a variety of distinct viewpoints, resources, and approaches to the table that may be applied to the issue at hand. Christian Terwiesch and Yi Xu made the groundbreaking discovery that ideation problems are well suited for distribution to a community of problem solvers located all over the world [16]. As a consequence of this, issues that call for the generation of original thoughts and ideas are great candidates for debate by a large audience in the digital domain.

Over the course of the last several years, governments have become increasingly open to the concept of using the Internet as a tool for public involvement and governance [17].

## 11.4 ISSUES IN CROWDSOURCING

Many companies are turning to crowdsourcing in order to find solutions to difficult technical problems. Some of these companies engage in direct interactions with members of the public, while others have resorted to using intermediaries or so-called "expert networks" that provide crowdsourcing platforms as a paid service [18].

Put your problem out there and wait for the masses to come up with a solution; at least that's how crowdsourcing sounds when we read it in a chapter. However, many companies have discovered the hard way that efforts using crowdsourcing may be plagued with significant challenges and risks. Despite the fact that they have great expectations and objectives, the corporate team may end up being dissatisfied since, unfortunately, the expenses may frequently exceed the rewards.

When we use crowdsourcing, we are almost always going to be collaborating with a group of people you have never interacted with before. It is standard procedure to keep some components of a problem, the aims of our firm, or our technology under wraps in order to prevent a competitor from acquiring an unfair edge over us. Even if the participants sign a non-disclosure agreement, we can't be certain of their names, histories, or jobs since none of that information will be disclosed. Because a large, anonymous group can only be trusted with a limited amount of information, we might be forced to withhold important details that could otherwise assist in finding a solution to our problem. As a result, the quality and breadth of the suggestions that we receive will be diminished as a result of this.

The solutions would be much more on target, actionable, and valuable if we were able to create something that still harnesses the power of a crowd's diversity, but with better control over confidentiality, allowing us to enhance the disclosure of information in order to be able to arm them with important information.

Given that we are attempting to reach out to a group of people that we do not know very well, and in many cases, there are many of them, it becomes very challenging to communicate with all of these participants in a meaningful way, in order to assist them in achieving a deep understanding of the problem that they are to solve. Given that we are attempting to reach out to a group of people that we do not know very well, and given that there are many of them, it becomes very challenging. Unfortunately, if we don't know what the problem is, you won't be able to devise a solution to fix it.

No matter how effectively you craft our problem statement for crowdsourcing, the resultant debate will be mostly unidirectional, with you pushing information out to participants and them receiving it. This is true regardless of how well we write your problem statement.

This makes it possible for everyone working on a solution to our problem to make assumptions, which raises the possibility that the end output will be insufficient since it will exceed the parameters that were initially established for the problem. It's possible that, all things considered, this is a waste of resources. Having access to dozens, or even hundreds, of possible solutions to our problem may appear to be a fantastic idea at first glance. However, when considering IP management, this may lead to a major headache that the majority of us would rather avoid: a high risk of IP contamination. The intellectual property and legal teams are going to get worked up about this one. As a result, nearly every concept that comes our way is potentially an invention, and as a result, it contains information about the idea that needs to be kept secret. It is possible that we may be required to analyze hundreds of top-secret technologies, placing you in danger of having confidential information revealed to us. If we choose to use a particular solution, awarding that solution to you will give you ownership of the intellectual property associated with that solution. But what about the other solutions? This becomes very difficult to control very quickly unless the terms of your crowdsourcing campaign provide you with the rights to every idea that is submitted (which will appear unjust to participants who are not compensated for their ideas). What is required of companies is a paradigm that not only protects intellectual property but also makes it possible for participants' best ideas to be implemented.

When it is time to award our rights, we find out that the person who first submitted the answer works for a university. They didn't give it much attention at the time, and they didn't go through the substantial intellectual property policy document that their institution had, maybe because they didn't anticipate being picked and reimbursed for their work. An examination of the intellectual property agreement at the university indicates that the institution asserts title to all inventions by the submitter. This makes the transfer of the intellectual property to the business either difficult or impossible.

The events that unfold are disastrous. Everyone comes out on the losing end of this scenario: the supplier of the solution does not get paid, the company does not get the solution that it requested, and worst of all, the organization is unable to use the solution at all. The perfect solution is no longer a viable alternative as a result of pollution.

If the university's intellectual property policy had never been made public or discovered, the submitter would have signed the IP assignment and the company would have started using the solution in their multimillion-dollar product launch. However, if the policy had never been made public or found, the submitter would not have signed the IP assignment. Think about the possible legal disaster that might be in store for the company in the near future. This is an issue that is rather frequent in the academic environment, but it may also arise with organizations and people that have contracts that are legally enforceable. The reality is that there are real risks involved if we are unable to determine who we are collaborating with.

Apart from these issues, there are major ethical issues in various domains where crowdsourcing is used. These are discussed in the next section.

## 11.5 ETHICAL ISSUES IN CROWDSOURCING

Crowdsourcing initiatives have been referred to as "crowd exploitation" and "digital slavery" by those who are opposed to the practice [19]. It would seem that crowdsourcing is a straightforward approach to obtaining access to high-quality labor at a cheap cost [20]. Businesses that make use of crowdsourcing get the advantages of the labor of a large number of individuals, but they do not have to pay those individuals as much as they would in a more traditional place of employment. According to these critics, the growth of the public has destabilized the professional class. This, in turn, has undone the years of work put in by professional organizations to raise pay, safety, and professional standards. On the other hand, there is a sophisticated complexity to the issue of exploited labor in huge groups, which makes finding a solution challenging [21].

Ethical dilemmas include questions such as what is beneficial, equitable, or appropriate, and therefore, what should or should not be done. These questions are, by their very nature, more fundamental than operational questions such as how to increase productivity.

It might be useful to conceive of the different theoretical frameworks provided for studies of ethics and morality as fitting into one of two major groups [22]. These categories are naturalistic and deontological. Establishing broad moral principles to function as the foundation for other strategies, such as rules, actions, and assessments, is the first tactic included in this method. When it comes to the study of business ethics, the word "categorical imperatives" is a phrase that comes up rather often. Kantian ethics is a school of thought that bases its moral judgements on what it terms "categorical imperatives." The categorical imperative that "act solely according to that maxim wherein you may at the same time wish that it should become a universal rule without contradiction" is the one that is most frequently referenced among the various versions of Kant's categorical imperatives, which can be found in many different places throughout his works. Regulatory documents of religious origin, such as the Torah, as well as national constitutions, may provide an example of the universalist worldview (like the United States Constitution). This strategy often results in difficulties in real-world economic and social contexts due to the fact that people might have vastly diverse perspectives on even the most basic ethical and moral norms. Whose morals, ethical principles, or religious beliefs ought to be regarded as the norm, and who has the power to make such a determination? The promotion of the development of regional ethical standards is the focus of the second proposed approach. In this particular instance, generalizations are less important than details. The problem with this kind of particularism is that it makes matters of morality and ethics seem to be relative, flexible, and maybe even arbitrary. Who are we to pronounce judgment on someone else based only on the preferences that we have for ourselves?

It has been suggested that a "third technique" that may overcome the impasse would be to adopt an approach to ethical theory that is more deliberative and discursive. These strategies strive to bridge the gap between the universalist and particularistic viewpoints by focusing attention on the (democratic) process by which such norms are formed. In most circumstances, the formation of ethical standards requires consideration of both universal and particular causes. Among the several potential possibilities, the "Discourse Ethics Theory" put out by Habermas [23], the preeminent advocate of the second generation of critical theory, stands out as the most notable. In their investigation of the moral implications of crowdsourcing, the authors discovered that Habermasian discourse ethics was applicable not just from a theoretical but also from a practical standpoint. They agree that Habermas's works have the potential to assist academics in investigating the moral conundrums brought about by activities using cutting-edge information technology (IT), in particular in environments where a variety of different values and cultural norms coexist. The study of the ethics of crowdsourcing offers particular obstacles, and the meditation on the criticism and debates indicated above was helpful in recognizing some of those issues. Habermas's discourse ethics may be applied to the study of the ethics of crowdsourcing. Given the relative newness of crowdsourcing practices and their global scope, the authors suggest that it would be hard to establish an initial set of values that is readily applicable to and across the many types of crowdsourcing activities. The only other option available is for everyone to communicate with one another, make an effort to understand what the other person is thinking, and come to a consensus about a code of conduct for crowdsourcing. Because of this, the investigation of the moral implications of crowdsourcing activities can be aided by the use of an important theoretical framework such as Habermas's theory of discourse ethics.

This philosophical standpoint calls for the ethical issues of crowd-sourcing in some of the domains. One is in the field of education.

The emphasis in education in the 21st century has shifted from the role of the teacher to that of the student, and one of the central goals of this shift is to provide students with opportunities to "pursue, scrutinize, and exchange ideas about themselves, their perspectives, and the times we live in" [24]. This interactive mode of education brings together teachers in a way that encourages two-way communication between teachers and students as well as interaction among students on a many-to-many level.

Conversations, cooperation, and collaboration are all beneficial to learning, understanding, and the ability to communicate newly gained knowledge. Despite the fact that students in a group are only beginning to get acquainted with one another, it is possible for collaboration standards to be established. It is not required for employees to be familiar with one another in order for them to be socially compatible with one another, particularly in virtual communities.

The usefulness of approaches that rely on the participation of large groups of people in education goes much beyond the scope of traditional, hands-on training. When the outcomes are favorable, it inspires the students to work harder, and it pushes them to aim for a conclusion that is even better than what they have already accomplished. The efforts of the students are obviously visible in the final product. Students that have a strong dose of competitive drive are willing to challenge themselves to their breaking point in order to produce more and better work than their classmates. As a consequence of this, the modifications to the educational system seem to be positive.

Students are able to acquire their own knowledge, which is often accomplished via a sequence of experiences that include trial and error, by drawing on the intellect of the class as a whole. Additionally, they get assistance or supervision in their attempts to recognize and create. During the first lesson of the Duolingo program, for example, students are introduced to assisted recognition activities. During following classes, students practice help production by using a vocabulary bank that has been customized to their target language. The language teachers who are in charge of supporting the study of a single foreign language will be responsible for actively overseeing their students' progress in learning that language while using enetCollect [25]. Previously, they had merely provided their students with passive assistance. Because it enables students to actively create their own knowledge, which is a fundamental component of constructivism, crowdsourcing is sometimes cited as an example of a kind of social media–enhanced, supervised constructivism.

In addition to the pedagogical and technological constraints, there are also a number of ethical preconditions that need to be satisfied before a project may employ crowdsourcing effectively. Since the introduction of the social web, students' rights to privacy have come a long way, and as a result, today's educational institutions face significant difficulty in protecting their students' rights to privacy. The recognition by Walter of the following three factors—"(1) a completely unwarranted premise that social media activity is completely anonymous; (2) that the characteristics of the Internet at a meta-level are indeed completely inconsistent with confidentiality; and (3) that one's expectation of anonymity does not entail affluent correspondence by definition"—can be of great benefit to education.

The activities that students do when participating in crowd-based education are extremely public, unless the students choose to participate in the system anonymously or conceal the nature of their contributions. Students are more likely to share personal information and participate in honest conversations when they are aware that their identities will remain concealed. However, disguised or anonymous access may also encourage students to be dishonest and lead to discussions about personal concerns that are overly open and honest. Certain students may become the focus of harassment and bullying due to their incompetence or lack of skill in a certain area. Before enrolling in a crowd-based course, it is important for students to carefully read the privacy policy so they are aware of what information about themselves will be shared with the class as well as who will have access to that information. This will allow students to avoid the problems described above. Statements of information responsibility need to be legally required, and they ought to be included in this policy.

It is possible that the risks associated with the intentional promotion of hate speech, the transmission of fake news, and, last but not least, the emergence of varied dogmas or ideologies may be reduced if the right to free expression is simultaneously encouraged and rigorously supervised.

It has come to light that malicious actors are increasingly taking advantage of crowdsourcing platforms, including the following: non-eligible participants (those who lack the necessary qualifications to take part in certain microtasks), fast deceivers (those who supply ill-fitting responses), rule breakers (those who provide incomplete answers), smart deceivers (those who enter unrelated words while still complying with all instructions), and the so-called gold standard preys.

If students are expected to grade test items as part of crowd-based learning, it is essential that they have a solid understanding of the rating scales that will be applied to their performance. Responses in the form of short answers or essays that divulge private or sensitive information, make excessive use of the right to free speech, or are plagiarized need to be penalized in the grading system. There has to be a method to weed out the findings from those who could be malicious or are otherwise untrustworthy in some other manner. If the abuse of knowledge continues outside of a situation that does not include crowdsourcing learning, then it has to be sanctioned. The dissemination of inappropriate content should be automatically filtered or it should be erased as soon as it is discovered by teachers or system administrators in order to prevent any potential damage caused by it.

A crowd-oriented learning platform is intended to supplement traditional classroom learning as well as learning that takes place online. It makes it possible to complete unfinished exercises that are designed to speed up the process of learning a language, as well as play fundamental educational games. Learning a language via crowdsourcing emphasizes healthy competition, collaborative effort, and support for one another. The approach that the group employs for teaching and learning is based on interaction between members of the group who work together. The production and maintenance of high-quality content, connection with students and other contributors through a crowdsourcing platform, and evaluation of student work are some of the obligations that fall on the shoulders of educators who use a crowd-based methodology in the classroom. The majority of teachers just do not have the time to devote to duties as weighty and time-consuming as these. Many teachers already feel emotionally depleted, and they find the new setting in the school to be especially difficult. Their decision to engage in crowdsourcing education will become an additional problem as a consequence of their collaborators' "various purposes, attitudes, and opinions," as well as the much-increased participation that results from the demand for a quick response. Involving the educators who have the greatest passion for the new educational paradigm, who will then be supported by administrators with greater experience, is essential for the effective implementation of the new paradigm on a voluntary basis. Oh, that there were more instructors in the classrooms like that! Participants in crowd-based education programs need to be adults who have a high level of accountability and who are dedicated to continuing their education and working for social justice. They should also be able to expect a greater degree of engagement and the consequences of their actions in an environment that is exceptionally open and dynamic. This is because the setting will provide both challenges and opportunities.

Before the whole system is deployed to real students, the pilot knowledge material, problem generators, and questions for evaluating student responses and knowledge should be produced by a number of professionals. These experts are aware of the locations where they may get reliable data, and they can put that knowledge to use by producing reports that are precise. According to [26], the finest instructors are those who are also excellent role models, have quick access to an enormous amount of materials, and are skilled at using technology that is on the leading edge. It is vital to bring in outside professionals in order to make the required modifications in order to make the curriculum and the content accessible to kids who have difficulty learning.

Another essential component of crowd-oriented education is the continuous and ever-changing participation taking place inside the system. Teachers may benefit from sharing their expertise with one another and assisting one another with concerns such as pupils' incompetent or incorrect use of a supplementary professional blog or discussion forum.

Educators have a responsibility to be vigilant and to take action that is fast, equitable, and compelling in order to safeguard their students from users who are dishonest or malicious. It requires a high level of concentration, in addition to ability and expertise. Teachers also have the extra responsibility of acting as "live mentors" for their classes, making themselves accessible to assist students whenever they may have questions or want assistance. It is possible that, in order to assist educators in doing their duties in an efficient manner, a library of previously carried out mentoring sessions may be constructed.

Applications that promote crowdsourcing provide users the ability to tap into the collective brainpower of the masses in order to generate original ideas, solve problems by applying previously acquired information, and evaluate the quality of suggested solutions or items. The open innovation process may benefit from a more fluid development of information, which may be made possible via collaborative effort. This may also serve as the basis for the process. You need to have an understanding of what the individuals in a crowd know and what motivates them in order to connect with them.

Voting is often used as a method to determine the merit of collectively conceived ideas that have been generated by a group of individuals [27]. The conclusions drawn from polls and votes not only provide managers with a justification for the decisions they make but also lend an appearance of democracy and justice to the operations of the organization. However, if the best-rated ideas were chosen via a voting procedure that was susceptible to manipulation, then it is possible that they do not accurately represent the views of the general audience. Ethically speaking, corporations have a responsibility to make the evaluation criteria crystal transparent and abstain from trying to influence or stifle the outcomes for their own gain. There are a variety of different ways in which crowds may be employed as assessors. Participants can provide feedback on both the work that is currently being done and the ideas that have been offered by others. The community may vote on a contest entry to choose the winner, contribute financial support for a project, or " like" or "Digg" a newspiece, for example. It is an excellent method for getting a sense of the general public's viewpoint as well as the degree of interest that a community has in a certain subject. As a result, there should be no space for manipulation or meddling in the voting area, and as a result, appropriate preparation is required. It is essential that the objectives of the website as well as the support of the crowd's participants and owners be completely clear. The promise of a free and open forum, where users could submit articles and comments and allow other users to "digg" their favorites, was the primary selling point of Digg when it was originally introduced to the public. After the publication of codes for high-definition compact disc players that overrode regional disc encoding, disputes broke out between site owners, organization stakeholders with an interest in regulating disc usage, and crowd members. These parties all had vested interests in the regulation of disc usage. The postings pertaining to disc codes were removed because of organizational demands and fears about being sued; nevertheless, the site owners subsequently gave in to public pressure and republished the posts, emphasizing their commitment to preserving an accessible forum for free debate.

The process of crowdsourcing has the potential to lower the value of knowledge and make it more vulnerable to exploitation. If the participants are not appropriately recognized and paid, it is possible that the information and skills that they have obtained will be misused. The negative impact that crowdsourcing may have on a professional's reputation might be observed on a bigger scale if one takes into account the fact that anonymous online contributors may have a lower feeling of worth as a result of their efforts not being recognized. Businesses may be able to justify their use of crowdsourcing by saying that consumers would profit from "better" products. However, this justification is only valid to a certain degree. Nevertheless, this is a poor justification that in no way justifies undervaluing the work that people have done.

If you want to harness the power of the crowd for innovation, you'll need to urge members of the audience to think creatively about how to solve problems rather than stick to traditional solutions. The "creativity from the crowd" phenomenon may be encouraged via the use of crowdsourcing since it enables the synthesis of different perspectives within a collaborative endeavor. As the size of the online community continues to expand, more individuals will be exposed to the problem. This will increase the possibility that the issue will be observed from a variety of viewpoints and that knowledge from different disciplines will be used to resolve the issue. It could be difficult to award credit for ideas and recognize individual contributions while working in a style that is so fluid and collaborative. It's possible that various sorts of problem solvers will come up with answers that aren't at all like what the seeker had in mind. On the other hand, not every unique or imaginative suggestion that is submitted in response to a crowdsourcing challenge ends up being put into action. Invention is only possible with a well-oiled production and distribution machine, and sometimes even the most brilliant ideas from the community are unable to be made a reality due to manufacturing, technical, or marketing hurdles. Innovation is only possible with a well-oiled production and distribution machine. Because members of the audience may have invested a significant amount of effort into solutions that ultimately weren't chosen, an organization should think about how it will handle ideas that are ultimately rejected, particularly those that have made it to the shortlisting stage. In other words, an organization should think about how it will handle ideas that are ultimately rejected.

It's possible that firms and individuals may have to spend a lot of money on crowdsourcing. Businesses may be able to save costs by delegating organizational tasks to a large number of employees and customers. Some people believe that Procter & Gamble was able to enhance idea generation and save a significant amount of money by turning to the public for assistance with research and development concerns. Additionally, by using crowdsourcing throughout the product development process, flaws and advantages of previously existing goods or services may be immediately disclosed, thereby reducing the need for user surveys and other, more costly kinds of marketing. It lessens the likelihood of incurring financial loss as a result of investing in a notion that, in the end, is not put into practice by the organization since the business had no interest in using it. The crowdsourcing community should not be prioritized above the staff people who are providing input. The fact that Netflix offered a million dollar incentive for the creation of a movie recommendation engine via the use of crowdsourcing exemplifies the broad variety of financial rewards that are achievable with projects that are completed through crowdsourcing. One specialist went to crowdsourcing in order to get full-time work, and as a result, he was successful in selling more than 100 designs for a total of $22,000. This is a small payment for the many hours of labor, ingenuity, and insight that were provided. It is presumed that users are just participating for the sake of enjoyment and the prestige of having their ideas regarded when they are depicted as inexperienced, which reduces the amount of pressure that exists for them to pay market pricing. Many of the jobs that are listed on crowdsourcing platforms may be done with very little knowledge or talent, and the money can sometimes be very little for the work that is done (only a few cents per work).

It is necessary to take into account intellectual property and copyright, and all contributors need to be made aware of their legal status in reference to any potential recompense they may get. The entity that is responsible for paying for the information will, in the vast majority of instances, also be awarded ownership of any intellectual property that is developed as a direct consequence of the crowdsourcing process. On the other hand, some intellectual property may be safeguarded by licenses issued by Creative Commons (creativecommons.org), which limit access to the work in question to only those individuals who satisfy certain requirements. If intellectual property (IP) protection measures are founded on the implicit premise that business partners are just interested in their own financial benefit, they may hinder innovation even if they are intended to prevent dishonesty on the part of business partners.

## 11.6 DISCUSSION

Despite the countless studies showcasing crowdsourcing's advantages and benefits, users of it should be aware of the actual or imagined hazards and drawbacks that the technology poses when it comes to ethics. Assessing the problems that might arise from using crowdsourcing as the first step in making a decision on whether or not to do so is recommended. Concerns like this may be helped to be better understood by asking questions like "Could the usage of crowdsourcing have any negative effects on anyone?" Possible problems include employees having the impression that they are being neglected or being led to believe that the incentives are of greater value than they really are. If crowdsourcing is both legal and effective, are there any additional considerations to take into account? Is it the case, for instance, that contributions from specialized groups are relied upon without appropriate recompense being provided? People have the right to ponder the same thing, especially given the fact that they can erroneously feel that their actions have no effect on anybody else.

In order for it to be used effectively for educational purposes and become a part of formal education, the entire process should be carefully organized, beginning with the selection of the experts, who will provide the initial body of knowledge and the pool of evaluation content; selecting the system developers with good presentation skills, who will train the "technology geeks" among the teachers; selecting the teachers who will learn how to use the platform and train their own students; and selecting students who will learn how to use the platform and train their own teachers. These are the most important requirements and responsibilities that must be fulfilled in order to ensure the platform for educational crowdsourcing operates efficiently and is maintained properly.

The user interface of the crowdsourcing website has to be easy to understand and get the hang of. The success of the platform is contingent on the platform's user-friendliness, its intuitive interactions, and the satisfaction of the platform's users. This is particularly important for more recent teachers, who could experience feelings of inadequacy and, as a result, be reluctant to use technology-enhanced solutions in their classrooms. Because extended use raises the danger of repetitive strain injuries, particular care in terms of human factors and ergonomics should be given to all users, including those who already have musculoskeletal diseases.

It is imperative that educators acquire the knowledge necessary to use the website in an efficient manner. This will be achieved by offering initial training to those educators who will catch up on the system fast and act as mentors to their colleagues who have less expertise. In the event that any problems arise that were not foreseen, it is possible that a small group of online technology experts will be hired to provide assistance. Software developers and teachers of languages other than English need to be included on the council of advisors. Everyone who uses the platform, as well as the people who design it and the committee that oversees it, has to contend with a widespread lack of interest. Each week, the best students will be recognized for their great contributions to the platform, which will be used to determine who receives this honor. The accomplishments of the teacher will get the same amount of recognition as the other successes. The winners will have the opportunity to brag about their accomplishments in public, which will remove any motivation for envy. For the sake of the end users, there will be a realistic amount of work for all parties concerned, such as something that can be finished in five days. This will allow the end users to both see and feel their development.

The enhancement of content obtained via crowdsourcing is highly dependent on the quality of the contributions that are made. The possibility exists that it might be damaged by several popularly held yet wrong assumptions, concepts, and points of view. Using crowdsourcing in traditional learning environments needs consistent effort on the part of the instructor. It is possible that it will be publicized in order to attract the attention of other educational institutions, which will then participate in a healthy competition to discover the most effective answers to the same challenges. There is also the prospect of broader people's access to educational opportunities. It's possible that the last phase in the process of generating and preserving possibilities and models is receiving institutional and financial support, sponsorship from companies that are willing to finance education, or commercialization of the idea.

Before a business can begin using crowdsourcing, it has to determine if it has an ethical policy and make sure that it is followed. As a component of this strategy, companies may find it beneficial to consider the kind of organizational environment that currently exists and to determine whether or not there is a healthy equilibrium between the requirements and expectations of the organization's internal stakeholders and those of its external stakeholders. A myopic vision of what is required inside the organization may result in myopia and an obsession with the organization's bottom line. Even though many businesses have an ethics code in place, they are nevertheless confronted with unethical problems. As a consequence of this, it is possible that it will be essential to reevaluate the code's applicability in the context of crowdsourcing. The majority of the time, the gap that exists between what is stated in the ethical code and what is really done may be traced back to the failure to successfully install ethical principles at all levels of decision-making. To encourage the development of an ethical culture inside a company, it is advised that official ethics initiatives be developed and carried out. Businesses have the ability to take public opinion into consideration by evaluating how the public would react to their activities in the areas of labor, intellectual property, and personal data.

To further expose the multiple facets of crowdsourcing, the next step is for managers and participants to participate in more holistic thinking and actively seek out input from a number of sources, including stakeholders. It could be helpful to inform judgments to get input from user communities and the audiences those decisions are meant for. It is anticipated that judgments that are more ethical would come from using the stakeholder perspective since it takes into consideration a wider variety of views. It is important to include the appropriate internal employees in this decision-making process, as they may have insights or resources that could be useful in coming up with a solution. It is important to do so because it is important to include the appropriate internal employees in this decision-making process. However, due to the common incidence of self-deception, putting an excessive amount of value on the organization's internal stakeholders might be problematic. In order to maximize one's personal profit, it is common practice to minimize a situation's ethical implications. People who fool themselves often believe that they are still acting ethically. It has been argued that ethics programmes are of limited value because they fail to take into account the enablers of self-deception, such as explaining an action as ethical when it is not, making the same unethical decision over and over again until it becomes second nature, making mistakes in identifying the causes of unethical practices (such as blaming the individual rather than the system), and the fact that humans have a limited capacity to see actions from the perspective of others. These enablers of self-deception include individual cognitive biases that have the potential to be reduced if alternative points of view are included throughout the decision-making process on ethical issues.

## 11.7 CONCLUSION AND FUTURE

This chapter deals with the major issues in crowdsourcing and the ethical issues involved, especially in the areas of education, knowledge, and economics. Because crowdsourcing is new, many questions remain. Crowdsourcing enhances the lives of consumers and participants, but detractors say it abuses individuals. Open source and co-creation systems may encourage agency, affecting future participation. As crowdsourcing expands, more in-depth investigations into many of its challenges are needed. Future workplaces will value the opportunity to acquire knowledge from outsiders. Further research is needed on how to acquire and apply these skills ethically at work. Businesses must invent new modes of communication and consumer interaction to stay up with customers' changing online habits. Organizational and participant perspectives should be considered. Companies that use crowdsourcing may wish to conduct interviews and surveys to learn how their employees feel about the practice, including if they feel their expertise is being ignored, how they feel about the company's decision-making process for involving participants, and how the organization treats crowdsourced information.

When ubiquitous computing becomes the norm, user-friendly crowdsourcing systems may become commonplace. InnoCentive and Mechanical Turk are two successful platforms that enable on-demand access to specialized problem-solving capabilities. In-house and ad hoc crowdsourcing applications will be replaced by comprehensive platforms. Crowdsourcing platforms will be seen as a usual corporate expense, like shipping and logistics or management consultancy.

## REFERENCES

[1] T. O'Reilly, *What is web 2.0*. O'Reilly Media, Inc., 2009.
[2] S. J. Andriole, "Business impact of web 2.0 technologies," *Communications of the ACM*, vol. 53, no. 12, pp. 67–79, 2010.
[3] O. Okolloh, "Ushahidi, or 'testimony': Web 2.0 tools for crowdsourcing crisis information," *Participatory Learning and Action*, vol. 59, no. 1, pp. 65–70, 2009.
[4] J. Howe *et al.*, "The rise of crowdsourcing," *Wired Magazine*, vol. 14, no. 6, pp. 1–4, 2006.
[5] J. Surowiecki, *The wisdom of crowds*. Anchor, 2005.
[6] D. C. Brabham, "Moving the crowd at threadless: Motivations for participation in a crowdsourcing application," *Information, Communication & Society*, vol. 13, no. 8, pp. 1122–1145, 2010.

[7] D. C. Brabham, "Crowdsourcing as a model for problem solving: An introduction and cases," *Convergence*, vol. 14, no. 1, pp. 75–90, 2008.

[8] E. Estell´es-Arolas and F. Gonz´alez-Ladr´on-de Guevara, "Towards an integrated crowdsourcing definition," *Journal of Information Science*, vol. 38, no. 2, pp. 189–200, 2012.

[9] D. L. Olson and K. Rosacker, "Crowdsourcing and open source software participation," *Service Business*, vol. 7, no. 4, pp. 499–511, 2013.

[10] Y. Benkler, "Peer production, the commons, and the future of the firm," *Strategic Organization*, vol. 15, no. 2, pp. 264–274, 2017.

[11] A. Vukicevic, M. Vukicevic, S. Radovanovic, and B. Delibasic, "Bargcrex: A system for bargaining based aggregation of crowd and expert opinions in crowdsourcing," *Group Decision and Negotiation*, pp. 1–30, 2022.

[12] S. Ellis, "A history of collaboration, a future in crowdsourcing: Positive impacts of cooperation on British librarianship," *Libri*, vol. 64, no. 1, pp. 1–10, 2014.

[13] T. Terranova and J. Donovan, "Media occupy social people Facebook Twitter movement online committee camp corporate," *Social Media Monopolies and Their Alternatives*, p. 296, 2013.

[14] J. W. Carey, "Historical pragmatism and the internet," *New Media & Society*, vol. 7, no. 4, pp. 443–455, 2005.

[15] J. Suler, "Computer and cyberspace 'addiction'," *International Journal of Applied Psychoanalytic Studies*, vol. 1, no. 4, pp. 359–362, 2004.

[16] C. Terwiesch and Y. Xu, "Innovation contests, open innovation, and multi-agent problem solving," *Management Science*, vol. 54, no. 9, pp. 1529–1543, 2008.

[17] G. Chatzimilioudis, A. Konstantinidis, C. Laoudias, and D. Zeinalipour-Yazti, "Crowdsourcing with smartphones," *IEEE Internet Computing*, vol. 16, no. 5, pp. 36–44, 2012.

[18] M. Vukovic, J. Laredo, and S. Rajagopal, "Challenges and experiences in deploying enterprise crowdsourcing service," in *International Conference on Web Engineering*, pp. 460–467, Springer, 2010.

[19] C. G. Harris, "Dirty deeds done dirt cheap: A darker side to crowdsourcing," in *2011 IEEE Third International Conference on Privacy, Security, Risk and Trust and 2011 IEEE Third International Conference on Social Computing*, pp. 1314–1317, IEEE, 2011.

[20] E. Awad, S. Dsouza, J. F. Bonnefon, A. Shariff, and I. Rahwan, "Crowdsourcing moral machines," *Communications of the ACM*, vol. 63, no. 3, pp. 48–55, 2020.

[21] A. Medlar, J. Li, Y. Liu, and D. Glowacka, "The critique of crowds: Using collective criticism to crowdsource subjective preferences," *arXiv preprint arXiv:2110.11744*, 2021.

[22] E. Bietti, "From ethics washing to ethics bashing: A view on tech ethics from within moral philosophy," in *Proceedings of the 2020 Conference on Fairness, Accountability, and Transparency*, pp. 210–219, 2020.

[23] J. Habermas, "Discourse ethics," in *Ethics*, pp. 146–153, Routledge, 2004.

[24] Y. Jiang, D. Schlagwein, and B. Benatallah, "A review on crowdsourcing for education: State of the art of literature and practice," *PACIS*, p. 180, 2018.

[25] V. Lyding, L. Nicolas, B. B´edi, and K. Fort, "Introducing the European network for combining language learning and crowdsourcing techniques (EnetCollect)," *Future-Proof CALL: Language Learning as Exploration and Encounters–Short Papers from EUROCALL*, vol. 2018, p. 176, 2018.

[26] A. Girimaji and T. Abdul Rahman, "Effect of storytelling on crowdfunding campaign success," 2019.

[27] A. Rossi, S. Vismara, and M. Meoli, "Voting rights delivery in investment based crowdfunding: A cross-platform analysis," *Journal of Industrial and Business Economics*, vol. 46, no. 2, pp. 251–281, 2019.

Printed in the United States
by Baker & Taylor Publisher Services